OXFORD STUDIES IN SOCIAL AND CULTURAL ANTHROPOLOGY

THE INTERPRETATION OF CASTE

OXFORD STUDIES IN SOCIAL
AND CULTURAL ANTHROPOLOGY

Oxford Studies in Social and Cultural Anthropology represents the work of authors, new and established, which will set the criteria of excellence in ethnographic description and innovation in analysis. The series serves as an essential source of information about the world and the discipline.

OTHER TITLES IN THIS SERIES

Organizing Jainism in India and England
Marcus Banks

Society and Exchange in Nias
Andrew Beatty

The Culture of Coincidence:
Accident and Absolute Liability in Huli
Laurence Goldman

The Female Bridegroom: A Comparative Study of Life-Crisis Rituals in South India and Sri Lanka
Anthony Good

Of Mixed Blood: Kinship and History in Peruvian Amazonia
Peter Gow

Exchange in Oceania: A Graph Theoretic Analysis
Per Hage and Frank Harary

The Archetypal Actions of Ritual:
A Theory of Ritual illustrated by the Jain Rite of Worship
Caroline Humphrey and James Laidlaw

The People of the Alas Valley: A Study of an Ethnic Group of Northern Sumatra
Akifumi Iwabuchi

Knowledge and Secrecy in an Aboriginal Religion:
Yolags of North-East Arnhem Land
Ian Keen

Unwrapping Christmas
Daniel Miller

The Arabesk Debate: Music and Musicians in Modern Turkey
Martin Stokes

THE INTERPRETATION OF CASTE

DECLAN QUIGLEY

CLARENDON PRESS · OXFORD

Oxford University Press, Walton Street, Oxford OX2 6DP
Oxford New York
Athens Auckland Bangkok Bombay
Calcutta Cape Town Dar es Salaam Delhi
Florence Hong Kong Istanbul Karachi
Kuala Lumpur Madras Madrid Melbourne
Mexico City Nairobi Paris Singapore
Taipei Tokyo Toronto
and associated companies in
Berlin Ibadan

Oxford is a trade mark of Oxford University Press

Published in the United States
by Oxford University Press Inc., New York

First published 1993
First issued in paperback 1995

British Library Cataloguing in Publication Data
Data available

Library of Congress Cataloging in Publication Data
Quigley, Declan.
The interpretation of caste/Declan Quigley.
p. cm.—(Oxford studies in social and cultural anthropology)
Includes bibliographical references.
1. Caste. 2. Caste—Asia, South I. Title. II. Series.
GN491.4Q54 1993 92–27757 305.5'122—dc20

ISBN 0–19–827882–9
ISBN 0–19–828027–0 (Pbk.)

Printed in Great Britain
on acid-free paper by
Biddles Ltd, Guildford and King's Lynn

To my parents
Gerry and Kathleen Quigley
and to
Ernest Gellner

ACKNOWLEDGEMENTS

I AM grateful to a number of people who have read part or all of the manuscript at various stages of its progress. Their comments and criticisms have been invaluable in helping me to formulate the argument. In particular, I would like to thank Pascal Boyer, Patricia Crone, David Gellner, Ernest Gellner, Gabriella Giannachi, Tony Good, John Hall, Caroline Humphrey, Eivind Kahrs, Rowena Robinson, Tom Selwyn, Vinay Srivastava, and Peter Webster. I am also indebted to the many students whose straightforward questions have encouraged me to write a book which is primarily for them.

Throughout the writing of this book I have been plagued by migraines and have made quite unreasonable demands on my doctor, Richard Irons, and his colleagues in the practice, Drs Jennens, Short, and Stevens. To all of them I am extremely grateful.

The research for this book was financed by a postdoctoral fellowship from the British Academy which I held in the Department of Social Anthropology, Cambridge University. During this time and for two subsequent years, while working as a lecturer in the department, I was affiliated to King's College as a Member of the High Table. I owe a huge debt to all of these institutions and to my colleagues who provided such a stimulating environment.

I would also like to acknowledge my gratitude to my copy-editor, Margaret Hardwidge, and to those at Oxford University Press who have been responsible for seeing the book through to publication.

The book is dedicated to my parents, whose support over the years has gone far beyond the call of parental duty, and to Ernest Gellner who has been a constant source of inspiration and encouragement.

CONTENTS

FIGURES

TABLE

1
The Problem before Dumont

The Entrenched View of Caste

THIS book offers a comparative approach to the explanation of caste, the institution which is often said to be the predominant feature of Hindu social organization. The argument will be that it is impossible to explain caste as the product of a particular ideology. Throughout her history, India has produced conflicting belief systems; some of these have attempted to legitimate caste organization, others to repudiate it. Among the ideologies which uphold caste, there is considerable dispute about what is being defended and why.[1] The problem, then, is to explain what these different belief systems are trying to come to terms with.

The view of caste which dominates both popular representations by Hindus themselves and descriptions by outside observers runs something like this:[2]

(1) The Hindu world is made up of a number of castes.
(2) Castes are closed social groups: one may only marry within one's caste and the children of the marriage belong to the caste of their parents. In this way the system is perpetuated *ad infinitum*.
(3) Castes are hierarchically ranked on a purity–pollution scale according to their traditional occupations.

Intensive historical and ethnographic investigations of caste-organized communities in India have repeatedly demonstrated

[1] '[T]here are exceptions to every rule of Hinduism and to every interpretation of caste' (Stevenson 1970: 25).

[2] See e.g. the entry on caste in the 1989 *Cambridge Encyclopedia of India* (the author is a highly experienced Indian anthropologist): 'Castes and families are, then, the building blocks of Hindu society. Membership of a caste is by birth . . . castes reproduce themselves through endogamy, that is, marriage within a defined group. Caste occupations are usually hereditary, particularly among artisan and service "jatis". Each caste stands below, above or on a par with others in a system of social ranking. While the top and bottom rungs of the social ladder are fairly well defined and occupied by the Brahmin and Shudra castes, there is much competition for the middle positions. According to traditional caste ideology, which is obviously the brain-child of Brahmins, the key to the rank order lies in the notion of ritual purity' (Madan 1989: 364–5).

that this three-line theory is at best inadequate, at worst wholly misleading. And yet it has remained remarkably resistant to attempts to modify it. In this book I will try to show why the three-line theory is false but why there are nevertheless good reasons, for Hindus and outsiders alike, to hold on to it as if it were true. The popular theory contains a certain amount of truth, enough to let one turn a blind eye to anything which it cannot explain. Unfortunately, the more information one uncovers, the more one finds aspects of Hindu society which either cannot be explained by the three-line theory or directly contradict it.

Initially the theory seems to have a certain attraction. It appears to account for the most striking observation about caste-organized communities—striking both to those who live in them and to those who do not. This observation is that Brāhmaṇs enjoy the highest status, Untouchables have the lowest status, and all other castes are in between. Adherents of the three-line theory argue that even if it does not explain everything, it explains this 'fact', the polarization of Brāhmaṇ and Untouchable, more adequately than any of the alternative theories which have been proposed.

As will become clear, however, one must be very cautious about the use of the word 'fact' in relation to caste. That Brāhmaṇs are sometimes priests is a fact; no one disputes it. That 'the supremacy of the Indian priest is an Indian fact' (Dumont 1980: 216) is not, however, beyond dispute. It is a claim which is soaked through with preconceptions about the nature of Hindu society and it is extremely contentious. There are, I will argue, very good grounds for rejecting it. If anything, the facts demonstrate again and again that the status of the Indian priest is extremely ambiguous.[3]

The debate about the nature of caste has generally led to a division between two main sets of protagonists whose only shared conviction is that members of the opposing camp are utterly misguided. Respectively, the two groups endorse a materialist and an idealist conception of history.[4] According to the materialist interpretation, caste is simply a rationalization, and obfuscation, of more base inequalities. High castes, it is noted, are generally wealthier than low castes; therefore the idiom of purity and impurity through which caste differences are expressed must be

[3] See Ch. 4 below.

[4] A recent bibliography of some of the main protagonists in this debate can be found in Krause (1988: 31).

'simply' a means of legitimating and obscuring the 'true' nature of social divisions.

According to the idealist explanation, caste is a cultural construct, the product of religious ideas: castes are higher or lower in relation to religiously conceived notions of purity and impurity. On this view, material considerations are largely irrelevant because caste is essentially an ideological framework for explaining universal problems of social order. As such, the underlying principle transcends local preoccupations regarding such matters as political organization or the regulation of land tenure and taxation. It also transcends local caste hierarchies because, it is argued, the structure of caste is to be found in a system of ideas and not in concrete manifestations of those ideas. The most lucid and consistent exponent of this view is Louis Dumont, and it will be examined in detail in the following two chapters.

The basic framework of the argument I will present was first proposed by A. M. Hocart in his essay *Caste: A Comparative Study*.[5] It is an argument which will appeal neither to rank materialists nor to rank idealists and this, I believe, is the reason why Hocart's book is often hastily dismissed, when not altogether ignored. Adopting the spirit of Hocart's interpretation, it will be suggested that there is a fundamental truth and a fundamental falsehood in both the materialist and idealist visions of traditional Indian society.

Along with the idealists, Hocart argues that caste ideology seeks to provide a transcendent foundation for the social order. Against them, however, he argues that caste society is only possible given a certain kind of political system—namely a kingdom—and there is nothing transcendent about this: kingdoms are the product of particular historical conditions. Along with the materialists, Hocart asserts that caste is indeed a means of regulating inequalities. Against them, however, he asserts that inequalities are not at all obscured in caste society; quite the contrary, they are very deliberately highlighted, glorified, and perpetuated. There is nothing shamefaced about caste.

In the light of material which has been published since his death in 1939, Hocart's theory of caste, though not without its problems,

[5] Hocart's book was first published in French in 1938, the year before his death, before being published in English in 1950. His theory is discussed in detail in Ch. 6 below.

still has much to offer. Not only does it offer a more plausible account of the relationship between Brāhmaṇ and Untouchable; it accounts for the relationships between all castes and for the way in which castes are internally structured. It is, to my knowledge, the only plausible theory of Hindu society in that it both explains indigenous ideas about caste and allows one to consider the historical and sociological constraints which have produced those ideas.

The Word 'Caste'

The word 'caste' can be used in a variety of ways—as a noun to denote an abstract principle or to designate a particular kind of social group, and as an adjective to denote the quality of this principle or the character of the group. In this book all of these usages will be retained but, before proceeding further, it is necessary to see where the concept comes from.

> The Portuguese seafarers who traded mainly on the west coast of India in the 16th and 17th centuries described groups they called castas (from which derive the English and French words caste), meaning 'species' or 'breeds' of animals or plants and 'tribes,' 'races,' 'clans,' or 'lineages' among men. (Marriott and Inden 1985: 348)[6]

There are two different issues here. The first is that the word 'caste' is a European invention. The second is the idea that castes are, in some fundamental way, unalike—as species are: '*jāti*, caste, is also "species" in the botanical or zoological sense' (Dumont 1980: 42). Each of these issues must be considered separately.

The word 'caste', as used in various European sources, is an extremely unhappy translation of two quite different indigenous concepts, *varṇa* and *jāti*, which are generally believed, both by Hindus and by outside observers, to correspond in some way. In a sense, the history of the debate about the nature of caste can be viewed as the attempt to discover what exactly the correspondence between *varṇa* and *jāti* is.[7]

The sense of *jāti* is of those people who are in some fundamental way alike because of their common origins, and fundamentally different from those who do not share these origins. One cannot

[6] See also Heesterman (1985: 180).

[7] See e.g. Srinivas (1962).

choose one's *jāti*; it is defined by birth. But one can choose whether one's *jāti* refers to a more or less inclusive group: this is going to depend on context. In one context, one's *jāti* is one's lineage; in another, it may be all the lineages with whom one can intermarry; in yet another, it may refer to those whose common ethnic or cultural heritage sets them apart from their neighbours.

Jāti is, of the essence, a relative term. The following definition gives some idea of the range and flexibility of the concept:

> One of the commonest words for genus in most Indian languages, *jāti*, is derived from an Indo-European verbal root meaning 'genesis,' 'origin,' or 'birth.' It is applied to any species of living things including gods and humans. Among humans, *jāti* can designate a distinct sex, a race, a caste, or a tribe; a population, the followers of an occupation or a religion, or a nation. (Marriott and Inden 1985: 349)[8]

This elasticity means that it is pointless to ask how many *jāti*s there are in any particular region. Unfortunately, this question is one of those most frequently asked by those who wish to quantify and classify in a definitive way. This has led to considerable confusion, even among those who are well aware that *jāti* is a relative term, as will be shown later.

The sense of *varṇa* is quite different. The basic idea is not of birth but of function, and not simply any function, but one which is necessary to ensure that social harmony and cosmic stability are maintained.[9] The term *varṇa* has a long history and dates back to the invasions of north-west India (contemporary Pakistan), beginning in approximately 1500 BC, by Aryans from Central Asia.[10] These Aryans are often referred to as Vedic, a word which

[8] The following more precise definition was given to me by a Sanskritist at the University of Cambridge: 'The word *jāti* derives from the verbal root *jan/jā* "generate, be born". The basic meaning would be "generating; birth" and it is indeed a common word for "birth; coming into existence". Another common meaning, particularly in technical *śāstras* such as grammar and logic, is "class; genus". (*Jāti* and the Latin word *genus* are etymologically related.) It is later used to denote generic qualities or properties constituting a class such as *gotva* "cow-hood" or *śuklatva* "white-ness" which refer to the classes of all cows and all things white respectively' (E. Kahrs, personal communication).

[9] '. . . the feature [of the *varṇas*] which most contrasts with the caste system is perhaps the stress laid on function rather than birth' (Dumont 1980: 69). The word *varṇa* is also commonly used to mean 'colour' though the significance of this is widely disputed—see e.g. Embree (ed.) (1988: 215–16).

[10] It should be understood that by 'India' I generally mean Greater India—i.e. the entire sub-continent including Nepal and Sri Lanka as well as Pakistan and Bangladesh—unless it is clear that I am referring to modern political units.

derives from the priestly ritual and literature with which they are primarily associated. The central idea of Vedic literature and ritual is that in order to safeguard the continuity of the universe, it is necessary to make sacrifices to the gods, and the concept of *varṇa* with which we are familiar today is inextricably tied to a sacrificial theory of human society.

The connection of *varṇa* with sacrifice first appears in a later hymn of the Rigveda (*ṛgveda*) which is generally believed to have been written about 1000 BC in the area around the Indus river.[11] In this hymn, four *varṇa*s are presented, *brāhmaṇa*, *rājanya* (later normally referred to as *kṣatriya*), *vaiśya*, and *śūdra*, each of which emanates from a particular part of the body of Puruṣa—'the lord of beings'—who is represented as a primeval god-man sacrificed at the beginning of time:

> When they divided Purusha, in how many different portions did they arrange him? What became of his mouth, what of his two arms? What were his two thighs and his two feet called?
>
> His mouth became the brāhman; his two arms were made into the rājanya; his two thighs the vaishyas; from his two feet the shūdra was born.
>
> (Rigveda x, 90: 11–12, quoted in Embree (ed.) 1988: 19)

In the later Hindu law book which is often referred to as the Code of Manu (*c.* 200 BC–AD 200) each *varṇa* is represented as fundamentally different in function. Just as the four *varṇa*s were created through an initial sacrifice, further sacrifices are necessary to maintain the order of the universe. In these, each *varṇa* is required to perform a particular function as its divinely ordained duty:

> Manu lays down that the duty of the brāhmaṇ is to study and teach, to sacrifice, and to give and receive gifts; the kṣatriya must protect the people, sacrifice, and study; the vaiśya also sacrifices and studies, but his chief function is to breed cattle, to till the earth, to pursue trade and to lend money; the śūdra's duty is only to serve the three higher classes—and 'it is better', Manu adds elsewhere, 'to do one's own duty badly than another's well'. This epigram, elaborated so beautifully in the *Bhagavad Gītā*, was the leading theme of most Indian social thought; for each man

[11] For a short description of the Vedas, see Dowson (1982). It should be noted that these texts were written over a long period of time and do not therefore have any single author.

there was a place in society and a function to fulfil, with its own duties and rights. (Basham 1971: 139)

It is very clear, then, that *varṇa* and *jāti* are two quite different concepts, yet both have been translated as 'caste'. What exactly is the correspondence between them? Perhaps the most widespread opinion is that *varṇa* is simply a theoretical category never actually encountered on the ground while *jāti* is the 'real' operational unit, the real caste. According to this view, which many Hindus themselves profess, the world is actually made up of units called *jāti* any one of which can, in theory, be slotted into one of the more embracing *varṇa* categories, or into the residual category of Untouchables.

The trouble with this opinion is that more often than not it fails to work when applied to actual situations. There is endless dispute about which *jāti* belongs to which *varṇa* and which does not. Often there is even dispute about who exactly belongs to which *jāti*, as the discussion in Chapter 5 will make clear.

These two difficulties—of defining *jāti* membership unambiguously, and of mapping *jāti*s on to functional categories such as the four *varṇa*s—are, I believe, features which are inherent in all caste systems. As a foretaste of the reasons why this should be so, consider the following hypothetical conversation. It is intended to illustrate the difficulties which outsiders encounter whenever they try to find out exactly which caste someone 'belongs' to. I have labelled the two parties to the conversation 'O' and 'I'—'outsider' and 'insider'. Who is an insider and who is an outsider is always a question of context; what these contexts are will be spelled out in greater detail as the argument unfolds.

For purposes of exposition, the conversation is in English and it quickly becomes apparent that there is a difficulty with the word 'caste' itself.

O: What caste are you?
I: We are *kṣatriya*.
O: Whom may you marry?
I: We may only marry other *kṣatriya*.
O: There are people in the next village who say they are *kṣatriya*. Presumably you can marry with them?
I: No. They are not like us, not the same caste.
O: But you said you were *kṣatriya* and they say they are *kṣatriya* so why can you not intermarry?

I: Well, in the first place, they *say* they are *kṣatriya* but how do we know they are? And in the second place, even if they are *kṣatriya*, they're not the same caste as we are, so we can't marry with them.

O: But who is the same caste as you?

I: Well, those people we can marry with.

The logic of this is not quite as circular as it might at first appear. As the conversation progresses, it becomes obvious that the word 'caste' is being used in two different senses—in the first place to refer to a *varṇa*, namely *kṣatriya*, and in the second place to identify another category which has yet to be specified. The insider is saying something like: 'We must marry people of the same *varṇa* (*kṣatriya*) but that's not enough. They must also belong to the same "caste".' Let's say he uses the word *jāti* for this second sense.

The outsider now realizes he could have avoided this misunderstanding if he had, in the first place, asked: 'What is your *jāti*?' instead of 'What is your caste?' He now understands that the insider has said something like this: 'Like many other people, our *varṇa* is *kṣatriya* but it is the *jāti* which must be taken into account when considering a marriage.' He continues:

O: So, you can only marry people belonging to your own *jāti*?

I: Yes.

O: Does your *jāti* have a name?

I: Of course—we are Rājputs.

O: So you can marry the Rājputs in the next village?

I: Oh no, we never marry them. They are not the same caste as we are.

O: But you are Rājputs and they are Rājputs so how can you not be the same caste?

I: Well, in the first place, they *say* they're Rājputs but how do we know they are? And anyway, even if they are Rājputs, they're not the same caste as we are, so we don't marry them.

O: So, whom *do* you marry?

I: I've told you that already—we marry the people who are the same caste as we are, the same *jāti*, the people we've always married.

O: But you've just said that your *jāti* is Rājput, yet there are some Rājputs you can't marry because they don't belong to your *jāti*. Surely this is a contradiction?

I: What one means by one's *jāti* depends on the context. In one sense, all Rājputs are alike and are different from those who are not Rājputs. In another sense, Rājputs are themselves divided into many different groups which do not intermarry *because* they are different.

Resorting to native terminology does not, then, provide a

solution: the Sanskrit or Hindi word '*jāti*' causes just as much difficulty as the English (or French) word 'caste'. The problem is rather to do with the quality of 'casteness' or '*jāti*-ness', or whether indeed such a quality can be said to exist at all. Thus the two major initial questions remain unresolved: (1) what do the groups which actually intermarry look like? (2) what, if any, is the correspondence between the way in which these are arranged and the way in which the four *varṇa*s are arranged? The questions look straightforward enough but the various answers which have been proposed have generated enormous dispute about the nature of Hindu society.

There are many ways into the problem of caste—from history, ethnography, the comparative study of religions, political theory, or kinship studies—but whichever path one chooses, one thing must be made clear from the beginning. To set out with the idea that castes are, in general, bounded groups with a fixed membership is to embark on a path of endless frustration from which many students of Hinduism have never escaped. Sometimes the boundaries of castes *are* relatively unambiguous; sometimes they are extremely fuzzy. Sometimes it is relatively straightforward to say who belongs to a caste and who does not; sometimes it is impossible. Later I will try to explain the reasons for this.[12]

There are those who argue that the word 'caste' should be abandoned altogether, so much confusion does it cause.[13] But, as I have shown in my hypothetical conversation, reversion to native terminology does not solve the problem. We are left with the difficulty of what to call the social groups one encounters on the ground. The conventions of caste, sub-caste, and *jāti* are too well established to be conjured away by mere academic wishful thinking, however well intentioned. And they are well established for good reason: for hundreds of millions of people these concepts are the primary means by which they identify themselves and others.

From the very outset, then, one is struck with an apparent dilemma. On the one hand, one has little option but to retain the word 'caste' or *jāti* in order to refer to actual social groups; on the other hand, these groups are not always bounded in the way in which castes are often thought to be. As if this was not awkward enough, there is another, related problem which concerns the

[12] See the discussion of hypergamy and isogamy in Ch. 5.

[13] See e.g. Baechler (1988: 16) and Levy (1990: 70–1).

relations between castes. Castes, it is generally thought, are always ranked one above the other—from the lowly Untouchables, who do polluting tasks, to the pure, priestly Brāhmaṇs. However, it frequently happens that two castes each claim superiority of status over the other.

Consider, for example, a group of people inhabiting a set of neighbouring villages, who call themselves, and are known to others, as the Potters. (Following the established convention, proper names which designate a caste group will be in the upper case—e.g. Potters—while occupations will be in the lower case—e.g. potters. Thus: 'the Potters of village *x* are not potters, but agricultural labourers'.) Perhaps these people did once derive their income from pottery but the development of factory-made glass, metal, and plastic products which are cheaper, more durable, and easier to clean, has made this particular craft redundant.

The Potters were thus obliged to seek alternative sources of livelihood: perhaps as farm labourers or as rickshaw-pullers, taxi-drivers, or minor government employees in a nearby town. Yet they continue to refer to themselves, and are referred to by others, as Potters. They marry only among themselves and are careful not to accept certain kinds of food from 'castes' which they consider 'lower', such as Tailors, even though many of the Tailors do not actually work cloth but are also farm labourers, rickshaw-pullers, taxi-drivers, and menial civil servants.

Perhaps, to make matters more awkward still, the Tailors claim superiority of status over the Potters and questioning members of other, disinterested groups fails to resolve the issue. Some people think Tailors are higher; others think that Potters are higher. Quite a few people have no idea which are higher and which lower and many do not seem to care particularly one way or the other. Everyone, however, including those who don't know and those who don't care, is agreed that they are of unequal status and should not intermarry.

Clearly the principle of identification is not based on current occupations. Perhaps it may not even safely be related to past occupations. Possibly these were given up many generations ago, so long ago that it is not at all clear if these occupations were *ever* actually performed by these groups. Nevertheless, even though there is no evidence that Potters were ever potters, nor that

Tailors were ever tailors, yet Potters and Tailors keep rigidly apart and will not exchange their women or certain kinds of food, nor will they share in each other's ritual. And no one from any other group is able to adduce an unambiguous, objective criterion to judge one way or the other who is higher and who is lower.

This is only one example among many of ambiguity in caste relations. On occasion, Brāhmaṇ priests are treated as if they they were as defiled as Untouchables.[14] Castes which are often referred to in the literature as 'dominant' (because they are the major landholders) enjoy high ritual status even though they frequently indulge in more impure activities, such as violence (conquest) and meat eating, or have laxer marriage rules, than those who are considered of lower status. It is possible for a group to enter a local caste system with high ritual status even though, before entering, its members have the most impure status of all—that of outsiders, barbarians.[15] One might indeed ask how social mobility is possible at all if status is ordained at birth?

These are just a few of the puzzling aspects of caste. The course of my argument will throw up many more for those who believe that higher castes are higher because they somehow approximate to priestly purity. Those who assert this are obliged to reduce the awkward features given in the previous paragraphs to the status of anomalies. Effectively they claim that their respective theories illustrate the 'true' nature of caste and that contradictory evidence only *appears* contradictory because one has not grasped the underlying structure of the system; or that it is a manifestation of some competing principle of social organization but one which is 'secondary' to that of caste; or that the principle of caste is itself secondary and the 'real' principle of social organization is something else.

The massive literature on caste will not be reviewed here. Rather, the argument will concentrate on what I consider to be the central issues and explore these through the work of a number of authors who have made significant contributions to the debate.[16] It

[14] The issue is examined in detail in Ch. 4.

[15] The word used is *mleccha* in Sanskrit and in Sanskrit-derived vernacular languages.

[16] Any selection is necessarily somewhat arbitrary. However, of those I have considered, a number have themselves made comprehensive reviews of the arguments of their predecessors—particularly Dumont (1980), Klass (1980), Parry (1979), and Raheja (1988*b*).

has now become clear, however, that the very definition of the word 'caste' is intensely problematic. One reason for this has been given: the two qualities most often associated with castes, namely unambiguous closure and unambiguous hierarchy, do not actually obtain. Is there then some other distinctive criterion which sets castes apart from other social groupings such as ethnic groups, classes, estates, or tribes? The answer, I will suggest, is an unqualified 'yes'.

Is Caste an Orientalist Construct?

Explanations of Indian society through indigenous cultural concepts have generally prevailed among the specialists and have filtered down into the popular imagination. There have, however, been dissenters from idealist interpretations of this kind. In an early attack on the position adopted by Dumont and Pocock in the first two issues of *Contributions to Indian Sociology*,[17] F. G. Bailey wrote the following:

> What the editors are advocating is not sociology at all, but a form of culturology. It is only as culturology that the subject can be made distinctively 'Indian' . . . There can be no 'Indian' sociology except in a 'vague geographic sense', any more than there are distinctively Indian principles in chemistry or biology. (Bailey 1959: 99)

In spite of Bailey's trenchant words, such 'culturology' is alive and well today. The attempt by Marriott and his students to construct an Indian 'ethnosociology' is but one in a long line of expressions of the argument that the only way to understand India is by adopting Indian concepts.[18] It should perhaps be added that idealist explanations of social institutions do not prevail only in South Asian studies. Anthropology generally has been moving increasingly in this direction.

In the following chapters one of my main aims is to point out the limitations of explanations of caste in terms of culture, or ideas, or meanings. The entire book can be read as a sustained critique not

[17] This position forms the subject matter of the following two chapters.

[18] See Marriott and Inden (1977) and the collection of papers in *Contributions to Indian Sociology*, NS 23(1) (1989). I would argue that the articles by Dirks and Raheja in this volume actually demonstrate the limits of ethnosociology and the need to introduce a comparative perspective.

only of Dumont's theory, but of all those who put the ultimate weight of their explanation of caste in terms of Hindu ideas. Recently a number of authors have added a new twist to the idealist interpretation of caste. Their argument draws on the deconstructionist idea that much of our current knowledge of other societies has been distorted by the employment of Western ideological constructs. There is both an epistemological and a moral critique here. In producing a false picture of other cultures, Western constructs are alleged to have shaped knowledge in such a way as to bolster the historical power structures engendered by colonialism.[19]

There is some ambiguity about what happens after the deconstruction of Western interpretations of other cultures. What seems to be offered is more of a manifesto for a change of perspective rather than any definitive picture of what the world will look like once this change has been effected.[20] Sometimes the suggestion is that we should revert to the old kind of idealist explanation—'let them speak for themselves'—but there is no clear consensus about this. One obvious reason for the lack of agreement is that many of the societies studied by anthropologists themselves provide a number of conflicting ideologies and the question of who speaks for the society as a whole is extremely problematic.

But if it is not entirely clear what is being prescribed, there is less doubt about what has been proscribed, for the new wave is nothing less than a moral crusade. It is essentially an expiation for the sins of our imperialist ancestors and woe betide those who would question the need for it. They run the risk of being branded as rednecks or, worse still, as guilt-free stalwarts of the ever more intrusive cultural imperialism of the West.

In the case of India, the principal defendant on trial by the deconstructionists is the concept of caste, and the allegation appears to be that caste is little other than the invention of European colonialists for their own glorification. According to this argument, the European obsession with caste derives for the most

[19] See e.g. the collection *Writing Culture* edited by Clifford and Marcus (1986).

[20] There are echoes here of Mannheim's *Ideology and Utopia*, certain versions of Marxism, and psychoanalytic theory: once one gets rid of some interfering mechanism, such as class interests or repressed desires, the truth will reveal itself, automatically as it were. See E. Gellner's (1974) *Legitimation of Belief* for a wicked exposé of this kind of theory.

part from a desire to find some mysterious other—the Oriental—who does not think quite the way we do and whose 'essential' nature is captured in his pernicious practices and beliefs.[21] The representation of Indians as prisoners of the outrageous institution of caste—addicted to hierarchy, ritual, concepts of purity and pollution, and other absurd theories of society and the cosmos—thus contributed to the political subjugation of the East while simultaneously reinforcing the rationality and moral righteousness of Western institutions.

The anthropologist's preoccupation with caste can then be seen as a derivative of more generalized Orientalist illusions. It is a product of the Western observer's peculiarly imperialist designs which aimed to subjugate the native through representation every bit as much as through military domination and economic exploitation. The native was (and remains) a titillatingly bizarre phenomenon to behold in the flesh and to record in text and photograph. Measured and exhibited, natives and their social structures were treated, like any other specimens, as objects.[22]

There is no doubt that the depiction of others as 'Other' easily lends itself to racism and other forms of stigmatization. Whether it *necessarily* does so, however, is another question. Most anthropologists today would, I think, argue that what they are looking for is the meaning in beliefs, actions, and institutions which, on the surface, look strange to the outsider's eye and therefore require explanation. They are looking for rationality, not irrationality, and Pinney's epitaph on the discipline as a whole would strike most as unjust. Drawing parallels with Foucault's (1971) study of the Western treatment of madness, he states that the claims to truth of anthropology 'rest precisely on the fact that it refuses to take seriously the beliefs of its objects' (Pinney 1988: 147).

There are a number of difficulties with this kind of deconstructionism. The most obvious is that we are left in a kind of intellectual limbo because it is no longer clear how one ought to proceed in order to understand other cultures and other eras. Should we take all beliefs seriously in the sense of according them equal explanatory value? This would be no mean feat given that beliefs incessantly contradict one another. What is more, if historical and ethnographic research by Westerners has now

[21] See esp. Inden (1986; 1990) and Quigley (1988*b*).
[22] See Pinney (1988) and Cohn (1987: 235 ff.).

become ideologically suspect, the theories of indigenous peoples must also be regarded as suspect because they have often been influenced by Western perceptions. Even if one could pinpoint some kind of uncontaminated and homogeneous indigenous interpretation of a society's institutions, two problems would remain. How would one evaluate its accuracy, and how could one translate this interpretation into a Western language without introducing the concepts which are held to produce an ideological distortion? Taken to its logical conclusion, the only option appears to be the abandonment of the comparative endeavour altogether.[23]

Inden's attack on Orientalist conceptions of India poses similar problems. His most extreme statement is that 'the intellectual activities of the Orientalist have even produced in India the very Orient which it [*sic*] constructed in its discourse' (Inden 1986: 408; 1990: 38). This indeed is the ultimate logic of the deconstructionist manifesto: it is no longer, as old idealism had it, that their ideas produce their universe. Now it is *our* ideas which produce their world. The problem remains: how do we gain access to that world without resort to an extreme relativism (or ethnosociology) which defies comparison?

More tangibly, Inden argues that the European obsession with caste as the dominant explanatory framework for Indian social organization precludes a consideration of political institutions generally and, in particular, ignores the pivotal role of kingship.[24] What makes this line of reasoning odd is that Inden quotes Hocart in admiration during the course of his argument, indeed claims that his own views are 'a critical extension of Hocart's' (1990: 229). Yet Hocart's theory, as will be seen in Chapter 6, is an explanation of caste *in terms of* kingship. The retention of the concept of caste as an explanatory framework for a kind of social organization which occurs under certain conditions does not preclude the consideration of kingship, or politics more generally. On the contrary, Hocart's theory shows that it is possible to have a theory of caste which combines considerations of power with those of ritual.

Inden's thesis is not, however, without merit. Cohn, in particular, has shown how the British attempted to reduce the

[23] Winch (1958) offers philosophical justification for such a course.
[24] See also Dirks (1987).

complexity of Indian society by slotting all groups into a neat series of caste-ordered pigeonholes:

> Attempts were made in the first census of 1871–2 to collect information on caste. The principle of organization was to try to place castes (*jatis*) in the four *varnas* or in categories of Outcastes and Aborigines . . . From the beginning of the census operations it was widely assumed that an all-India system of classification of castes could be developed. (Cohn 1987: 243)

For the 1881 census, Cohn notes that the then Lieutenant-Governor ordered that any confusion about a caste's social position should be resolved by referring to a list drawn up by 'the outstanding Indian Sanskrit scholar of the time' (ibid.: 245).

There were two mistakes in this colonial understanding of caste. The first was the confusion of the *varṇa* system with caste system*s*. There is no such thing as *the* caste system, only so many political units each of which is divided into different castes. (These units do, however, have a basic common structure which is illustrated in Chapter 7.) The second mistake is the assumption that there is one unambiguous interpretation of the *varṇa* system which outstanding Sanskrit scholars have access to. The *varṇa* system is a set of ideas developed to explain an early division of labour, but these ideas have always been interpreted in different, contradictory ways. According to Dumont, for example,

> It is generally agreed that the opposition [between pure and impure] is manifested in some macroscopic form in the contrast between the two extreme categories: Brahmans and Untouchables. The Brahmans, being in principle priests, occupy the supreme rank with respect to the whole set of castes. (Dumont 1980: 46–7)

But there is actually a great deal of disagreement about this—as is demonstrated by the frequent portrayal of priests as vessels of impurity, which is discussed in Chapter 4. Brāhmaṇs can *be* Untouchables, and Untouchables, as ritual specialists, are priests.

The only thing which the conflicting interpretations of the *varṇa* categories have in common is that the various functions which the *varṇa*s represent must be kept separate. In particular, the functions of king and priest must be kept separate. One way of defining these functions on which everyone might agree is to say that the role of the king is to create social order by making boundaries, while that of the priest is to manipulate these boundaries through ritual and so give them enduring legitimacy.

Both functions can be, and have been, interpreted as the crucial ones for maintaining social and cosmic stability. I will argue that the separation of the two functions implies their interdependence, and the frequently made claim that caste organization derives its rationale from one of them alone obscures this.

A related question, which deserves serious consideration, concerns the representation of caste as a timeless, 'traditional' social order which conceives of little flexibility or change in pre-colonial South Asia. Since the late 1960s, some historians have been painting a rather different picture which suggests that the inflexibility which has tended to be associated with caste was largely an artefact of the colonial period. It is not only the construct of caste which has been challenged. So too have the representations of those institutions which have been widely portrayed as underpinning 'the traditional caste system'—in particular, the so-called *jajmānī* system and the 'traditional' self-contained village community centred on a local dominant caste.[25]

Fuller puts the argument particularly strongly, arguing that 'the [*jajmānī*] system so well described by Kolenda [1967] is largely a figment of the anthropological imagination' (1989: 34). He suggests that the local power of dominant castes increased during the early colonial period as a result of the political and economic infrastructure which the British established (Fuller 1977: 110). There is a certain ambivalence in his argument, however. On the one hand he asks 'whether the "traditional" caste system is not also a creation of the British' (ibid.: 111). On the other, he appears to contradict himself when he writes that 'although the caste system in itself may not have altered so much, its connections with other systems within the total society, particularly the agrarian system, have altered fundamentally' (ibid.: 112). It is not entirely clear what is meant by the phrase 'the caste system in itself' but it is clearly implied that some kind of caste system existed prior to British representations of it.

In a similar vein, Bayly has urged caution in treating pre-colonial India as unchanging: 'Caste, for instance, was not an immutable "given" of Indian society. Castes were constantly in the process of formation and change, notably in periods such as the eighteenth century when political authority was very fluid' (Bayly 1989: 11–12). Moreover, it is transparently obvious that not all of

[25] See e.g. Fuller (1977: 107 ff.; 1989), Cohn (1970: 45) and Bayly (1988: 11–13).

India was in the grip of caste. The social organization of tribals and nomads in particular was decentralized and governed by kinship principles which were antithetical to hierarchical notions of purity and pollution.

That this latter feature was obvious to British administrators is evident in the census reports which were entitled 'The Tribes and Castes of . . . [such and such a region]'. The colonial administration was always perfectly aware that it was dealing with (at least) two fundamentally different kinds of social organization. By spilling so much ink on caste, anthropologists working on India have sometimes given the impression that other forms of social structure in India were insignificant. But one should be careful not to build a straw man here; the identification was normally made between Hinduism and caste, not between India and caste.[26]

While it is my aim in this book to sketch out a basic model of how caste systems work, it is not my intention to suggest that this model is inflexible. Quite the contrary; I am perfectly aware that there are endless variations on the basic theme. For example, where there is hypergamy, the structure of the units which exchange women in marriage is quite different from the situation where there is isogamy. In fact, in the case of hypergamy it is often impossible to specify group boundaries with any precision at all. It is also the case that over time a caste group (i.e. a set of intermarrying lineages) may fragment for various political, economic, and demographic reasons. Alternatively, two groups which did not previously intermarry may begin to do so—in order to form political or trading alliances, for example. They may then be considered as one caste by others even though they continue to observe other kinds of internal discriminations. Any understanding of how caste works must be flexible enough to take these variations and complications into consideration.

Whatever the variations, however, caste systems only exist given certain conditions. The purpose of this book is to spell out what these conditions are. For example, caste organization literally evaporates when one reaches a certain altitude in the Himalayas. The reason is not to do with altitude *per se*, of course; people do not think differently merely because they live at 5,000 or 6,000 feet above sea level. The reason is to do with the kind of

[26] The identification of Hinduism and caste is also false—there are various sects which do not embrace caste—but it is more understandable.

social organization which can be sustained by an economy which, because of the infertile terrain, produces little or no agricultural surplus. Here, then, is one clue: caste organization depends on an agricultural surplus. This is obvious enough: if some groups or individuals are not themselves food producers, then their food must be produced by others. But if this is obvious, it nevertheless has to be considered in relation to the other ingredients which make up caste systems.

Another clue comes from the fact that caste does not exist in Western, industrial society. This is the starting point for the most celebrated modern theory of caste, that of Louis Dumont, which will form the subject of the following two chapters. What I will try to show in these chapters is that while Dumont's theory is ingenious, its basic premises are flawed. In Chapter 4 I will give one powerful empirical reason why Dumont's theory is false—namely, that the opposition of pure and impure which he claims to be fundamental to caste is at times collapsed. The category of persons which is claimed to represent the most pure can also represent the most impure!

Chapter 5 adds ethnographic flesh to the argument by looking at some of the connections between caste and kinship. An exhaustive survey of this field would itself require several volumes; my aim in this chapter is simply to point out that there *is* a connection between kinship and caste. Again, this may seem obvious to some, but this is not always understood by non-specialists.

Chapter 6 is a presentation, and critique, of Hocart's theory which explains caste in terms of kingship and its associated ritual. This leads on to the concluding chapter in which a general model of the social structure of caste systems is presented. The perspective of this model is comparative rather than Indological and the central theme of my argument is contained in this methodology. In order to understand caste, one must step outside Brahmanical representations which focus on ideology in one particular cultural context.[27]

The book is directed both at specialists and at those who know little about caste beyond some common platitudes. In order to

[27] Ernest Gellner's model of complex agrarian societies is taken as the starting point here but a similar approach is taken by a number of historical sociologists; Crone's (1989) *Pre-Industrial Societies* provides an introduction to this literature and a very useful bibliography.

facilitate this, I have focused on a small number of texts which have, in my opinion, made particularly significant contributions to the debate. This should make it easier for the non-specialist to follow the argument as well as allowing more immediate access to some of the relevant literature. The experts may at times feel that I could have pruned the exegesis of others' works, but this is hazardous if one is to get at the underlying assumptions which they make when they string discrete pieces of evidence together. Throughout, as will be seen, I am at pains to show that the assumption which underlies virtually every analysis of caste is a matter of doctrine, not of sociology. If one begins with this assumption—that 'Brahmins are the highest caste'—one will never understand how caste systems work.

2
Dumont's Theory of Caste

Epistemology and Sociology

WITHOUT doubt the single most influential contribution to the study of caste since the end of the Second World War has been Louis Dumont's *Homo Hierarchicus*.[1] In this chapter a descriptive synopsis of Dumont's position is given while the following chapter presents a critical analysis of his theory. While Dumont has posed the problem in a uniquely penetrating way, there is a fundamental difficulty with his underlying approach to sociological explanation which inevitably renders his solution untenable. The insights to be gained from Dumont's theory come from the questions he asks rather than from the answers he proposes.

The forcefulness of Dumont's argument stems partly from the remarkable epistemological consistency his work has displayed throughout his intellectual development. In order to understand his theory of caste, one might begin with his more recent studies of individualism before reading *Homo Hierarchicus*. This is because there is a thread in his ideas which reaches full maturity in his later work where he becomes increasingly theoretical and philosophical, and where he examines modern ideology in more detail.[2] The underlying problem is already contained in his work on India but it is often missed or dismissed—as Dumont himself has often been at pains to point out.

Mary Douglas, in her introduction to the first English-language edition of *Homo Hierarchicus*, broached this issue when she formulated Dumont's central concern: 'India is only the ground, the experimental range, for an ambitious exercise in the sociology

[1] Dumont's output on India has been prolific. The essential theory of caste is, however, contained in *Homo Hierarchicus*, particularly since the 1980 publication of the 'Complete Revised English Edition' which, unless otherwise stated, is the edition I will refer to. The 1980 edition contains a new preface in which Dumont replies to his critics, and a 'postface' entitled 'Toward a theory of hierarchy'. It also contains three appendices which were published in the original French edition but omitted from the first English translation. These appendices, which are reprints of earlier articles, are in fact central to the overall argument.

[2] See esp. Dumont (1977) and Dumont (1986).

of knowledge. The central problem is the old, familiar one of objectivity' (Douglas 1972: 12). This is where one must begin. Dumont uses India as a *particular illustration* of a much more wide-ranging social philosophy which is intended to illustrate the nature of traditional society generally. Having isolated what it is that makes traditional society, Dumont believes that this can be used as a mirror to explain what it is that makes for the distinctiveness of modern society: this has been his preoccupation since the 1970s.[3] However, he also believes that modern Western ideology and traditional ideology are fundamentally incompatible (in a way I shall shortly delineate). The problem, then, is whether one can *validly* make sense of one with the other. If we are prisoners of a historically unique cultural and conceptual framework, how (if at all) can we legitimately analyse other cultures which do not share our framework, our world-view?

Dumont's opening remarks in *Homo Hierarchicus* on the validity of comparative sociology are often glossed over or ignored by those who are in a hurry to get to the ethnography on India. A common attitude among students is that his introduction is at best unoriginal and at worst irrelevant. The charitable opinion is that Dumont is simply establishing his intellectual legitimacy in a French lineage which includes Rousseau, Durkheim, and de Tocqueville. The uncharitable opinion is that his introduction is an unnecessarily long-winded discourse on the philosophical relationship between the individual and society which says nothing new and is a tiresome distraction from the central issue—the study of caste in India. As for professional anthropologists who do not specialize on India, they seem in general to be overwhelmed by the complexity of caste, and leave it well alone.

Homo Hierarchicus, it must be said, is a genuine attempt to bridge the chasm between the specialists and others. However, unless one comes to terms with Dumont's opening salvo about the underlying premises of comparative sociology, the rest of his argument about caste will never fully make sense. Dumont's initial approach may be summed up in the following four propositions which are related in such a way that each makes sense only in terms of the others:[4]

[3] There are many similarities between Dumont's project and Weber's: see e.g. D. N. Gellner (1982; 1988).

[4] These summary propositions are my own distillations of Dumont's argument. The exact quotations will be produced in the course of the argument.

(a) Traditional society is holistic: modern society is individualistic.
(b) Because we (moderns) are individualistic, we always perceive hierarchy in terms of inequality: traditional society perceives hierarchy in terms of holism.
(c) 'The principle of hierarchy is the *attribution* of a rank to each element in relation to the whole' (Dumont 1980: 91; emphasis in original)—this is what 'holism' means.
(d) In order to understand traditional society, we must transcend our individualistic ideology and embrace the holistic vision. Comparative sociology (anthropology) is impossible without this transcendence.[5]

In the modern West, Dumont argues, inequality is generally perceived as 'exploitation', or 'discrimination', or 'segregation': it is unjust, morally indefensible. This perceived injustice provides us with our primary motivation to explain inequality wherever we find it. It also produces a tendency in sociological theory to reduce ideology to more material factors. Thus ideology (or, to be precise, other people's ideology) is, more commonly than not, perceived as 'superstructure', or as a 'reflection' of some other more fundamental forces, or—the least charitable interpretation of all—as a 'fiction' which masks the 'real' organizational principles of society.[6] This view of ideology displays in full vigour that the modern mind is most of the time as parochial as the traditional and is generally incapable of escaping its own introverted system of values.[7]

Dumont argues that any evaluation of caste divisions as

[5] Comparative sociology and anthropology are treated as synonyms by Dumont, a practice which will be followed in this book. Traditionally, there has been a difference in their frames of reference. In so far as sociology has concerned itself with modern industrial society, comparative sociology has, implicitly or explicitly, taken as its central problem the difference between modern society and traditional society. In so far as anthropology is the study of mankind, it has, implicitly or explicitly, taken as its central problem the difference between man and other forms of animal life. 'Comparative sociology' is actually a tautology since sociology is, by its very nature, comparative. However, since this is often not understood, the compound term will be retained to designate sociology which makes the comparative theme explicit.

[6] For an appraisal of this kind of reductionism, see Crone (1989: 137–43).

[7] See Dumont (1980: 3) 'Another way of remaining shut in on ourselves consists in assuming from the outset that ideas, beliefs and values—in a word, ideology—have a secondary place in social life, and can be explained by, or reduced to, other aspects of society.'

iniquitous is inappropriate because it introduces a concept of individualism which is foreign to the traditional Indian world-view.[8] The orientation of caste ideology is to the whole, not to the individual, and we cannot imperialistically impose our values on theirs. Traditional societies like caste India are, of course, hierarchical, but much more revealing is that they make a *virtue* out of being hierarchical. According to Dumont,

> Our task is to make possible the intellectual transition from one ideology to the other, and this we can do through the inclusion in our comparison of the non-ideological residue, which is revealed through comparison, and through comparison only. (Dumont 1977: 18)

In order to make this transition possible, we must know exactly how we are constrained by our own ideology: 'to isolate our ideology is a *sine qua non* for transcending it . . . otherwise we remain caught within it as our very medium of thought' (ibid.: 27). In other words, having isolated our ideology from others and having demonstrated that it is uniquely individualistic, we must somehow transcend it. The barrier to understanding other (holistic) ideologies is being caught within our own individualistic world-view, so that barrier must be raised.

Where and how does the holistic character of traditional society manifest itself? According to Dumont, one must look at values because: 'a certain consensus of values, a certain hierarchy of ideas, things and people is indispensable to social life' (Dumont 1980: 20). Holism and hierarchy are thus defined in terms of each other:

> So we shall define hierarchy as *the principle by which the elements of a whole are ranked in relation to the whole*, it being understood that in the majority of societies it is religion which provides the view of the whole, and that the ranking will thus be religious in nature. (ibid.: 66, emphasis in original)

In other words, in order to understand any particular traditional society, one must understand its system of values in the holistic fashion that this system is conceived by the people themselves.

Dumont is not saying that traditional societies are holistic, full stop: that Western society is individualistic, full stop. What he is arguing is that the two types of society differ in their ultimate

[8] Here one might cite in particular the work of Berreman: see his (1979) *Caste and Other Inequities: Essays on Inequality*.

values. In the final analysis, traditional ideology places the highest moral value on the idea of society: modern ideology places the highest moral value on the idea of the individual.[9]

The Distinctiveness of Caste

Let us now move on from these opening considerations of Dumont's on the way in which we must proceed in order to understand traditional society in general. Using the particular example of caste India, he shows how this approach is to be implemented. To the initial four propositions, which deal with the nature and method of sociological inquiry, can now be added two further propositions which distinguish the Indian case. These are:

(e) The principle of hierarchy in 'the caste system' is the opposition of the pure and the impure: 'superiority and superior purity are identical: it is in this sense that, ideologically, distinction of purity is the foundation of status' (Dumont 1980: 56).[10]

(f) 'The fundamental characteristic of the caste system for comparison [is] the hierarchical disjunction between status and power' (ibid.: 232).

Let us take each of these principles in turn.

The principle of hierarchy in 'the caste system' is the opposition of the pure and the impure. Dumont begins by recalling the three essential characteristics of 'the caste system' set out by Celestin Bouglé in his book *Essais sur le régime des castes* (first published in 1908). These features are separation, interdependence, and hierarchy: *separation* in matters of marriage and contact, whether direct or indirect; *interdependence* such that each group has in theory, or by tradition, a profession from which its members can depart only within certain limits: *hierarchy* which ranks the groups as relatively superior or inferior to one another.

[9] In *From Mandeville to Marx* (1977) (the French edition was more revealingly entitled *Homo Aequalis*), Dumont maps out the progress of the transition from traditional to modern ideology through the eyes of the philosophers and economic historians who first became aware of it. The argument is, of course, extremely problematic—see e.g. Macfarlane's (1978) hypothesis on the prevalence of individualism in pre-modern England.

[10] As noted in Ch. 1, it is more accurate to speak of the *varṇa* system (singular) and caste system*s* (plural).

Building on Bouglé, Dumont insists that these three principles are reducible to a 'single true principle'—namely, the opposition of the pure and the impure. He explicitly states that the fundamental opposition of pure and impure is not the *cause* of all the distinctions of caste, but rather that it is their *form* (1980: 45). It is the idiom through which Hindus understand their own society:

I do not claim that the opposition between pure and impure is the 'foundation' of society except in the intellectual sense of the term: it is by implicit reference to this opposition that the society of castes appears consistent and rational to those who live in it. In my opinion that fact is central, nothing more. (ibid.: 44)

But is it merely a question of form? A few pages later, Dumont would appear to say something rather different: 'The opposition of pure and impure appears to us the very principle of hierarchy, to such a degree that it merges with the opposition of superior and inferior: moreover it also *governs* separation' (ibid.: 59; emphasis mine). Here it would seem that the opposition of pure and impure is not simply the way in which caste is rationalized, internalized by those who practise it; it is the way in which caste is *shaped*. It is not simply that people understand their relations with others in terms of relative purity; they *act* in accordance with that understanding. But Dumont's point about causality here has a different emphasis: while the oppositional principle of pure and impure is ideologically pre-eminent, the existence of this principle itself depends on something else. It depends on what he calls the disjunction between status and power and he is undoutedly correct to claim that: 'It is, as always, the relation between the ideological and empirical aspects which is at stake' (ibid.: 45).

The fundamental characteristic of the caste system for comparison is the hierarchical disjunction between status and power. This is really the central issue in Dumont's theory of caste, and the most hotly contested. According to Dumont, the opposition between pure and impure is sustained by the disjunction between ritual status and secular power which characterizes Hindu society. His argument is this: within 'the caste system' there are two competing sources of authority—the spiritual authority of the Brāhmaṇs, and the temporal authority of the kings (more prosaically, the power-holders or, at the local level, the politically dominant caste). In the ideology of caste, he argues, temporal authority is subordinated to, encompassed by, spiritual authority.

Dumont claims that this disjunction of power and status is *implicit* in the hierarchical opposition of pure and impure: 'Thus in the theory of the varnas one finds that status and power are differentiated, just as the general consideration of hierarchy seemed to require' (ibid.: 72). And again, 'the existence of the theory of the pure and the impure presupposes at least the relationship established in the varnas between priesthood and royalty' (ibid.: 74). This formulation, that the disjunction of status and power is *required* by the opposition of pure and impure, allows Dumont to fend off those who claim that much of the evidence about caste suggests otherwise. He himself agrees that the observable facts do indeed contradict the theory: 'In theory, power is ultimately subordinate to priesthood, whereas in fact priesthood submits to power' (ibid.: 71–2). There is, he says, a 'confrontation of ideology with observation' (ibid.: 77). But he has no doubt as to where one should stand on this confrontation:

> first we shall be concerned with the ideology, which easily accounts for the overall framework; secondly, finding the concrete factor, power, in the 'middle zone', a factor not immediately accounted for by the theory of purity, we shall consider it in its turn. (ibid.: 76)

If the observable facts can be brushed aside so easily in this manner, what exactly is the empirical content of Dumont's claim? His position on the disjunction between power and status is set out most clearly in an earlier article entitled 'The Conception of Kingship in Ancient India', which is reprinted as an appendix in *Homo Hierarchicus*.[11] The first point made here is that in most of the traditional societies where kingship is found, it has a magico-religious character as well as a political character. In the later Vedic texts known as the Brāhmaṇas, however, 'the Brahmans' were claiming that they had a monopoly over the entire realm of religion—that is, not only over the performance of ritual, but over the entire domain of moral and spiritual values.[12] As a corollary of this, those who were politically powerful—in shorthand, the

[11] Dumont (1962), and reprinted in Dumont (1970) and Dumont (1980).

[12] Dumont (1980: 67, 72). I have put 'the Brahmans' in inverted commas because this label confuses two very different concepts which must always be separated if one is to understand caste—*varṇa*, i.e. function (*brāhmaṇ*), and *jāti*, i.e. caste or kinship group (Brāhmaṇ). It would be pedantic to include inverted commas every time Dumont uses this expression. Instead I will simply omit the diacritics, as Dumont does, whenever I want to show that the usage is his. The distinction between Brāhmaṇ and *brāhmaṇ* is discussed fully in Ch. 4.

kings—were to have no brief whatsoever in the matter of moral values; they were to confine themselves to purely secular affairs: 'the king has lost his religious prerogatives . . . power in India became secular at a very early date' (ibid.: 71, 76).

Dumont's theory of caste is an attempt to answer one question: how and why do Brahmans enjoy a monopoly on the religious domain? Or conversely, why is it that those who are politically and economically powerful allow them to enjoy this privilege? Historically and conceptually, this alleged monopoly is the basis of what Dumont considers the essential feature of the caste system—the disjunction between status and power. To answer how and why this state of affairs came about, he proposes a theory, one which seems to fit with the evidence he produces but, much more importantly perhaps, one which fits very nicely with his general theory of the nature of traditional society. It is a kind of contract theory and it is beautifully simple.

Somewhere in Indian history, Dumont argues (it is not clear exactly when but it must be before the texts called the Brāhmaṇas were written, since in these it is presented as a *fait accompli*), the Aryan kings made a contract with their priests, the Brahmans. Thenceforth Brahmans would not only do as before—namely, perform fire sacrifices to the gods and recite the long ritualistic formulae for which they were famous—but would assume exclusive responsibility for the entire 'magico-religious' domain:

> the hierarchical disjunction in question has seemed to us to provide an explanation, a causal one in this case, of many of the system's features. The decisive step in its historical establishment was probably when the Brahmans were attributed the monopoly of religious functions as against the king. (ibid.: 213)

But why should the kings be so magnanimous? Why should they happily relinquish control over the religious domain when this is, on Dumont's theory, superior to and encompassing of temporal power?

Dumont's answer is that in return for their religious monopoly, three things were to be expected of the Brahmans. The first was that they would guarantee the spiritual welfare of their political masters. They were to serve as personal priests (*purohita*) and perform sacrifices on behalf of their political patrons (*yajamāna*). The second condition of the Brahmanic monopoly was that priests and kings conjointly would stand above the rest of society. While the Brahmans, as religious specialists, would naturally consider themselves religiously superior, the kings insisted on being accorded second place in the social hierarchy. In submitting to priesthood, says Dumont, royalty shares in it (ibid.: 72). The king *must* be given second place or 'his dignity and the usefulness of his function' would be denied altogether (ibid.: 77).

The third condition was that the priests would guarantee the transcendental purity of values (Sanskrit: *dharma*). By making the magico-religious function the unique preserve of a specialized class (the Brahmans), whose sole duty in life was to protect and glorify it, *dharma* (duty, order, morality) could be seen to stand unequivocally apart from the treacherously impermanent world of *artha*—instrumentality, wheeling and dealing, profit and loss, conquest and subordination. The Brahmanic guardianship of the religious domain would render it permanent, transcendent, the ultimate source of unquestionable authority.[13]

The fact that there are many different Brāhmaṇ castes which are associated with different traditional functions and do not intermarry is a problem which is not broached by Dumont in any detail.[14] For him, the essential feature to note is that the Brahmanic status, in general, is the fount of the hierarchical principle of purity–impurity. More precisely, this principle springs from the contrast between Brahmans and Untouchables:

> It is generally agreed that the opposition is manifested in some macroscopic form in the contrast between the two extreme categories: Brahmans and Untouchables. The Brahmans, being in principle priests, occupy the supreme rank with respect to the whole set of castes. (ibid.: 47)

The rest of humanity is not, of course, one undivided mass. It has already been pointed out that the kings, the politically powerful, should stand together with the Brahmans above the rest of society. Since the priests ultimately depend on the material support of their patrons, these patrons are accorded second rank in the hierarchy.

[13] Hinduism, of course, has no Bible or Koran, nor had it any Prophet or Son of God, to provide 'The Truth'. Instead there is a multitude of texts from which one can find justification for just about any philosophy one chooses—including atheism and anti-casteism. In a sense, it is misleading to speak of Hinduism as a single religion at all—see e.g. Potter (1989).

[14] See e.g. Dumont (1980: 356–7, fn. 24 f.).

Other ranks in the society are divided according to the hierarchical principle of purity and impurity—with impurity being defined by Dumont as the irruption of the natural world into the social world and the contamination of the latter by the former. Those who deal professionally with natural, impure substances—e.g. faeces, dead bodies, menstrual blood, cut hair etc.—are designated the lowest position: 'the elementary and universal foundation of impurity is in the organic aspects of human life and from this the impurity of certain specialists (washerman, barber . . .) is directly derived' (ibid.: 55). It is axiomatic for Dumont's theory that the rest of society—those who are neither specialists in purity nor specialists in impurity—can be ranked along the pure–impure axis which has Brahmans at one end and Untouchables at the other: 'Note that so far superiority and superior purity are identical; it is in this sense that, ideologically, distinction of purity is the foundation of status' (ibid.: 56). The actual criteria of purity are, however, various—for example tolerance of widow remarriage, or diet (which can always be manipulated to set one's own group apart)—and this quickly generates a complicated system of ranked groups. Using whichever criteria are to its own advantage, each group can find others who are inferior. The process of differentiation is potentially capable of infinite extension and refraction.

Status, Power, and Encompassment

Dumont's theory of caste has certain virtues. It is simple, elegant, and internally consistent. It also accords with certain ancient Hindu texts and Dumont believes this gives it historical authenticity. He maintains that it explains the feature of caste society which outsiders find most problematic—the fact that those who are the most powerful politically and economically do not necessarily enjoy the highest status, while those who do enjoy the highest status (the Brahmans) may be poor and have little political clout.

For Dumont, the distinguishing feature of caste society is that status is superior to, and encompasses, power. What does Dumont mean by 'encompassment'?

As the mantle of Our Lady of Mercy shelters sinners of every kind in its voluminous folds, so the hierarchy of purity cloaks, among other differences, its own contrary. Here we have an example of the complementarity between that which encompasses and that which is encompassed, a complementarity which may seem a contradiction to the observer. (ibid.: 78)

The underlying idea here can be interpreted as a restatement of Durkheim's central argument in *The Elementary Forms of the Religious Life* (1915): in order for society to be possible, there must be some shared system of values, a *conscience collective*. This is a universal necessity of human society, an *a priori* sociological truth.

In our society, Dumont says, the encompassing nature of individualism inevitably leads us to conceptualize social relations in terms of that which most threatens our individualistic values—namely political and economic power. This is because inequalities of power habitually, inexorably, establish inequalities of status—that is, differences in the relative values of individuals. For us moderns, whatever the historical reasons for the emergence of our ideology, such relative evaluation of individuals has become increasingly unacceptable. Our obsession with inequalities of wealth and power stems directly from our obsession with equality of status.

India, and traditional society generally, argues Dumont, has a quite different obsession. It is not concerned with maintaining an equality of status among individuals; it is concerned with maintaining itself. The idea of society (of holism) is more highly valued than the idea of individualism because individualism is of the essence schismatic. In caste society, says Dumont, what gives 'the system' its rationale, what provides an overall, encompassing framework for ordering all social relations, is the opposition of the pure and the impure: '*The whole is founded on the necessary and hierarchical coexistence of the two opposites*. One could speak of a "synthetic *a priori*" opposition' (ibid.: 43; emphasis in original).[15]

The Structuralist Interpretation of Caste

So far I have given the skeleton of Dumont's theory of caste, his theory of traditional society, and the philosophy of sociological

[15] There is a more abstract formulation of the notions of hierarchy and encompassment in Dumont's (1980) 'Postface' to *Homo Hierarchicus* (pp. 239–45). See also N. J. Allen's (1985) discussion.

knowledge on which these are premised. There is one further aspect of his study of India which must be considered and this is his methodological approach. Having determined the true nature and function of caste, what prescriptions does Dumont give for investigating it? His answer is that one must look at caste in structuralist terms, that is, in terms of relations, and the logic of those relations. One must be especially careful not to 'substantialize' caste, to conceptualize 'the caste system' as an aggregate of so many 'castes' divided into so many 'sub-castes'. This, argues Dumont, is a 'substantialist fallacy': caste does not work like this. The argument can be summarized in a seventh, and final, proposition:

(g) The structure of the caste system is to be found in the relations between the elements, not in the 'substantialist' nature of the elements themselves.

My own view is that this structuralist approach to caste is as uniquely penetrating as it is poorly understood.[16] Indeed my subsequent argument will be that Dumont does not fully understand its consequences himself and that the rest of his theory actually weakens the structuralist interpretation he advocates. First, however, it is necessary to elaborate a little on what Dumont means by structuralism.

> in the middle region [of 'the caste system'] in particular it is often difficult to rank one of two given castes absolutely in relation to the other. Happily, things change if one considers the principles whereby the castes are ranked in a more or less exact order. Underlying this order is found a system of oppositions, a structure . . . We shall speak of structure exclusively in this case, when the interdependence of the elements of a system is so great that they disappear without residue if an inventory is made of the relations between them: a system of relations, in short, not a system of elements. (Dumont 1980: 39–40)

There is, then, no general agreement on the order of castes, but everyone felicitously agrees that there ought to be *some* order.[17] So what is the *principle* which underlies that belief? That principle, says Dumont, is the oppositional idiom in which differences of

[16] As Dumont acknowledges (1980: 41), his structuralist interpretation owes a great deal to Evans-Pritchard's (1940) study of the segmentary nature of Nuer kinship and political organization.

[17] Note the implication that all castes *must* be ranked in a more or less exact order. This is something I will dispute later.

status are expressed—namely, purity and impurity. It is this simple opposition which structures relations between all 'castes'. Because of the fact that there is a 'multiplicity of concrete criteria' for evaluating purity and impurity, it is not always clear who is higher and who is lower but the principle itself is indisputable (ibid.: 57).

This raises an immediate problem. I have pointed out what Dumont calls the 'substantialist fallacy'—namely, the tendency to consider 'castes' as concrete, discrete groups. Yet, in the preceding argument, Dumont appears to be doing precisely the same thing himself: '. . . the principles whereby *the castes* are ranked in a more or less exact order' (emphasis mine). The question of whether or not castes are real 'substantial' groups is never fully clarified by Dumont—which is unfortunate because a great deal depends on the resolution of this problem.

On the one hand, Dumont wants to dismiss the common dichotomy of caste and sub-caste by insisting that this is always a relative matter. Among others, he cites in admiration Ketkar, Blunt, O'Malley, Ghurye, and Mayer[18] in support of the structuralist idea that there is no privileged level at which groups called castes exist:

> it is useless to claim to make a choice of level in order to define the 'real group' . . . seen from the outside, from the overall point of view or from that of another caste, it is the caste which appears; seen from the inside, it is segmented at least into subcastes and, in practice, into territorial fragments of the subcaste. The diverse characteristics of the caste are not borne by a 'group' at a unique level but by groups at different levels of segmentation. (ibid.: 63)

It is only our modern empiricism, he argues, which propels us to seek out and find bounded units—things with 'substance'.

What we ought to be looking for, Dumont insists, are the underlying principles which are not dependent on context—for structure, not substance:

> Substantially, we reduce everything to a single plane of consideration: the individual man, or the nation, or the caste. Structurally, the caste appears in certain situations and disappears in others in favour of larger or smaller entities. Here there is not, as in our universe of the individual, a privileged level. In particular, we shall see that the various properties of caste are attached to different levels of the phenomenon. (ibid.: 42)

[18] Ketkar 1909; Blunt 1931; O'Malley 1932; Ghurye 1932, 1950; Mayer 1960.

What exactly any particular group looks like is something which Dumont does not go into in any detail. Indeed he makes a virtue out of this, insisting that one must distinguish 'between theory and practice, between ideology and that which is yielded by observation, without sacrificing one to the other' (ibid.: 64).

As we have seen, however, Dumont is not entirely consistent in his exhortation to avoid the substantialization of castes. The need to confront the facts presented in various census and ethnographic reports raises the problem of what to call the various groups which they identify as castes and sub-castes. In a rather convoluted footnote, Dumont first implicitly endorses the use of the terms 'caste' and 'subcaste', then says that the 'real group' is something else, something which is produced (it is not clear how) by 'the territorial factor':

> We can agree with Mayer [1960] in saying, roughly, that relations within the village are relations between different castes (except for relations within the local group of the subcaste, which are agnatic relations in this case), whereas relations within the caste are always relations within the subcaste (except for rare relations between different subcastes of the same caste), and unite people from several villages. In one passage (p. 9) Mayer, interpreting Blunt, seems to say that caste and subcaste, having different attributes, are groups of different kinds. Actually these attributes, some external, the others internal, are complementary. I would rather say that there are not two groups, but that the 'real group' which some have sought to discover is constituted by the complicated configuration of the 'caste', the 'subcaste' (etc.), as qualified by the territorial factor. I am not a member of two different groups, I am a member of one complex group which has different aspects and functions at different levels. (ibid.: 361, fn. 26d)

That the complex question of the constitution of 'real groups' is never settled by Dumont should not be taken as an oversight: the 'territorial factor', as he calls it, is an 'empirical' fact and, as such, is secondary. For Dumont, the study of caste is the study of ideology and here 'the ideology ignores territory as such' (ibid.: 154).

The question of the sense in which bounded, substantial 'castes' can be said to exist or not, and under which circumstances, will be discussed again later.[19] For the moment, we may note only that

[19] See Ch. 5 below.

Dumont has made a singularly important contribution to our understanding of the principle of caste in insisting on its quintessentially relational nature. It is the difficulty of defining what a caste is in isolation, of establishing its boundaries, which leads Dumont to look at the system as a whole, and the way in which this system is structured. This is a crucial advance on the majority of rival explanations.

Dumont's View of Empiricism

Either power must be accommodated within the theory of caste, as here, or else the theory of caste must be brought under the notion of power and 'politico-economic' relations . . . It is a matter of approach: at the empirical level, territory effectively encompasses the castes, as will be recalled shortly; at the conceptual level, representations or ideas encompass what is not directly represented, as we have tried to make clear. The fact remains that the empirical approach is a misconstruction of Indian civilization: it amounts to assimilating *dharma* to *artha* . . . (Dumont 1980: 388, fn. 71a)

What exactly does Dumont mean in this quotation? Who is he chastising and what sin have they committed? He is chastising those who see caste as an ideological distortion, a ritual idiom which obscures the 'real' forces which shape society—those of power and economics (it being agreed by both sides to the dispute that in traditional India political power and economic superiority are effectively the same thing, a question of control over land). His argument is that this reductionism on the part of the economic determinists (those who assimilate *dharma* to *artha*) is specious because of the disjunction of status and power. The fact that Brahmans are everywhere superior in status though often materially dependent makes nonsense of the theory that status follows on from power and can therefore be explained in terms of it.

As an illustration of the position he is attacking, Dumont quotes F. G. Bailey who argues that there is a general correspondence between wealth and political power on the one hand and caste ranking on the other:

But the correlation is not perfect, since at each end of the scale there is a *peculiar rigidity* in the system of caste . . . in between these two extremes, ritual rank tends to follow their economic rank in the village community. (Bailey 1957: 266–7, quoted in Dumont 1980: 76; emphasis added by Dumont)

Dumont pours scorn on Bailey's characterization of the rigidity of the poles as 'peculiar'. On the contrary, he argues, it is the very feature of caste which encapsulates the logic of the whole system. This can only be grasped, he insists, by focusing on ideology rather than concrete manifestations of power because 'by keeping to the level of power, one is prevented from understanding the essential characteristic of the Indian system. This characteristic is the subordination of power' (Dumont 1980: 76).

'[At] the empirical level, territory effectively encompasses the castes . . .'. Here, Dumont is taking a slightly different swipe at the purveyors of *Realpolitik*. When one looks at caste on the ground, what one sees is a number of groups of different status who interact in a more or less restricted locality. Not very far away, the configuration may be slightly different: some groups may be missing, others present; some of the groups may have a different status in one locality than in another; groups with the same ritual function may be known by different names and/or refuse to recognize each other as status equals; perhaps they will even speak different languages or perform their rituals differently; they may have different forms of dress, jewellery, or architecture. In a society where the vast majority are peasants, local affiliations are extremely important.

Dumont does not at all deny the significance of the variations in social organization according to territory. The way that caste is articulated in one territory may not be (is frequently not) exactly the same as in another. But this is, for him, simply a matter of empirical variation. The underlying *principle*, the opposition of the pure and the impure, is the invariable structuring basis of caste society. The solution to understanding caste, he insists, cannot be found by looking at any particular local hierarchy. It is the very *idea* of hierarchy which is the fundamental unitary theme. In other traditional societies this may be expressed in a variety of ways: in Hindu society, argues Dumont, hierarchy is always at bottom expressed in terms of purity and impurity. This opposition encompasses rival expressions of hierarchy such as those phrased in terms of inequalities of power.

Dumont's Critique of His Critics

Dumont's theory of caste has been attacked from so many different directions that it is difficult to know where to begin—except perhaps with the observation that not one single criticism has caused him to alter his perspective. He has gone to great lengths to clear up misunderstandings of his theory but one is never left with the impression that he is trying to wriggle out of an earlier position. Dumont is convinced that he is right, that his critics generally only half-understand what he is saying and that their alternative explanations of caste are at best partial and at worst completely beside the point.

Dumont believes that his theory of caste has two advantages over its rivals. The first is that it is consistent. The second is its explanatory power: if some facts appear to contradict the theory, this is only because one has not grasped the underlying principle. Dumont has not only been consistent about his own theory; he has been consistent in his view of the alternatives on offer.[20] Totally undisturbed by his critics, Dumont's evaluation of them in the preface to the 1980 edition of *Homo Hierarchicus* is very similar to the sentiments he expressed more than twenty years earlier when the book was first published. Then, reviewing the contributions of others who had had carried out intensive fieldwork in the sub-continent since 1945, he remarked:

> . . . direct observation does not put an end to views which are Westernistic, atomistic, materialistic, behaviouristic, and which lead, for example, to the confusion between caste and racism . . . [The] chief manifestations [of this] are: the reduction of the religious to the non-religious; the tendency to take the part for the whole, either *the* caste instead of the system, or one aspect (separation *or* hierarchy) instead of all the aspects together; finally and especially at this time, the under-estimation or the reduction of *hierarchy*, the failure to consider it or the incapacity to understand it . . . this is the stumbling block, the main

[20] Some idea of the range of disputes spawned by Dumont's work can be gleaned from two sets of collected papers: *Journal of Asian Studies* (1976, XXXV, No. 4) and T. N. Madan *et al.* (1971). See also Dumont (1980: 340, fn. 6) for a further list and the 1980 preface of *Homo Hierarchicus* for his own evaluation of his critics.

obstacle to the understanding of the caste system. (Dumont 1980: 32; emphasis in original)

Without denying the validity of this criticism, I will argue in the following chapter that Dumont's own approach to caste produces an equally obstructive stumbling block.

3
The Problem with Dumont's Solution

Why the Problem is not Simply about Caste

THE argument in this chapter will be that Dumont has misunderstood the relationship between status and power in Hindu society. From the viewpoint of Brahmanic ideology, these are indeed necessarily disjoined; from the viewpoint of comparative sociology, however, they are necessarily *conjoined*. Dumont's error springs from one misconception concerning the nature of comparative sociology and another concerning the nature of power. This is clear from the very introduction to *Homo Hierarchicus*.

Dumont may be correct that the alternatives to his theory, both before and since, are at best partial explanations. But his own partiality produces a more intractable difficulty: it prevents him from considering evidence which appears to contradict his theory and thus, naturally, from considering alternative explanations of that evidence.

In Dumont's eyes, certain elements of his theory are empirically demonstrable (e.g. that the ideology is pre-eminently articulated in terms of purity–impurity), while the theory as a whole appears to be perfectly consistent. Thus any elements of his theory which are not demonstrably true should, nevertheless, be true by extension. This is Dumont's last line of defence from which, to his own satisfaction at least, he effectively disarms his critics. Contradictory evidence—for example, that power does not in fact submit to status—is always explained away as an obscuration of the 'true' underlying principle.

The first objection one might make to this argument is that theories which have no *possible* counter-examples can only be vacuous.[1] While there has been immense debate among philo-

[1] Karl Popper's *Conjectures and Refutations* (1963) is often regarded as the seminal work on this issue. See also E. Gellner's *Legitimation of Belief* (1974).

sophers of science about the criteria of testability, the idea that a hypothesis must at least *in principle* have a counter-example is incontrovertible. This is purely a question of formal procedure. However powerful Dumont's theory may appear, it is methodologically indefensible.

If Dumont had not been so influential, one might be tempted to abandon further consideration of his theory of caste at this point. Whatever its methodological deficiencies, however, the theory appeals to many anthropologists of South Asia because it seems to capture the way in which Hindus themselves often represent caste through concepts of purity and pollution. Moreover, it does so in a fashion which is highly consistent.

It is the very quest for ideological consistency which is, I believe, Dumont's downfall. The version of caste values which he presents is *too* consistent, much more consistent, it should be said, than the versions which Hindus themselves normally present.[2] It amounts to an idealized statement of priestly values and, because it is idealized, it leaves a great deal unexplained.[3] It does not explain, for example, how it is possible to go against priestly concepts of purity while still upholding the practices and institutions which underpin caste organization. (The high ritual position of 'impure' dominant castes is the most obvious illustration of this.) Nor can it cope with the fact that certain versions of Brahmanism stress renunciation at the expense of caste.[4] The existence of caste among non-Hindu groups is yet another problem.[5]

It is not that these are areas which are outside Dumont's frame of reference; on the contrary, he systematically considers all of them in turn. It is rather that his approach forbids him from seeing caste other than through the eyes of the Brāhmaṇ priest. I will first try to show why this is so and then examine the implications of his approach for the relationship between status and power in traditional Indian society.

[2] Some illustrations of these inconsistencies are given in Ch. 4.

[3] Berreman (1979: 155–63) makes this point forcefully.

[4] See also Ch. 4 where I will argue that the equation of caste ideology with Brahmanic ideology is impossible to defend. Dumont is not, of course, the only one to make this equation.

[5] Without leaving South Asia, one might think of the Muslim Swat Pathans in Pakistan (see Barth 1959, 1960; Dumont 1980: ch. X) and the Buddhist Newars of Nepal (see Toffin 1984).

The Sociological Bridge between Traditional and Modern Societies

Dumont is undoubtedly correct in saying that modern society places a historically unique premium on the individual. However, while he initially distinguishes between the fact of modern individualism and the sociological (holistic) explanation of that fact, he then conflates the two, thus causing irreparable damage to his argument.

Dumont (1980: 5) characterizes the holistic approach of sociology as the 'sociological apperception'—and claims that anyone who does not grasp this will likely be reading *Homo Hierarchicus* in vain (ibid.: 8). This apperception, he argues, is inextricably and uniquely a product of the modern world. Its roots, however, are elsewhere: 'while sociology as such is found in egalitarian society, while it is immersed in it, while it even expresses it—in a sense to be seen—it has its roots in something *quite different*: the apperception of the social nature of man' (ibid.: 5; emphasis added). This apperception, he argues, has been especially prominent in the work of his French predecessors, Durkheim and Mauss.

My contention, starkly phrased, is that while Dumont states precisely what the 'sociological apperception' is, and the conditions under which it develops into the discipline of sociology (the same conditions which give rise to modern individualism), the implications he draws out are completely misleading. The first hint of this has already been given in the italicized words 'quite different' in the preceding quotation. What he means is elaborated on at the end of the second section of his introduction to *Homo Hierarchicus*. There is a nice irony here when Dumont accurately paraphrases Durkheim and then immediately turns his essential argument upside down. From this point on, the reader who possesses the 'sociological apperception' will find *Homo Hierarchicus* rather puzzling:

> As Durkheim said, roughly, our own society obliges us to be free. As opposed to modern society, traditional societies, which know nothing of equality and liberty as values, which know nothing, in short, of the individual, have basically a collective idea of man, and our (residual) apperception of man as a social being is the sole link which unites us to them, and is the only angle from which we can come to understand them.

This apperception is therefore the starting-point of any comparative sociology. (ibid.: 8)

There are a number of problems here. The first is that there is no shortage of historical examples of oppressed peoples in traditional societies seeking to liberate themselves from their oppression and employing ideology as one means among others to this end. Efforts to improve one's caste status or to escape from the constraints of caste altogether are illustrations of this in India, and the literature is full of examples. The phenomenon of status emulation dubbed 'Sanskritization' by Srinivas (1956) was noted earlier by Hutton: 'By organization and propaganda a caste can change its name and in the course of time get a new one accepted, and by altering its canons of behaviour in the matter of diet and marriage can increase the estimation in which it is held' (Hutton 1963 [1946]: 98). The rejection of caste can be seen in early Buddhism and Jainism, medieval mass conversions to Islam and Sikhism, more recent conversions to Christianity and the adoption of communism, and in the plethora of renunciatory sects scattered throughout India.[6]

It is not traditional societies which know nothing of equality and liberty, but ideologies, whether traditional or modern, which claim to have a unique blueprint for social order and prescribe repression for those who would choose a different path. To some extent this is true of every ideology, a fact which creates an insoluble dilemma for modern liberalism. Even the most extreme form of individualism necessarily subordinates the individual to the collectivity. This, after all, is the whole point of ideologies—to regulate individual behaviour for the common good. In any case, while the individual may be uniquely highly valued in the modern, industrial world, and while there may be increasing antagonism towards all holistic belief systems, the rise of nationalism is powerful evidence that the issue is far from resolved.[7]

All ideologies, however, including those which are convinced of their benignity, seem invariably to be challenged by systems of belief which promise the individual an alternative, and express this alternative in terms of enhanced dignity or status. This is always

[6] For brief characterizations of South Asia's main religious movements and suggestions for further reading, see Robinson (ed.) (1989). On renunciatory groups, see e.g. Burghart (1983).

[7] See esp. E. Gellner's *Nations and Nationalism* (1983).

galling to fundamentalists but it is a fact of life that every society produces alternative manifestos for promoting political harmony and the moral good. And this fact is as transparent in India's history as it is elsewhere.

It is Dumont's characterization of the sociological apperception as 'residual' which leads him into difficulty on this question. Durkheim's point was that the development of this apperception was *not* residual: it was new, uniquely new, a product of the modern condition, of our ideological freedom.[8] Normally, traditional man so took his social condition for granted that he was incapable of seeing it; to see it one must be able to imagine an alternative, and this alternative was precisely what was missing in the pre-modern world.

If exceptions to this rule occasionally occurred, they were indeed exceptional. The work of the fourteenth-century Islamic scholar Ibn Khaldun is perhaps the most outstanding example. But what was not in general possible (and in many places still is not possible) was the institutionalization of the sociological apperception—the generalized recognition that the agnostic claims of professional sociologists (historians, anthropologists, etc.) have greater legitimacy when it comes to explaining social formations than any interpretation which depends on faith or dogma. This is not a residual phenomenon; historically it is very recent.

It is probably true that one of the main motivations behind a great deal of sociological and anthropological inquiry is a sense of profound discomfort with inequalities, both in our own society and in others. Dumont argues that looking at India in terms of inequality is inappropriately individualistic, but the motivation to explain inequality and the nature of that explanation are analytically separate. Proper sociological explanation makes no value claims with regard to the relation between the individual and society.[9] It is holistic in the sense that explanation requires putting

[8] See e.g. Lukes (1975: 66–85).

[9] There are problems here with various 'critical' sociologies/anthropologies—Marxist, feminist, or whatever. I would argue that such aspirant sociologies are incapable of incorporating a genuinely comparative perspective. They have a built-in self-legitimating prejudice which prevents them from throwing their own ideology into relief. Recent attempts to construct an 'ethnosociology' of India (Marriott 1989) or an 'Islamic anthropology' (Ahmed 1986) are similarly doomed. The whole point about sociology and anthropology is that they cannot be qualified; to do so is to compromise their legitimacy.

things in context, in relation to the whole: it is taken as axiomatic that social institutions never exist in isolation. But genuine sociological explanation makes no *a priori* assumptions (nor 'synthetic *a priori*' assumptions) about the precise mechanisms through which institutions actually are connected in particular societies at particular times. This is a matter of observation and record.

The essence of sociological method is comparison—comparison of social constraints and historical conditions. Social anthropology is, as Dumont points out (1980: 7), the discipline which has taken the comparative perspective furthest, and in so doing demonstrated the uniqueness of modern society. The first premise of anthropology is that knowledge of other societies, including knowledge of their ideologies, is not only possible but valid. Another way of saying this is that knowledge of other societies is not relative, that is, it does not depend, indeed must not depend, on understanding other societies through their ideologies alone.[10]

The main difficulty with Dumont's prescription for transcending modern individualism is that it leads inevitably to relativism. Effectively he sets up an opposition between two possibilities which he sees as the only possibilities—the modern, individualistic view and the traditional, holistic view. By rejecting the former, he has no alternative but to adopt the latter. The traditional holistic perspective is, however, fundamentally incompatible with the *sociological* holistic perspective. Far from underwriting the theory and methods of comparative sociology (anthropology), Dumont denies the very possibility of comparison, whatever his aspirations to the contrary.

Dumont is led into this position by joining his characterization of sociology as a residual apperception of the traditional holistic perspective to his characterization of society as a hierarchy of values: 'To adopt a value is to introduce hierarchy, and a certain consensus of values, a certain hierarchy of ideas, things and people, is indispensable to social life' (Dumont 1980: 20). It is no doubt true that a harmonious society only endures when those who live in it at some level share certain basic values. The trouble is that societies of any complexity are rarely, if ever, harmonious. Dumont's contention that one can meaningfully characterize

[10] A range of arguments, for and against relativism, can be found in two collections—Wilson, ed. (1970) and Hollis and Lukes, eds. (1982).

Hindu society, or even 'the caste system', in terms of a consensus of values is extremely problematic.

At most one might agree that the underlying orientation of traditional India is holistic, that is, anti-individualistic, though even this raises enormous difficulties. But to invest this holistic orientation with any particular content, such as the Brahmanic opposition between pure and impure, and claim that this is the predominant feature of Hindu culture to which everyone subscribes, immediately raises the problem that one can find innumerable instances where this ideology is quite flagrantly flouted or ignored.

In the end, Dumont's explanation of caste merely substitutes one set of values (individualism, secular equality) with another (conformism, priestly hierarchy). Yet Hinduism and Brahmanism have always been characterized by ideological pluralism, an endless tendency to produce schismatic, oppositional movements.[11] Many of these movements are hostile to the ascendancy of the priest.[12] While Dumont is censorious towards Western individualism because he sees it as *the* obstacle to grasping the holistic character of traditional society, he is extraordinarily benign not just to traditional ideology in general but to one particular ideology (a version of Brahmanism which makes the priest supreme) at the expense of its rivals. It is this selective benignity which damns relativism above all else.

Power and Legitimacy

Let us now turn to Dumont's two central propositions regarding caste: the opposition of purity and impurity, and the disjunction of status and power.

For Dumont, as we have seen, the opposition of the pure and the impure is the principle of hierarchy in 'the caste system'. As it stands, this formulation is problematic because the opposition of pure and impure is a universal feature of human societies. The

[11] Derrett has made the same criticism of British administrators: 'It will be insufficient to proceed as the British, misled by medieval jurists' tendentious reliance on mīmāṃsā techniques, often did, viz. pretending that the sages spoke with one voice, when there were, in fact, a great many unresolved alternatives' (Derrett 1973*a*: 36).

[12] The following chapter gives some illustrations of this.

reason for this has been brilliantly explored by Mary Douglas in her book *Purity and Danger* (1970), and it is regrettable that she did not exploit her own insight further when she wrote the introduction to the first English-language translation of *Homo Hierarchicus* (Dumont 1972). Had she followed her own theory of liminality and pollution, Douglas might have come closer to the nature of caste divisions.

Douglas's insight, derived from the seminal work of Durkheim and Mauss (1963), is that ideas of purity are essentially about boundary maintenance and are found in all systems of classification. Whatever threatens cognitive categories is inherently dangerous and must somehow be controlled: anything which is anomalous, which crosses classificatory divisions. Similarly, anything which threatens to unmask man's image of himself as 'socially pure', of standing above nature, must be controlled: the ingestion of food (a natural substance, at least before the chemical industry took over), bodily emissions, sickness, decay, and finally death itself—the most dangerous transition of all from man's social state to whatever lies beyond.

All societies exhibit elaborate rules and taboos with respect to those processes which most threaten our social 'purity' by demonstrating our natural 'impurity'. That which is impure, which most clearly identifies us with nature, must be circumscribed, ritualized, avoided, or propitiated—whichever strategy renders it less dangerous. The point here is that since the preoccupation with purity is in some sense a human universal, it cannot be used, as it stands, to explain a particular case such as caste India:

> . . . the idiom of purity is only too well known to us. It is liable to dominate our transactions with one another whenever other kinds of social distinction, based on authority and wealth, are not clear. Purity and impurity are principles of evaluation and separation. The purer must be kept uncontaminated by the less pure. (Douglas 1972: 16)

Thus far, the same applies to caste society.

Unfortunately Douglas follows Dumont from this point on, though her rather literal interpretation would, one suspects, leave the French anthropologist a little uneasy:

> In India the idiom of purity is used whenever the organic erupts into the social domain and particularly when ingestion of food is concerned. Demarcation, ranking and the separation of organic life from the social,

that is enough to give a complete system of occupational ranking. Any occupation which deals more directly with organic processes is ranked lower than one which deals with them less directly, and all are lower than priesthood which by definition is concerned with the spiritual. (ibid.)

Dumont does indeed say that in caste ideology 'impurity corresponds to the organic aspect of man' and that the Hindu proscription of impurity 'in fact sets up an opposition between religious and social man on the one hand, and nature on the other' (Dumont 1980: 50–1). But he argues, as was pointed out in the previous chapter, that the opposition of pure and impure is not itself the *cause* of 'the caste system'. It is the way in which social relations are pre-eminently understood and articulated.

Of course people act in accordance with the way in which they understand their relations with others, so in this sense the opposition of pure and impure regenerates and sustains those relations. But the fact that this principle is predominant ultimately depends, he claims, on the disjunction of status and power which he believes to be the unique feature of Hindu India. It is this disjunction which is the pivot of his theory of caste; it is also, I believe, completely misleading.

Why is this so? In the first place, the disjunction is a feature of Brahmanic ideology and not of caste organization. In the second place, the disjunction between power and authority (which is what is really at issue here) is a feature of all ideologies; it is not at all peculiar to caste. Finally, Dumont's concept of power is too ambiguous to be useful as a tool of sociological analysis, simultaneously legitimate (in relation to force or dominance) and illegitimate (in relation to religious authority). I will very briefly consider each of these three problems.

(i) In order to save the idea that there is an *ideological* disjunction between status and power, Dumont's proposition ought to be reformulated along the following lines:

Brahmanism defines this-worldly interest (*artha*), which kings represent, as morally subordinate to the divine order (*dharma*), which *brāhmans* represent.

Brahmanism, of course, presents its own values as 'the truth'—unchallengeable, timeless, transcending the vagaries of the 'real' world. The authority of its values must be seen to rest on something other than either simple domination or the whimsical pronouncements of any particular religious specialist. And they must, in some way, appear to be self-evidently the *only* legitimate values.

But what Brahmanism represents as divine, unalterable truth, sociological comparison quickly demonstrates to be contingent on a peculiar conjunction of factors thrown up by particular historical conditions. What Brahmanism cannot do (because to do so would be to deny its own legitimacy) is to explain what those conditions are, and why caste is not timeless as the ideology of Brahmanical purity would have us believe. Any adequate explanation of caste must go beyond its unconditional Brahmanical validation.

(ii) There is nothing peculiarly Hindu about the philosophical subordination of power to status. On the contrary, this is an inescapable feature of all ideologies: means are subordinate to ends, instrumental action is subordinate to ultimate values, might is subordinate to right.[13] The opposition of power and authority is the first principle of legitimation. Power must always submit to status (the hierarchy of values) if it is to become recognized as legitimate—that is, as authority and not mere coercion.[14]

As a matter of sociological observation, however—and in contrast to philosophical self-legitimation—status (authority) and power are not opposed or disjoined. There can, of course, be power without authority but it is always, as Weber and history have taught us, unstable. There cannot, on the other hand, be status (authority) without power. The very concept of authority is premised on the idea that there is some relation of unequal power which would be problematic if not legitimated. One might summarize this by saying that the ideological disjunction of status and power derives from their sociological conjunction.

If this is always the case, as I believe it is, then the disjunction between status and power cannot possibly be the crucial distinguishing feature of caste society.

(iii) These problems with Dumont's theory of caste stem from his definition of power:

> It is exclusively political power that is in question, the political domain being defined as 'the monopoly of legitimate force within a given territory'. Power is thus legitimate force . . . It has the advantage of

[13] I would dispute Dumont's assertion (1980: 303) that the equivalence of ends and means with *dharma* and *artha* respectively is misplaced.

[14] The classic text on this is Max Weber's *Economy and Society* (1968).

corresponding quite well to Indian notions: power is roughly the Vedic *kṣatra*, the principle of the Kshatriya varna (literally 'the people of the empire'); it is force made legitimate by being subordinated to the *brahman* and the Brahmans. (Dumont 1980: 153)

In other words, 'power', as used by Dumont here, is assimilated to 'temporal authority'.[15]

Dumont's prime concern is to distinguish temporal authority from spiritual authority, as they are distinguished in the texts called the Brāhmaṇas. This is not simply an academic matter of faithfully recapitulating ancient Indian philosophy. It is the absolute distinction established in the Brāhmaṇas between the authority of the priest and the authority of the ruler which is, Dumont believes, the fundamental characteristic of the caste system.

A point which must be emphasized in connection with the varnas is the conceptual relationship between Brahman and Kshatriya. This was established at an early date and is still operative today. It is a matter of an absolute distinction between priesthood and royalty. Comparatively speaking, the king has lost his religious prerogatives: he does not sacrifice, he has sacrifices performed. In theory, power is ultimately subordinate to priesthood, whereas in fact priesthood submits to power. Status and power, and consequently spiritual authority and temporal authority, are absolutely distinguished. The texts called the Brahmanas tell us this with extreme clarity, and whatever has been said to the contrary notwithstanding, this relationship has never ceased to obtain and still does. (ibid.: 71–2)

This is an extremely revealing paragraph. What exactly does Dumont mean in saying that the relationship between spiritual authority and temporal authority 'has never ceased to obtain and still does'? Does he mean that this has always been the case in principle or in practice, or both? If priesthood 'in fact' submits to power, then in what sense are the two distinguished?

Dumont's difficulties spring from the fact that while he sometimes uses power as a synonym for *legitimate* force, at other times he equates power with dominance pure and simple. Criticizing others who use terms such as 'secular status' and 'ritual dominance', he argues that status and dominance should be absolutely distinguished to refer respectively to the religious

[15] In the original French text the word used is *pouvoir*, which is distinguished from *force* (1980: 74).

sphere and the political sphere. Note well that here he seems unsure about whether this applies only to the *varṇa*s or to castes as well: 'We prefer to maintain a fundamental distinction between the two [i.e. status and dominance], a distinction which, as we have seen, is built into the theory of the varnas itself, *if not into the theory of the castes*' (ibid.: 162; emphasis added). If not into the theory of the castes? The footnote which accompanies this baffling statement confuses the issue still further.

> The extension of the term 'dominance' to the religious level seems even less defensible than the extension of 'status' to the non-religious level. Whereas on the present view it is absolutely necessary to distinguish clearly, in the very terminology, between these two levels, we have noted that in certain conditions power surreptitiously becomes the equal of status. In such cases one could speak of indirect or derivative status (where the authors under discussion say 'secular status'), and say for example (previous note) that dominance entails a certain superiority of derivative status. (ibid.: 392, fn. 74g)

My suspicion is that this failure of plain language reveals a certain conceptual confusion. Now we have three positions: 'theoretically' power submits to status; 'in fact' status submits to power; 'in certain conditions' power 'surreptitiously' becomes the equal of status.

What exactly are the conditions in which power 'surreptitiously' becomes the equal of status? The example which Dumont gives appears to indicate that it is whenever a question of caste must be adjudicated on.

> When, in a village, members of a dominated or dependent caste come to ask a notable of the dominant caste to settle a difference, they recognize his authority as arbiter or judge. Thus we pass here from power to authority. If force becomes legitimate by submitting to Brahmanic ideals, and thus becomes power, then as can be seen from our example, power is invested with judicial authority by those subjected to it. Thus acknowledged, and in some way internalized by its subjects, power becomes equal, in a specific sphere, to authority *par excellence*, i.e. religious authority: just as the Brahmans have authority in religious matters, so the dominants have authority in judicial matters. (ibid.: 167)

In practice, then, it would seem that in everyday caste affairs power is *always* equal to authority and there is nothing surreptitious about it at all.

The reason for this confusion is straightforward enough.

Dominance and authority are quite different, and to try to get round this by defining power as 'legitimate force' is to introduce an ambiguity which raises more problems than it solves. It is because Dumont attempts to accommodate a particular Brahmanic version of *its* authority that he ends up in this position. He is left claiming that power is authority in relation to force but something less than authority in relation to authority *par excellence*. *Kṣatra* does indeed have the same ambiguous quality as power. *Kṣatra* is ambiguous for the same reason that power or temporal authority is always ambiguous—because it is the legitimation of something which ultimately defies legitimation. The legitimation of coercion has to be ambiguous or it would not succeed.

Dumont is right that the realms of *dharma* and *artha* are absolutely opposed, as the qualities *brahman* and *kṣatra* are. And he is right that ideologically *artha* must be subordinate to *dharma*: this-worldly self-interest cannot be its own justification. What is obfuscated by Dumont is that temporal authority *is* authority and not mere dominance. From the viewpoint of any particular ideology, political rule can be either legitimate or coercive. If it is legitimate, it is because it submits to the transcendent authority of that ideology. It is always the case that when rule is not legitimated by transcendent values it is regarded as coercion. There is nothing unique about Hinduism in this respect.

There are three mistakes in Dumont's approach to these matters. The first is to write as if one particular ideology is the truly representative one of Hinduism. The second is to suggest that power has a morality of its own. While power may have an amoral dynamic of its own, it cannot have an independent morality. This would be a contradiction in terms. The third mistake is to claim that the priest's authority is somehow transcendent. The priest can *claim* that his authority is transcendent but in fact it depends on his position in a structure and, in particular, on his relation to the king or dominant caste. The priest *derives* his authority from this relation just as the king derives his authority from it also. One might parody Dumont by saying that authority is an attribute of relations between different functions rather than a substantial entity.

European interpretations of traditional India have always tended to assume that caste is a product of priestly values of purity and impurity. What Dumont has done is to take this assumption as a premise and build a systematic theory around it. It is the systemic nature of his argument, its internal coherence, which gives his theory its appeal rather than any external fit with observable reality. Everyone can find facts which the theory does not fit, even Dumont himself. The problem is that his theory is so consistent internally that it is difficult to see what a *systematic* alternative explanation might look like.

Some of what Dumont says is manifestly true—anyone who is familiar with Hindu culture will immediately point to the preoccupation with purity and pollution. All over the sub-continent the connection between caste membership and purity is repeated. The connection is made by Brāhmaṇ and non-Brāhmaṇ alike and often by those who are not even nominally Hindu—Muslims, Christians, Buddhists, and members of various sects, some sober, some ecstatic, but all of them somehow opposed to 'conventional' Brahmanism.

If, as many believe, Dumont has misrepresented the character of Hindu India, how can one say this without accusing all Brāhmaṇs of deliberately distorting the truth and without accusing everyone else of being gullible enough to go along with their fabrication? This would be an extraordinary claim. But it would be even more fantastic if Dumont were right. According to him, caste is the uniquely Indian expression of a pure form of hierarchy in which the values of the king, of politics, are subordinated to the purer values of the priest which alone reflect the social whole.

If this were so, we would have to credit Brāhmaṇs with singular powers of imagination and persuasion: the imagination to conjure up the disjunction between status and power which is alleged to be peculiar to Hindu India, and the ability not only to achieve consensus about this among themselves but to persuade the rest of society into meekly accepting a fabrication which made them subordinate to their priests. And all this over a vast land mass with hugely varied ethnic populations and over a timespan of more than two millennia. Ultimately Dumont's theory fails because its initial premise is implausible.

Structuralism

Dumont's structuralist method remains to be considered. In one sense, his proposition that the logic of caste is entirely relational should be endorsed wholeheartedly. This is because any attempt to give a general definition of what castes *are* runs into insuperable difficulties. As was seen earlier, however, Dumont was not entirely successful in his attempt to do away with castes altogether and nor, indeed, has anyone else been. There are good reasons for this and much of Chapter 5 will be given over to this problem.

Dumont's particular difficulties with the nature of caste affiliation stem from his systematic misrepresentation of the fact that being a Brāhmaṇ by caste does not imply being a priest, or being related to priests, even if the local ideology sees things this way. This misunderstanding might have been avoided had he respected his own interdictions against conceiving of the caste system in terms of 'substantial' entities—in his case, of turning purity into a priestly substance.

There is at least some excuse for regarding castes as substantial entities because there are situations when the boundaries of caste membership are relatively well defined. There is no excuse at all, however, for substantializing purity. By making purity a priestly substance, something which priests have, Dumont demonstrates that he has simultaneously misunderstood the connection between caste and ritual functions and the connection between caste and kinship. Purity is a relational concept, not a substance. Purity is the absence of impurity and this is an entirely relative matter—in any culture. The question is: what is impurity relative to?

In order to answer this question, it is necessary to go back to the beginning. We have, however, made progress because we know that Dumont's solution to the problem of caste cannot be the correct one. His solution, which at first sight seems so coherent and impressive, in fact merely hides the real problems under a series of circular propositions which preclude reference to the actual, lived world of caste. We are back to the beginning, but not quite. One option has now been removed since the equation of caste with Brahmanic ideology does not hold. The problem can thus be phrased in a different way. If caste organization cannot be explained in terms of Brahmanic ideology, how is it to be explained?

4

The Pure Brāhmaṇ and the Impure Priest

The Ideal *Brāhmaṇ* in the Real World

THIS chapter will consider the claim that Brāhmaṇs stand at the top of the caste hierarchy because of their purity. This is much more problematic than Dumont and others would have us believe because at least six different Brahmanic personae, with dramatically conflicting characteristics, manifest themselves in the Hindu world. On a scale of decreasing ethereality they may be presented as follows:

(1) The Brāhmaṇ as renouncer	divorced from the social world
(2) The Brāhmaṇ as spiritual preceptor	minimally tied to the social world
(3) The Brāhmaṇ who is not a *brāhmaṇ* (see text below)	in the social world but unconnected with priestly activity or renunciation
(4) The Brāhmaṇ as personal priest	intermediary between powerful patrons and the gods
(5) The Brāhmaṇ as temple priest	intermediary between the masses and the gods
(6) The Brāhmaṇ as death priest	intermediary between this world and the forces of decay and destruction

Note again the distinction between upper and lower case (and here also the use of italics) to distinguish caste (Brāhmaṇ) from profession or function (*brāhmaṇ*; Sanskrit: *brāhmaṇa*).[1] Note also

A slightly different version of this chapter was published in French in the journal *Recherches Sociologiques* (1992).

[1] See also Ch. 2. This is exactly the same distinction as one finds in English between Smith (family name) and smith (profession). In the same way that Smiths, more often than not, are not smiths, Brāhmaṇs, more often than not, are not *brāhmaṇs*. And just as there may be no proof that today's Smiths were ever smiths

the choice of words 'on a scale of decreasing ethereality'. Whether or not one considers this to be a hierarchical scale, it is certainly not an unambiguous hierarchy. Renouncers are very often considered to be superior to priests, both by themselves and by others. But priests often assert the reverse, while different kinds of priests compete for status among themselves. Similarly, priestly Brāhmaṇs and Brāhmaṇs who perform secular occupations also often claim superiority over each other.

The starting point for discussing these contesting claims is a difference of opinion between Dumont and Heesterman about the nature of the 'ideal' Brāhmaṇ. In fact it is often not at all clear whether these authors mean the ideal Brāhmaṇ, or the ideal *brāhmaṇ*. Dumont most often seems to mean the ideal Brāhmaṇ; Heesterman most often seems to mean the ideal *brāhmaṇ*. In both cases, however, what is always implied, when not stated explicitly, is that Brāhmaṇs (i.e. members of Brāhmaṇ castes) enjoy their exalted status in the caste hierarchy because of their association, real or imagined, with the ideal *brāhmaṇ*. This equation of Brāhmaṇ with *brāhmaṇ* quickly leads to confusion, as the following discussion will show. In order to demonstrate the problem, I will follow the argument of both Dumont and Heesterman indicating clearly when caste is meant (Brāhmaṇ) or when profession or function is meant (*brāhmaṇ*), or whether both are meant at the same time.

As has already been made clear, Dumont's theory of caste rests on what he believes is the uniquely Indian disjunction of status and power. Essentially this is a theory of the supremacy of the Brāhmaṇ caste, and for Dumont this is synonymous with the supremacy of the priest over his political lord or king. In general, while some anthropologists (though remarkably few) have been rather uneasy about the alleged Hindu disjunction of status and power, the supremacy of the Brāhmaṇ is seldom doubted. The proposition that Brāhmaṇs are the highest caste is the first thing most people learn about caste, and few regard it as contentious.

We can call Dumont's explanation of the Brāhmaṇ's superiority

or related to smiths, there may be no proof that today's Brāhmaṇs were ever *brāhmaṇs* or related to *brāhmaṇs*. Conversely, an English smith need not, of course, be a Smith. The question of whether a *brāhmaṇ* is automatically a Brāhmaṇ is the central question of this chapter. See also the discussion of Hocart's position on this question in Ch. 6 below.

the priest's version: 'The Brahmans, being in principle priests, occupy the supreme rank with respect to the whole set of castes' (Dumont 1980: 47). Dumont is, of course, well aware that not all caste members follow their alleged hereditary profession and he explains this discrepancy by arguing that:

> the link between caste and profession is primarily a matter of status, that the important thing is the hereditary profession provided it is not contradicted by following too inferior a profession, and that the system has probably always carried with it some plasticity of this sort, whilst the village specialities, ritual or other, constitute its solid core. (ibid.: 97)

In any case, Brāhmaṇs must be in the social world of caste because it is primarily in relation to them (as priests) that the axial principle of purity–impurity derives its meaning: 'The Brahmans, as priests superior to all other men, are settled in the world comfortably enough' (ibid.: 273). In belonging to the social world, to the hierarchy of castes, the Brāhmaṇ is thus opposed to the renouncer. The renouncer does not adhere to the values of caste and for this reason Dumont often refers to him as an 'individual-outside-the-world'.

Dumont does not deny, however, that the renouncer has a historically important role to play in informing and enriching Brahmanic thought:

> . . . the secret of Hinduism may be found in the dialogue between the renouncer and the man-in-the-world . . . In fact the man-in-the-world, and particularly the Brahman, is given the credit for ideas which he may have adopted but not invented. Such ideas are much more relevant and they clearly belong to the thought of the renouncer. Is it really too adventurous to say that the agent of development in Indian religion and speculation, the 'creator of values', has been the renouncer? The Brahman, as a scholar, has mainly preserved, aggregated, and combined; he may well have created and developed special branches of knowledge. Not only the founding of sects and their maintenance, but the major ideas, the 'inventions' are due to the renouncer whose unique position gave him a sort of monopoly for putting everything in question. (ibid.: 270, 275)

One might object that there is a certain amount of sophistry involved here. The renouncer is 'outside-the-world' yet his ideas have been the most significant in shaping Hinduism. Moreover, as Dumont acknowledges, the renouncer is tied to others by accepting alms and preaching (ibid.: 185). If he does not 'in fact' escape complementarity with others who are in the world, in what sense does he 'really' leave society?

Dumont anticipates this question by appealing to the values of caste:

The answer is simple: that this occurs must simply be stated as a fact, even if it means that in this case what agents imagine is more important than what the outside observer describes as really happening, that ideas are more important than behaviour. Moreover, the objection rests on a misunderstanding: to leave society is to renounce the existing role which one is given by society (as member of such-and-such a caste, father of a family, etc.) and to adopt a universal role which has no equivalent in the society; it does not involve ceasing to have any actual relationship with its members. Naturally enough, from the point of view of the sociologist the renouncer is *in* the society in the sense that society shapes his relationships as well as the others'; but the renouncer is a man who leaves his social role in order to adopt a role that is both universal and personal; this is the crucial fact, both from the subjective and the objective point of view. (ibid.: 185, emphasis in original)

Readers may judge for themselves whether this is a sophistic argument or not.

Fortunately, Heesterman's counter-argument does not rest on philosophical questions about the determination of who is to be included and who excluded in the explanation of sociological phenomena. It is instead a direct appeal to religious texts, to written evidence. Heesterman believes that these texts demonstrate that the picture of the Brāhmaṇ which Dumont presents is contradicted again and again by Brāhmaṇs themselves.

Heesterman's most celebrated article opens with the assertion that 'In Hindu society, the brahmin stands supreme' (Heesterman 1985: 26).[2] It has generally been assumed, he argues, that this pre-eminence derives from his priestly capacity and his monopoly over the performance of Vedic ritual. In fact, believes Heesterman, the source of his supremacy appears not to be priesthood but precisely the opposite—the abstention from priestly activity, or renunciation.

According to Heesterman, it is only by escaping from the transient and polluting affairs of the everyday social world that the ideal 'brahmin' manages to achieve a state of transcendent purity. Above all, he argues, the ideal 'brahmin' must not be a priest

[2] Originally published in 1964 in slightly different form.

because priestly activity is a source of degradation and *impurity*; in fact, priesthood is the quintessential source of impurity!

In order to demonstrate why this should be so, Heesterman draws a distinction between classical and pre-classical ritual:[3]

> In the classical system of ritual, as presented in the brāhmaṇas and the sūtras, the pivot of the ritual is the *yajamāna*, the patron at whose expense and for whose benefit the ritual is performed. He is supposed to incorporate the universe—he is identified with the cosmic man, Prajāpati. The ritual culminates in his ritual rebirth, which signifies the regeneration of the cosmos . . . the ritual is the domain of absolute purity; the brahmin ritual specialists are pure and the yajamāna has to undergo a purificatory ceremony, the *dīkṣā*, in order to be admitted to the ritual. (Heesterman 1985: 26–7)

In the older, pre-classical pattern, however, the *yajamāna* enters the ritual charged with impurity which he then transfers to the priest. In this case,

> The yajamāna, who has undergone the dīkṣā, is not pure, but on the contrary is charged with the evil of death to which he has to submit in order to be reborn . . . Being tainted by death, the dīkṣita has to divest himself of his impure self . . . By means of the various offerings and the gifts (*dakṣiṇā*) which represent the parts of his body, he disposes of his impure self. Thus he is reborn pure, 'out of the sacrifice.'
>
> In this light, the relationship between patron and officiant is of a nature diametrically opposed to what the classical theory of the pure ritual wants it to be. The function of the brahmin officiant is to take over the death impurity of the patron by eating from the offerings and by accepting the dakṣiṇās. (ibid.: 27)

The 'brahmin' of the pre-classical ritual and the 'brahmin' of the classical ritual are thus two very different personae. Heesterman sometimes refers to the transition from one to the other as the 'axial breakthrough' and it is clear that this transition is for him the beginning of caste. In the pre-classical situation, the 'brahmin' is a priest who performs a necessary (and necessarily perilous) function for a patron. In the classical situation, the 'brahmin' has escaped from his dangerous and degrading role; he is no longer a priest accepting the death impurity of his patron.[4]

[3] Heesterman normally only italicizes a Sanskrit word the first time he employs it: this will not always be obvious from these quotations.

[4] There is some ambiguity in Heesterman's account as to whether this escape applies to all 'brahmins' or merely to the 'brahman' (spelt with an 'a') who 'is

In the classical ritual, the patron (*yajamāna*) has already been purified. Acutely aware of the dangers inherent in accepting a patron's gifts and thereby his impurity, the 'brahmin' has made his sacrificial services 'superfluous' (ibid.: 39). Or, put another way, the patron has become his own priest with the result that death and impurity no longer circulate between the parties, in the words of Mauss quoted by Heesterman, as 'prestations totales de type agonistique' (ibid.: 31). The prototype of the self-contained sacrificer is the original cosmic man—Puruṣa—who sacrificed himself at the beginning of time and from whom the four *varṇa*s are supposed to emanate. He is the 'primordial sacrificer, victim and officiant' (ibid.: 39) on whom the classical *yajamāna* should model himself.

The 'brahmin' of the classical ritual can thus be seen in two ways which, in effect, amount to the same thing. On the one hand, he is a renouncer: he has renounced his priestly duty of sacrificing for powerful patrons, essentially of submitting to a ritual death in order that his patron might be reborn. On the other hand, he has interiorized the ritual—he sacrifices for no one but himself. If the *yajamāna* has become his own priest, the 'brahmin' has become his own *yajamāna*. The functions of *purohita* (domestic priest, literally 'he who stands in front') and *ṛtvij* (sacrificial officiant) have been dispensed with:

> The renouncer can turn his back on the world because he is emancipated from the relations which govern it. He is a world unto himself, or rather, he has resumed the oppositions of the world in himself; there is no duality for him anymore . . . He has resumed the sacrificial fires in himself, and so he is able to perform the ritual in himself and by himself. (ibid.: 39)

Not surprisingly, then, the Brāhmaṇ who continues to act as a *purohita* or *ṛtvij*—i.e. who performs rituals for others in exchange for payment or gifts—is viewed with some contempt:

> Service with a king is even ruled out for the proper brahmin. For the learned brahmin, the king is as great an abomination as ten brothels or even as the keeper of ten thousand slaughter houses . . . the purohita cannot be a proper brahmin because he is stuck in the sphere of

recognized as the most important of the officiants' and whose function 'is to redress the faults committed in the ritual' (1985: 27), rather than actually to perform the ritual. However, the implication seems to be that the 'brahman' epitomizes the ideal which all 'brahmins' should aspire to.

antithetical relations where he has to exchange his purity for the impurity of his patron. (ibid.: 38)

Thus the classical 'brahmin' has two choices and two only.[5] He can revert to the old pattern through which he perpetually absorbs the death pollution of others, or he can fuse with his patron. This second solution, as Heesterman notes, effectively means that if the 'brahmin' is not to compromise his purity, he can sacrifice only by and for himself or with other 'brahmins', and this indeed is the preferred solution for the ideal 'brahmin':

. . . the highest place in the hierarchy of sacrifices is taken up by the sacrifice 'without dakṣiṇā,' according to *Gopatha Brāhmaṇa* 1.5.7. Such sacrifices are the *sattras* of the classical ritual. In the sattra only brahmins participate. They unite their sacrificial fires and thus are actually assimilated with each other and are fused into one single unit. (ibid.)

On occasion, the 'brahmin' who performs rituals for others is not considered by the Brahmanical texts to be a real 'brahmin' at all but is seen as equal to a *kṣatriya* (ibid.).

But if the 'brahmin' cannot be a priest for others, who can? The answer, says Heesterman, is that priestly functions 'are more often than not fulfilled by non-brahmin castes, for instance, by the potter, or castes have their own ritual functionaries' (ibid.). Here the connections between sacrificial ritual, the removal of impurity, and caste begin to emerge: 'Death and impurity having been "assimilated away," the ritual has become the domain of absolute purity. The brahmin's world is a pure world and consequently his place in the hierarchy is the highest' (ibid.: 35). Since the 'brahmin' can no longer handle impurity, this must be dealt with by others:

The hierarchy, which originally was, in principle, rearticulated at the periodic agonistic ceremonies, now becomes permanently settled. Evil, impurity, does not circulate anymore between the parties but is fixed at the lower levels of the hierarchy. Disposal of impurity becomes a hereditary speciality. In other words, we touch here the principle of caste ideology. (ibid.)

We can now return to Heesterman's opening statement: 'In Hindu society, the brahmin stands supreme'. What is not clear in

[5] Heesterman suggests that there are three choices—antagonistic complementarity of patron and priest, fusion of the two, and interiorization of the ritual by the 'brahmin'. But, as he himself acknowledges, the third of these is simply the logical extension of the second.

this statement is whether he is referring to religious specialists or to any member of a Brāhmaṇ caste. This ambiguity is typified by the following kind of statement:

> In fact the brahmin when serving a patron must either relapse into the ancient system of exchange and reversal or become one with his patron. The latter solution, however, tends to render his relations with a patron outside the brahmin caste all but impossible. (ibid.: 38)

What he appears to be saying is that Brāhmaṇs (i.e. members of Brāhmaṇ castes) are superior not because they are priests, but because the ideal Brāhmaṇ is a renouncer and all Brāhmaṇs to some extent share in this whether or not they actually earn their livelihood as priests. The supremacy of the Brāhmaṇ is in spite of his association with priesthood, not because of it.[6] In my terms, Heesterman's pre-classical 'brahmin' is a *brāhmaṇ* (i.e. a priest) while his classical 'brahmin' is a Brāhmaṇ (i.e. a member of a Brāhmaṇ caste). A Brāhmaṇ may in fact sometimes be a *brāhmaṇ*, but *ideally* he should not be. The Brāhmaṇ who functions as a *brāhmaṇ* continually threatens his purity.

The real world is not, of course, organized to accommodate Brahmanical theorizing so conveniently. Most Brāhmaṇs cannot afford the luxury of abstaining from patronage; they are required to enter into relations with others in order to provide their daily bread, or rice. They are not necessarily constrained to work as priests and, in fact, they may well be constrained either by economic necessity or by ignorance of ritual procedures to choose some other livelihood.

For the moment, however, let us consider those Brāhmaṇs who are actually *brāhmaṇs*. Do they see their calling as inherently pure, as Dumont claims, or inherently polluting, as Heesterman claims? The answer, one will hardly be surprised to hear, is both. Precisely the same kinds of ambiguities emerge from recent ethnographic reports on priesthood in India as from Heesterman's interpretation of ancient texts. Contemporary Brāhmaṇs are also acutely aware of the perils of priesthood: this is not simply some archaic invention lost in Vedic scriptures, but very much a live issue.

Convincing ethnography on this subject comes from Parry, who has carried out extensive fieldwork among ritual specialists in Benares. Parry's pen is also aimed at Dumont's equation of

6 Parry (1980: 89), discussed below, comes to the same conclusion.

priesthood with purity. The truth of the matter, he says, is precisely the opposite:

> The priest's status is highly equivocal; and he is seen not so much as the acme of purity as an absorber of sin. Just as the low caste specialists remove the biological impurities of their patrons, so the Brahman priest removes their spiritual impurity by taking their sins upon himself through the act of accepting their gifts. (Parry 1980: 89)

While most of Parry's evidence is taken from the Mahābrāhmaṇ death priests, he emphasizes that his characterization of the tainted priest applies 'to the entire range of priestly occupations followed by the Brahmans of Benares' (ibid.).

Relating his Indian material to Marcel Mauss's celebrated essay (1970) on gift exchange, Parry insists that what degrades the Hindu priest is his acceptance of gifts and he cites Heesterman as an authoritative source: 'More specifically the gift is held to embody the sins of the donor, whom it rids of evil by transferring the dangerous and demeaning burden of death and impurity to the recipient (Heesterman 1964)' (Parry 1986: 459). It should first be pointed out that there is actually an interesting difference between Heesterman's analysis and Parry's, which illustrates Brahmanical attempts to minimize the degradation involved in accepting gifts. When Heesterman refers to gifts which pollute the recipient, he uses the word *dakṣiṇā*. Parry refers to these gifts by the word *dān* (Sanskrit: *dāna*) and cites other ethnographic reports to confirm this usage.[7]

One might first ask if they are actually talking about the same thing. It has frequently been reported that ritual payments to priests consist of two separate parts—*dāna* and *dakṣiṇā*. Malamoud, for example, writes of a 'différence entre le don, *dāna*, et la *dakṣiṇā* proprement dite' (1976: 169). He claims that, strictly speaking, *dāna* is a gift to the gods while *dakṣiṇā* is a payment to priests, and argues that both Heesterman and Gonda[8] fail to make this distinction. However, everyone seems to agree on the obligatory nature of the *dakṣiṇā*: the patron of the sacrifice is obliged to give it and the priest is obliged to accept it:

> Le sacrifice désire la *dakṣiṇā*, la *dakṣiṇā* comble le sacrifice. Malheur à qui célèbre un sacrifice sans payer de *dakṣiṇā* . . . c'est sur lui que retombe

[7] Principally Gloria Raheja's doctoral work—the reader should now refer to the book she has published since Parry's article was written (Raheja 1988*a*); this book is discussed below.

[8] See Gonda (1966).

tout le péché du monde . . . sans *dakṣiṇā*, le sacrifice est incomplet et qu'un sacrifice incomplet est un sacrifice nul. (Malamoud 1976: 164–5)

Given this sense of ritual obligation, Malamoud's contention that *dakṣiṇā* should be narrowly interpreted as a salary, 'un achat de service' (ibid.: 169), seems difficult to sustain.[9] From his own description, it is the *dakṣiṇā* which makes good the sacrifice and creates an inseparable bond between patron and priest. Heesterman makes this argument forcefully:

The function of the brahmin officiant is to take over the death impurity of the patron by eating from the offerings and by accepting the dakṣiṇās . . . the brahmin is not allowed to refuse the dakṣiṇā; indeed Manu 4,249 deprecates a brahmin who refuses a gift. (Heesterman 1985: 27)

If my understanding of Heesterman is correct, the concept of *dakṣiṇā* provides a particularly revealing link between classical and pre-classical ritual. *Dakṣiṇā* is the most significant vestige of the agonistic character of the pre-classical exchange of death for rebirth. Recognizing the dangers inherent in their acceptance, the *brāhmaṇ* 'does not accept the dakṣiṇās in a direct way but by "turning away" from them and assigning them to various deities' (ibid.: 37).

The receipt of *dakṣiṇā* is, then, simultaneously dangerous but obligatory. The only worthy recipient of the gift in the first place is someone who is ritually pure. But by accepting the gift, he defiles himself in relation to the giver. The sequence is as follows:

(1) the patron demeans himself by admitting that he has impurities which he must shed;
(2) he finds a worthy recipient on whom to dump his impurities;
(3) he demeans the recipient in so doing and simultaneously raises his own status above that of the recipient; at the moment of the ritual there is an exchange of statuses symbolically expressed in the exchange of 'gifts'.

It would appear that when a distinction is made between *dāna* and *dakṣiṇā*, one or the other is considered polluting, but not both. One idea seems to be that *dāna* is voluntary, a pure gift, and therefore its receipt does not compromise the officiating priest or, at any rate, he is not compromised any more than he has already been by taking the *dakṣiṇā*. If his patron is generous, all well and

[9] See also Good (1982).

good; if he is miserly, then this is also well and good. In any event, the good Brāhmaṇ stands aloof from considerations of material reward. One might say that the Brahmanic motto is 'poor but pure'. The generous patron, of course, establishes his nobility in the eyes of all but the important point is that he does not do so at the expense of the Brāhmaṇ, or so it is claimed. Another idea, more common in ethnographic accounts, is that *dāna* is polluting, while *dakṣiṇā* is simply a nominal payment on top.[10]

Often, however, it would appear that no distinction is made between *dāna* and *dakṣiṇā*. Both are seen as payments for ritual services and both imperil the recipient. Put another way, the distinction is either ignored or appears to be seen as an academic rationalization of the Brāhmaṇ to salve his own conscience and status. According to Malamoud's interpretation, the priest can accept his patron's *dāna* without risk because this is for the gods rather than for him. But in practice this claim seems to be viewed by many, including many Brāhmaṇs, as so much humbug.

The equation of priesthood with impurity is perhaps particularly pronounced for castes like the Mahābrāhmaṇs who are most prominently associated with the pollution of death. But in some sense every priest is tainted by death pollution whatever rationalization or obfuscation of this predicament Brāhmaṇs have conjured up through the ages:

> Most Mahabrahmans would like to abandon the priesthood. The fact that few, if any, of them will ever be able to do so is a product of material circumstances that force them to subordinate their scruples about the profession to the needs of their families. But the spiritual price they pay for their domesticity is high. Precisely this dilemma faces all the various groups of Brahman priestly specialists, for the acceptance of *dan*—the gifts made to the Brahman—is a perilous matter. To be sure, the *dan* associated with death is particularly noxious. But as every Benares Brahman would agree, all *dan* is debilitating . . . *I stress that my observations here relate to the whole range of priestly specialists represented in the city and not just to the Mahabrahmans*. (Parry 1980: 102; emphasis in original)

Lest it be thought that Parry has over-stated his case by taking as his main sample priests who specialize in death impurity, let me now turn to Fuller's study of temple priests in the Minakshi temple, Madurai, South India.

[10] See e.g. Fuller (1984: 66 ff.).

The Nāyaka dynasty which controlled Madurai collapsed in the early eighteenth century and the city then came under the intermittent control of various Muslim chieftains before the region fell to the English East India Company in 1801. While the British at first took an active interest in managing temple affairs, in 1833, 'the Company's Court of Directors in London, responding to pressure from Christian missionaries and their supporters, ordered the government in India to withdraw from its investment in religious institutions' (Fuller 1984: 12–13). This withdrawal was finally implemented in an act passed in 1863 through which temples were handed over to local management committees.

On many occasions—for example when *prasāda*[11] is distributed during festivals—the temple priests (known as Adiśaivas) have to take second place to the temple officials whom Fuller sees as fulfilling the traditional function of the king. The priests dispute this order, arguing that 'the Nāyaka kings were the last legitimate rulers and protectors of the Minakshi temple' (ibid.: 109–10).[12] According to them, neither the British nor the subsequent management committees can be regarded as rightful guardians of the temple. As Fuller points out, this invocation of a kingly past, which alone provides for a legitimate order and 'which provides a yardstick against which the present is judged defective, depends upon the premise that kingship is an essential element in the total structure within which gods and human society are situated' (ibid.: 135).

The question of who should precede whom in the social and moral order does not only arise in the relationship between the temple's priests and officials. The Adiśaiva priests regard themselves as superior to non-priestly Brāhmaṇs and, 'of course', to all other castes. Non-priestly Brāhmaṇs, however, regard themselves as superior to all priestly Brāhmaṇs whether these are temple priests or domestic priests. Monks and temple priests also claim superiority over each other, though popular opinion generally sides with the monks (ibid.: 59).

As regards the general populace, 'most non-Brahmans appear to be unaware of [n]or interested in ranking within the Brahman

[11] *Prasāda*: offerings made to a deity which are then redistributed to the devotees.

[12] See also Barth (1960: 140): 'Politically powerful Pakhtuns can denigrate the sacred status of Saints and claim rank equality with them; Saints on the other hand are adamant in their claim that all Saints *ipso facto* rank higher than all Pakhtuns.'

caste' though 'non-Brahmans (like many ordinary Brahmans) widely despise Brahman priests' (ibid.: 50). Temple priests are generally thought to be ignorant and incompetent; domestic priests are held to be grasping. In return, the priests have a 'generalised dislike of the devotees which is—in their own eyes—a natural reaction to the supposed fact that ordinary devotees collectively detest the priests' (ibid.: 131). Indeed 'the Brahmanhood of Adiśaivas (and other priestly groups) is sometimes denied' (ibid.: 64).

Fuller concludes with the observation that 'the notion that priestly Brahmans are relatively inferior is an ideological construct, which is no more logical, coherent or well-founded than its converse' (ibid.: 163). He does, however, clearly believe that priestly Brāhmaṇs *are* generally regarded as inferior and says that the concept of hierarchy which the temple priests have constructed, arrogating to themselves an exalted status, has not 'genuinely challenged the "orthodox", Brahmanical ideology underlying the caste system' (ibid.).

There is, then, he seems to believe, an 'orthodox' ideology underlying the caste system, though given all the competing claims to status to which he draws our attention, it is not exactly clear what this orthodoxy looks like. At one stage he endorses Heesterman's claim that ' "it is the ideal image of the brahmin that is the mainspring of brahminical prestige" (Heesterman 1964: 31, n. 52) and conversely is at the root of the Brahman priests' relative lack of it' (Fuller 1984: 64). But he concludes by saying that the explanation for the traditional inferiority imputed to priestly Brāhmaṇs 'has to be sought in the historical development of the relationship between priests and the more powerful non-priestly Brahmans' (ibid.: 163). He himself denies having the competence to undertake such an explanation.

If, on the basis of the writings of Heesterman, Parry, and Fuller, we were to construct a composite league table ranking various kinds of Brāhmaṇs in relation to one another, we would come up with the kind of order suggested at the beginning of this chapter. There seems to be a general agreement that the 'highest' Brāhmaṇs are those who do not perform priestly functions. Among these, the purest is often said not to belong to the ordinary world of social relations at all; he does not work for others and does not accept any form of reward. He is, in all senses, a renouncer. Then there is the Brāhmaṇ who functions as a spiritual guide but not as a sacrifical priest—he is often referred to as a *guru purohita*.

The status of Brāhmaṇs who have secular rather than spiritual occupations is a matter which we have to regard, for the moment, as *sub judice*. It would be impossible for all Brāhmaṇs to earn their livelihood as priests; there simply would not be enough patrons of means to go round. Traditionally, the majority of non-priestly Brāhmaṇs would have been (and perhaps still are) landowners and government servants. Today they cover a whole range of other, generally literate, professions—as doctors, lawyers, engineers, teachers, office staff, or whatever. Nowadays the occupation of priest is poorly paid and the better educated Brāhmaṇ will seek a more rewarding position. In any case, many Brāhmaṇs seem to believe that the occupation of priest has always been somewhat degrading and is best avoided if at all possible.

This brings us to those Brāhmaṇs who actually work as priests. Of these the 'highest' is generally regarded as the family priest (*purohita*) who performs sacrificial rituals for wealthy patrons to mark life-cycle events such as birth, caste initiation, and marriage. But in so doing, he is often said to absorb the 'impurity' of the patron which is embodied in the payments which the priest receives for his services. He is widely regarded as superior to the temple priest who effectively absorbs the pollution of all and sundry, or at least all who are admitted to the temple to make offerings to the gods. Then there is the funeral priest who absorbs the most dangerous pollution of all, that of death. But even this is not the lowest group because the funeral priests must have their own funeral priests (see Parry 1980: 91). And below them are the funeral priests to low castes who do not rate as Brāhmaṇs at all.

The association between priesthood and the absorption of perilous substances is found in north India and in south India, in cities and in villages (see below), in the earliest known literature on priesthood down to the most recent reports from the field. It applies to all priests whether they specialize in death ritual, temple ritual, or domestic ritual. It applies even to the king's priest; in fact some accounts state that this is the most dangerous occupation of all.

Priests and 'Others' as Vessels of Inauspiciousness

All of the accounts given so far ultimately explain the Brāhmaṇ's supremacy in terms of Brahmanical theorizing. Gloria Raheja, in her book *The Poison in the Gift* (1988*a*), the main findings of which are summarized in Raheja (1989), and in a tightly argued review article on caste, kingship, and dominance (1988*b*), adopts a very different perspective. In her eyes, the predominant model of intercaste relations is neither in terms of a hierarchy of purity and impurity, nor does it have as its conceptual pivot the Brāhmaṇ.[13] Instead she argues for the 'centrality' of the dominant caste, a centrality that was, in the pre-colonial period, assumed by the king and which was (and still is) enacted ritually as much as politically.

In order to see how she comes to this conclusion, it is necessary to know a little about the village of Pahansu, Uttar Pradesh, where she conducted extensive fieldwork. The dominant caste in Pahansu are the Gujars: they are one of fifteen castes in the village but comprise 55 per cent of all households and own 98 per cent of the land. The emphasis of Raheja's field research was on the nature of different kinds of prestations both between and within castes, with particular attention being given to those transactions in which Gujars were involved. (By 'prestation' is meant an exchange which might involve the transfer of either material goods or immaterial substances, particularly inauspiciousness, or both.)

Six castes depend almost entirely on shares of the Gujars' grain for their livelihood. Additionally, with one exception (the merchant Baniyas), all the other castes receive payments from the Gujars 'for the performance of various ritual services, mostly on the occasions of festivals, marriages, births and deaths' (Raheja 1988*a*: 19). These payments, which the other castes are *obliged* to accept, are known as *dān*. Not only do all these other castes receive *dān*; they all give it as well—either to other castes or to specific relatives. The relatives in question, who are again obliged to accept, are daughters and sisters who have been given away in marriage and their conjugal families.

Like women of other castes, married Gujar women also accept *dān* from their natal families. With one exception, however, Gujar

[13] For a hostile reaction to Raheja's relegation of the Brāhmaṇ, see Toffin (1990).

men never accept *dān* from anyone, not even from their wife-giving affines. The one exception is the gift of the virgin bride herself—*kanyā dān*. There are a number of fascinating issues buried here. More often than not, *kanyā dān* has been cited as the Indian exemplar of the 'pure gift' for which nothing may be taken in return: 'Not even a glass of water may be accepted [by the wife-givers] in a village to which one of the daughters of the lineage has been given in marriage' (Parry 1986: 461).[14] Raheja, however, suggests that *kanyā dān*, like all other forms of *dān*, is permeated with inauspiciousness and danger, and she provides convincing evidence that this danger is apparent to all concerned. Immediately following his acceptance of the bride, the husband makes a gift of *dān* to his own family priest 'to remove the faults caused by the acceptance of a wife' (Raheja 1988*a*: 136).

Several authors have noted that among hypergamous north Indian castes, where the ideology of *kanyā dān* is pronounced, the exchange of women sets up an inequality such that givers rank lower than receivers.[15] Moreover, the inequality is perpetuated over time, the wife-givers sending a one-way flow of prestations to their daughters' conjugal families. Raheja argues that this is not the case among Pahansu's Gujars. While they do conceive of affinal relations as being asymmetrical, they do not consider this asymmetry to be a hierarchical one: 'In affinal as in intercaste prestations, Gujars thus stress the ritual centrality of the giver of *dān* rather than his hierarchical position vis-à-vis the recipient' (ibid.: 121).[16]

According to Raheja, Gujars 'regard it as extremely significant' (ibid.: 20) that their men never accept forms of *dān* other than *kanyā dān* and believe it is this which, above all, expresses their dominant status *vis-à-vis* other castes. She goes to considerable lengths to argue that while other castes also give *dān*, the Gujars are the givers *par excellence* and that this fact is the linchpin of intercaste relationships:

In Pahansu, the centrality of the Gujars in the local configuration of castes, as well as their role as *jajmāns* of the village, is not simply an empirical fact of their dominance and landholding in the village and in the region, but is implicated in the ritual life of the village in ways that are

[14] See also Dumont (1980: 138).

[15] See esp. Vatuk (1975).

[16] The issues of hypergamy and affinal relations generally will be explored in greater detail in the following chapter.

only peripherally concerned with purity and impurity and a hierarchical ordering of castes. (ibid.: 28)

Indeed, in effect her argument is that political (and economic) institutions, such as dominant caste patronage or *jajmānī* relations, are *always* expressed in a ritual idiom. To divorce politics and ritual is to do damage to the way in which both are conceived—ritual is always political; politics are always ritualized: 'the organization of castes around the king or village-level *jajmān* is not simply a matter of political power but of the ritual maintenance of the ordered life of the realm' (Raheja 1988*b*: 504).

As she acknowledges, Raheja's view of caste relations owes much to McKim Marriott in so far as it emphasizes that these are generated by various kinds of transactions (Marriott 1959, 1965, 1968, 1976). However, her analysis differs from Marriott's in two related ways. The first is that she confines herself to what can be more or less directly observed whereas Marriott ultimately depends on questions about hypothetical situations posed during constructed interviews. The second, as noted already, is that she relegates the importance of hierarchy.

Marriott's analysis revolves around transactions between different castes in various media—food, water, women, services. The most significant of these media for the purposes of the present argument is *kaccā* food. Depending on the region, *kaccā* food refers to foods cooked in water—typically boiled rice, or breads cooked without oil or butter. In other words, it is the kind of food normally eaten every day with one's own immediate family, those who share the same kitchen. The acceptance of *kaccā* food from others is generally regarded as a matter requiring the utmost care.

According to Marriott, members of a dominant caste would accept *kaccā* food from Brāhmaṇs but Brāhmaṇs do not accept *kaccā* food from non-Brāhmaṇ dominant castes, nor indeed from anyone else. Similarly, Marriott argues, all other castes will accept *kaccā* food from those groups which they consider 'higher' but not from those they consider 'lower'. By taking all possible permutations into consideration, he then constructs a hierarchical transactional matrix. Brāhmaṇs are at the top because they accept *kaccā* food from no one else; other castes are ranked by 'adding up' their transactions, givers taking precedence over receivers.

Raheja counters this approach with the following pithy observation about the Gujar dominant caste in Pahansu: 'Theoretically, they say, they *could* accept *kaccā* food from a Brahman, but the most significant point is that they never accept anything at all from Brahmans' (1988*b*: 508; emphasis in original). Brāhmaṇs, on the other hand, accept a whole host of prestations from the Gujars, and not only from them. Raheja recalls a conversation with a Washerwoman who said: 'Just as Gujars do, we too give grain to our "workers" . . . to Barbers, to Brahmans, and to Sweepers' (1988*a*: 245). For many non-Gujars, Raheja says, 'the fact that their pattern of giving and receiving approximates, more or less closely, that of the Gujar *jajmān*s is of greater importance than their hierarchical position vis-à-vis other castes in the village' (ibid.).

Raheja's second disagreement with Marriott follows on from this observation on the difference between a hypothetical ordering of all castes and the actual way in which each caste constructs its relations with others through different kinds of transactions. In particular, she argues, Marriott's work 'does not focus at all on the extremely numerous individually named prestations through which the ritual centrality of the dominant caste is constituted' (ibid.). What Raheja seems to say is that while castes *can* be ranked in a hierarchical fashion, she herself found little evidence that they were normally represented in this way. Because of this, the most significant question is not (as the protagonists themselves maintained) whether such a hierarchy derives from actual and hypothetical transactions (Marriott) or from inherent attributions of purity and impurity (Dumont). The fact, insists Raheja, is that in most contexts hierarchy is not stressed at all. What is stressed is the institutional and conceptual centrality of the dominant caste, not the hierarchical superiority of the Brāhmaṇ.

Raheja's position depends on a distinction she and others have made between impurity on the one hand and inauspiciousness and evil on the other.[17] She argues that the crucial feature of impurity (e.g. that caused by birth, death, or menstruation) is that it cannot be removed through transferral to a recipient (ibid.: 46). It simply goes away after a specified time or is washed away by the individual concerned. In any case, it is not, as Dumont would have it, the pre-eminent idiom in which intercaste relations are expressed. This, apparently, is her reason for not discussing purity and pollution in any depth.

[17] See also Marglin and Carman (eds.) (1985) and Parry (1991).

The predominant representation of intercaste relations, she argues, is rather in terms of obligatory transfers of the cumulative inauspicious qualities—sin, evil, death—which are generated by *all* connections between individuals:

Inauspiciousness flows . . . through the 'connections of the body' . . . between persons, and when these connections are transformed (at birth) or attenuated and created anew (at marriage) inauspiciousness flows over, as it were, and must be channeled or removed. The inauspiciousness of death is largely a result of the dead person's continued existence as a disembodied *pret* . . . (ibid.: 147)

Inauspiciousness is moved on with the help of prestations, normally referred to as *dān*, and 'each type of inauspiciousness requires a particular ritual, a particular type of *dān*, and a particular recipient' (ibid.: 48). Recipients should normally be qualified to accept *dān* by being married (ibid.: 91–2) and there are certain times when the receipt of *dān* is avoided—for example during pregnancy or when a prospective donor is in a state of birth or death pollution—in order to avoid the accumulation of danger.

According to Raheja,

Gujars certainly do not see the giving of these prestations as a matter of hierarchical status; they give such prestations, in the course of a wedding, to the groom, to the Barber, to the Sweeper, and to the Brahman, and they do not interpret the gifts in terms of the relative superiority or inferiority of these recipients. It is, rather, the obligation of the recipients, as *pātra* [vessels], to accept these prestations for the well-being and auspiciousness of the *jajmān*, the family of the bride. (ibid.: 147)

Like Parry, Raheja states that the recipients of *dān* ' "digest" the sin, the evil, and the inauspiciousness of the *jajmān*, his household, and the village' (ibid.: 248). However, she contradicts Parry's claim that 'On an ideological level, the notion of *dan* puts all the stress on the merit and prestige to be derived from giving to superiors' (Parry 1979: 283). Here Parry is in agreement with Heesterman in suggesting that the reluctance of the Brāhmaṇ to accept *dān* stems from the belief that the ideal Brāhmaṇ should not do this if he wants to maintain his superiority. Similarly, Trautmann (1981: 287) has argued that the Brāhmaṇ is reluctant to accept the 'inferior essences' of the donor which are embodied in his gift.

Raheja insists that this kind of explanation is inadequate

because '*dān* is given, not only to Brahmans, but also to Barbers, to Sweepers, to Doms and Dakauts, to anyone who happens to pass by a crossroads, to one's married daughters and sisters and their husbands, and to many other recipients' (Raheja 1988*a*: 188). All of these groups are aware that the receipt of *dān* is dangerous because it involves the acceptance of the donor's inauspiciousness. Therefore, she says, the receipt of *dān* 'cannot simply be a matter of relative superiority and inferiority' (ibid.). A more plausible explanation lies in the fact that the main purpose behind *dān* prestations is to transfer inauspiciousness to those who are 'other', and others may equally be Brāhmaṇs or Barbers, married daughters or their husbands, or 'anyone who happens to pass by a crossroads'.

In Raheja's interpretation of caste, then,

> hierarchy is not the encompassing cultural value; rather it is one contextually stressed way of construing caste in the village, and it exists alongside the values of auspiciousness and inauspiciousness that are associated with the central–peripheral, 'royal' model of intercaste ritual relationships . . . And it is the central–peripheral model that is the most prominent in everyday village talk and in the prestation patterns that constitute the most significant aspect of intercaste relations. Caste is not necessarily or fundamentally about hierarchy in Pahansu. (1988*b*: 512)

To what extent a sense of hierarchy remains present in Pahansu is never made entirely clear. Raheja does not believe that a hierarchical ordering based on the opposition of purity and impurity is completely absent: 'As I began to see it wasn't that "centrality" had displaced hierarchy but that these were two contextually differentiated ways of constructing intercaste relationships and configurations of caste in the village . . .' (1988*a*: 32). Yet she produces only one context in which hierarchy, as she defines it, is manifested. This is in terms of transactions of food much along the same lines as Marriott proposed, although an important rider is added: in such situations the crucial question is 'Who did the cooking?' rather than 'Who is the donor?' because the preparation of food is seen in some sense to embody the qualities of the cook (ibid.: 241):

> hierarchical considerations generally prevent a Brahman from accepting *kaccā* food prepared by lower-caste cooks. In terms of a hierarchical order constructed from analysis of the media of such transactions, then, the

Brahman as 'optimal transactor' emerges as hierarchically superior to all other castes. (Raheja 1988*b*: 508)[18]

According to Raheja, when the members of a Gujar household want to make a prestation to a Brāhmaṇ which involves the preparation of a meal, they may present him with two options and are not concerned which of these he chooses. He may either accept *pakkā* food which they have prepared themselves,[19] or he can take the uncooked ingredients for a *kaccā* meal 'since hierarchical considerations generally prevent a Brahman from accepting prepared *kaccā* food from a Gujar cook' (1988*a*: 241). She continues with the observation that:

The hierarchical aspects of the relationship between Gujar and Brahman are thus evidenced in these acts of giving and receiving, but they tell us nothing of why the prestation had to be made to begin with; the donor–recipient relationship and the meaning of the prestation itself remain obscure if we attend only to the relative rank of the persons involved in the transaction, or to the media in which the prestation is made. (ibid.)

Alongside the other two models of intercaste relations—hierarchy and centrality—there is, says Raheja, a third which is repeatedly manifested in a different congeries of prestations under the umbrella rubric of 'mutuality'. Apart from *dān* prestations, which always involve the transfer of inauspiciousness, there are many other exchanges which do not carry this perilous load:

Dān is always given to those who are seen as 'other' (*dūsre*) precisely in order to 'move away' (*haṭānā*) the inauspiciousness afflicting the *jajmān*. Yet these same recipients are, in other contexts, said not to be 'other' but 'one's own people' (*apne ādmī*) and are given prestations that imply a mutuality of services rendered and payment received, or simply a 'sharing' that is deemed appropriate among 'one's own people' or 'tied together brothers' (*lagū-bandhū bhāī*) and 'sharers' (*hissedār*). (Raheja 1989: 88–9)

[18] See also 1988*a*: 240: 'When asked by the anthropologist about the giving and receiving of *pakkā* and *kaccā* foods and other media of this type, villagers responded that such considerations indicate "dispositions about high and low" (*ū̃c-nīc kā bhāv*) and "touching and not touching" (*chuāchūt*). In these contexts, the terminology reflects hierarchical distinctions of "high caste" (*ū̃cī jāti*) and "low caste" (*nīcī jāti*), or juxtaposes "big" castes and "little" castes (*baṛī jāti* and *choṭī jāti*).'

[19] *Pakka* food refers to foods cooked in oil or clarified butter. Such foods are commonly prepared at feasts or other situations where members of different castes are present and there are generally somewhat looser restrictions governing their acceptance than is the case with *kaccā* food.

Whereas the ideology of *dān* stresses the 'obligation' to accept it and the inauspiciousness that accompanies it, the ideology of shares and payments stresses the 'right' to receive them and there is no implication that any inauspiciousness is involved.

There are two primary contexts in which prestations are said to be given to 'one's own people'. The first is the distribution of grain at harvest time, referred to as *phaslānā*; the second is payments made for ritual services performed during calendrical and life-cycle rituals, referred to as *neg* and *lāg*. The vocabulary used for these payments emphasizes sharing, reciprocity, and mutual dependence. In these contexts, the recipients are never referred to as *purohit* and *kamīn*[20] as they would be when they accept *dān*.

It should, however, be pointed out that there is an ambiguity in Raheja's account of 'mutuality'. She tends to stress the symmetry of the relationship—a precise *quid pro quo* of payment for services rendered. But it would appear that the expression 'one's own people' is used rather one-sidedly by those who are in a position to make such payments. Since land is the predominant form of wealth, and since the Gujars own virtually all of it, it is primarily they who employ the services of others: 'Several points should be noted concerning this enumeration of the "shares" of the harvest given by the Gujar *jajmān* to those he calls his *gharelūs*, those who are "of the house" and who are nourished and sustained by the grain of his fields' (1989: 90). One of these points is that 'shares' of the harvest or other forms of wealth are always given to those who are 'attached to us, joined to us' (ibid.: 91). Whereas the recipients of *dān* are conceived as 'others', the recipients of *phaslānā*, *lāg*, and *neg* are referred to by terms which emphasize inclusiveness—'tied together brother', 'of the house', or 'sharer in the dowry' (ibid.). But what is not made sufficiently clear is that this attachment is decidedly unequal. To be joined to 'us' means to be joined to *jajmān*s who can afford the attachment; to be a *jajmān* is to be the patron of the services of others.

Raheja herself writes that: 'In Pahansu, Gujar dominance is absolute' (1989: 98). Through owning virtually all of the land, they are regarded not only as *jajmān*s in respect of their own domestic and agricultural rituals, 'but also in relation to the ritual life of the

[20] 'In return for the performance of their specific services, Barbers, Washermen, Sweepers, Carpenters, and Ironsmiths receive, as *kamīn*s of their Gujar *jajmān*s, payments of grain . . .' (Raheja 1988*a*: 18–19).

village as a unit at the annual ritual for [the village deity] Bhūmiyā and at many other times throughout the year' (ibid.). Self-consciously echoing Hocart, Raheja several times (describes the Gujar dominant caste as sacrificial protectors of the village, and likens this role to the duty (*dharma*) of the traditional Hindu king, the *kṣatriya*, whose position as guardian of the kingdom is assured only through the repeated performance of munificent sacrifices.[21] Moreover, like Hocart, Raheja cites the antiquity of this conception: 'In the very first verses of the Laws of Manu . . . [it] is the *dharma* of the Kṣatriya to give *dān* for the protection of the universe and the people of his realm, and it is the *dharma* of the Brahman to accept *dān* (ibid.: 97).

Raheja summarizes her own findings with a model, reproduced here as Figure 1, which depicts the three different ways in which intercaste relationships are represented in Pahansu.

There are three main observations to be made about this model. The first is that configurations B and C are incomplete. It is not only the Gujars who have others attached to them, whether as 'one's own' or as 'other'. Power is never absolute and even in Pahansu, where the Gujars own 98 per cent of the land, they are not the only ones who are able to command the services of others. *Every* caste has others to remove their inauspicious qualities, even the lowliest and poorest. If other castes cannot be found to do this, then the function is performed by married daughters and wife-taking affines. Raheja does not give us enough information to build up a complete picture of these relations for all castes, but the question of whether one caste can call upon another to absorb its inauspiciousness seems to depend primarily on whether they have the economic resources to do so.

Where the Gujars can call on all other castes (except the merchant Baniyas) at some time or other, none of these castes can call upon the Gujars to reciprocate. The fact that Gujars and Baniyas do not accept each other's inauspiciousness seems to reflect their economic independence from each other. The only form of inauspiciousness which the Gujars will accept is that which accompanies the gift of the bride. This seems to indicate that marriage alliances are the only kind of dependence which they are prepared to acknowledge. They are obliged to exchange their

[21] On Hocart's theory of caste and kingship, see Ch. 6.

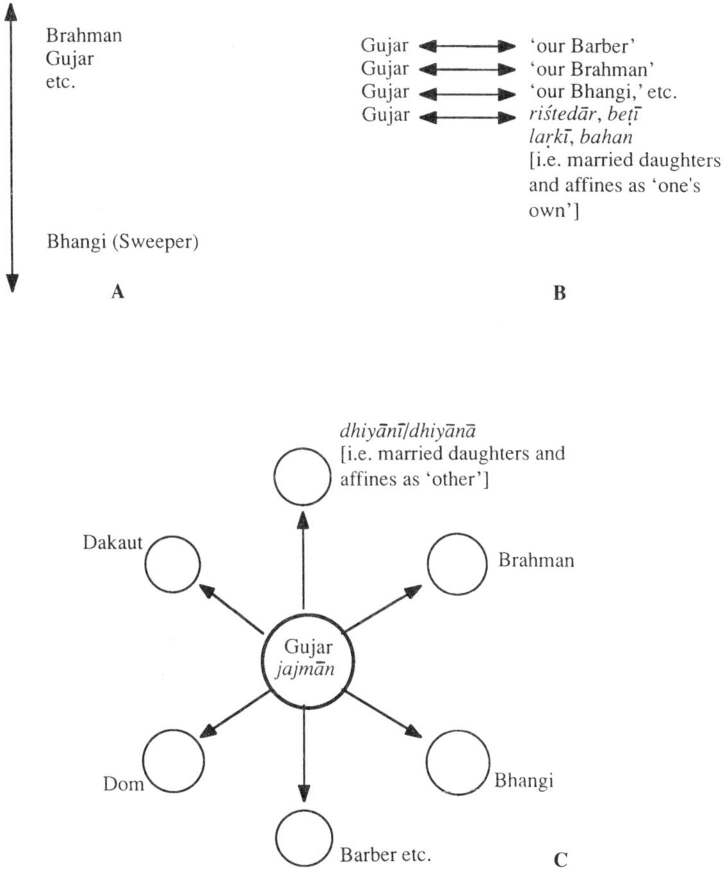

FIG. 1. Raheja's model of orderings of caste and kinsmen in Pahansu (1988*a*: 243) A. Hierarchical ordering B. Ordering of 'mutuality': Gujars and 'one's own people' C. Ordering of 'centrality': the oriented flow of inauspiciousness to those who are 'other'

daughters for those of other Gujar lineages but are not obliged to enter into any other form of transaction.

All exchanges, in so far as they set up relationships between the parties involved, are seen as inherently dangerous.[22] The danger

[22] As I have written in a short review of Raheja's book (1990), the general implication of Raheja's argument seems to be that society is built up on a never-ending sequence of poisonous exchanges. T. N. Madan (1991: 293) has recently

lies in the receipt of something, or someone, which puts one party in a position of dependence on another. The Gujars are, of course, dependent on other groups to remove the inauspiciousness which their dominance generates just as these other groups (except the Baniyas) are dependent on the Gujars for their material well-being. But these relationships, precisely because they are between those who are (economically and politically) dominant and those who are dominated, are decidedly unequal.

The second observation on Raheja's model is that only two of the configurations (B and C) include relations between households and their married daughters (and/or the daughters' conjugal families).[23] In the case of B, where mutuality is stressed, these relatives are conceived of as 'one's own'. In the case of C, where the transfer of inauspiciousness is stressed, married daughters and affines are conceived of as 'other'. This point needs to be stressed because in her summary article (1989), Raheja omits married daughters and affines from her representation of the configuration stressing mutuality—as shown in Figure 2. This omission is probably meant to simplify a complicated picture for the purposes of a short article, but it is very unfortunate because it obscures one of the central findings which emerges from Raheja's material. This is that there is a continuity between the way in which caste relations and kinship relations are conceived, and to separate the two as if they belong to different orders of reality is to introduce a distinction which is often difficult to sustain.[24]

In the next chapter I will examine in detail the relationships

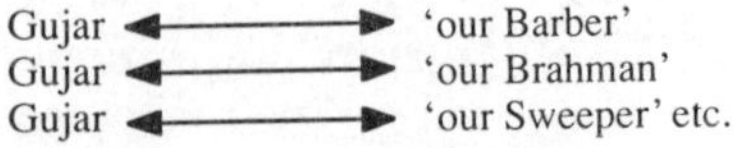

FIG. 2. Raheja's ordering of 'mutuality': Gujars and 'one's own people' (1989: 94)

written that, 'if gift-giving is inauspicious in *all* cases, and if the gift is the basis of social life, the conclusion would then follow that social life is inauspicious in its very foundations. This obviously is unacceptable.' Madan's final statement seems to me to be arguable.

[23] The work of Lynn Bennett (1983) is very pertinent here.

[24] The point has been made by others (see the following chapter) but has generally failed to make a strong impression on the dominant view of caste.

between caste, kinship, and affinity. For the remainder of this chapter I wish to concentrate on the various ways in which relations between castes are represented and, in particular, to highlight the position of the Brāhmaṇ caste. As will become clear later, however, this is directly pertinent to the question of how caste and kinship are connected. It will also explain why married daughters and affines are included in Raheja's configurations B ('mutuality') and C ('centrality') but not in configuration A ('hierarchy').

This brings me to the third observation on Raheja's tripartite model of intercaste relations. What is at issue here is the concept of hierarchy. Raheja follows Dumont and Marriott in arguing that a hierarchical ordering of castes always implies that Brāhmaṇs are at the top. Yet she also states that the supremacy of the Brāhmaṇ is an idea which is rarely stressed in everyday contexts. Its most explicit formulation is in the context of the giving and receiving of cooked foods, and then the crucial consideration is who has cooked the food rather than who has offered it. However, since members of the dominant caste never accept anything from Brāhmaṇs, including *kaccā* food, any superiority of the Brāhmaṇs is rather hypothetical.

Nevertheless, Raheja continues to insist that the Brāhmaṇ is indeed hierarchically superior in some way. She compares the position in Pahansu with that revealed in the South Indian temple myths analysed by Shulman:

> The king's duty, his *dharma*, was to protect the realm. He did this, according to the texts, by absorbing the sins and evil of the people, principally the unavoidable evil of the sacrificial remains, evil that accumulates in any ritually ordered life [Shulman 1985: 85]. In order, then, to rid himself and the kingdom of this burden of evil, he was compelled to shower gifts upon the Brahmans, who, like the North Indian priests discussed by Parry and Raheja, had to 'digest' the poisonous residues or transfer them onward. (Raheja 1988*b*: 514)

Evil, argues Shulman, 'seems to preexist, perhaps even to condition the emergence of the powers of royal splendor and prosperity (*śrī*)' (1985: 68). Its expulsion is of paramount importance for the well-being of the kingdom, and the vessel used to take it away is the Brāhmaṇ priest.

Raheja's conclusion on Shulman's interpretation of Hindu kingship and priesthood is rather odd: 'In the medieval South

Indian polity, then, as well as in the contemporary North Indian village of Pahansu, the Brahman priests are hierarchically pre-eminent, but at the same time they must absorb the evil of their sacrificial patrons' (Raheja 1988*b*: 514). How exactly Raheja extracts this idea of hierarchical pre-eminence from Shulman's characterization of the Brāhmaṇ priest as an absorber of the evils of the kingdom is mysterious. Even the extraction of the supreme Brāhmaṇ from her own ethnographic material seems somewhat tendentious given her insistence that it is, to all intents and purposes, a concept which is rarely aired, and then only hypothetically.

The only conclusion one can come to is that Raheja, in spite of her powerful case against Dumont, Marriott, Heesterman *et al.*, cannot escape the notion that in some contexts status does indeed encompass power. This, after all, can be the only explanation of the Brāhmaṇ's superiority. But we have seen already the difficulties inherent in such an argument, many of which Raheja herself draws attention to. When Heesterman, for example, writes that 'the brahmin stands supreme', he is obliged, like Dumont, to argue that caste 'exclusively refers to the values of purity. As a matter of principle, it lacks common ground with the world of power relations' (Heesterman 1985: 187).

In order to explain how the 'brahmin' escapes from the earlier agonistic exchange of life for death, and from the world of power relations in general, he calls on the notion of an 'axial breakthrough'. But the evidence for such a breakthrough is palpably tenuous when, right up to the present day, Brāhmaṇ priests are still being referred to as those who digest the sin, evil, and death of others. In this regard, the conclusion of Parry, who insists on the continuing latter-day perils of priesthood, is distinctly peculiar. He narrates the following story:

> When in the early days of the British Raj a Funeral Priest was sentenced to death for murder, the learned Pandits advised the High Court that his execution would constitute Brahminicide and the sentence was commuted. But despite their unequivocal status as Brahmans they are treated much like Untouchables in many contexts. I have heard them described by the Hindi word *acchut* which means just that; and no fastidious person of clean caste will dine with them. In theory they should live outside the village and to the south of it—that is, in the direction of death. The Mahabrahmans themselves explain that they participate in the *sutak* (or death pollution)

which afflicts their *jajman* (patrons); and that since they have many *jajman* they are—as it were—in a permanent state of death pollution. (Parry 1980: 94)

But having repeatedly emphasized the Mahābrāhmaṇ's unenviable status. Parry then retreats from what would appear to be the obvious conclusion: 'The Mahabrahman, then, is regarded with a mixture of fear and contempt . . . But having said all this . . . *He is after all a Brahman*' (ibid.; my emphasis).

Like Heesterman, what Parry seems to be saying is that in the final analysis, 'after all', the status of the Brāhmaṇ is not ambivalent; it is unequivocally high whatever evidence there is to the contrary. It would appear that the first proposition which we have all repeatedly imbibed since the days when we read our first book on caste is beyond question. And that proposition is, of course, that 'Brāhmaṇs (or Brahmans or Brahmins) are the highest caste'.

The trouble is that this proposition is extremely questionable, as the evidence of Heesterman, Parry, and others cited in this chapter makes abundantly clear. One might say with just as much conviction that since the function of the Brāhmaṇ priest is to be the vessel of other people's impurity, he is essentially indistinguishable from those who remove pollution but who are normally seen as belonging at the bottom of the caste hierarchy. This is particularly evident in the case of the Mahābrāhmaṇ and there is more than one irony involved in the difference of opinion between Parry, who describes the Mahābrāhmaṇ as being 'after all, a Brahman', and Dumont, who says he is 'in fact an Untouchable of a particular kind' (1980: 58).[25]

Even Raheja, who challenges the notion of the 'axial breakthrough' whereby Brāhmaṇs achieved their alleged superiority, undermines the force of her otherwise exceptionally cogent argument by insisting on the difference between a concept of hierarchy based on impurity and a concept of centrality based on inauspiciousness. Had she relied on her own ethnography more ruthlessly, Raheja might well have concluded that there is good reason to ignore the Brahmanical (or Dumontian) hierarchy based on purity and pollution.

Manifestations of 'hierarchy', Raheja first warns us, are rare:

[25] This is a good example of the difficulties Dumont gets himself into by arguing that the empirical approach to India is a mistake.

'although as we have seen there are perhaps hundreds of specifically named prestations in Pahansu, there are few situations in which these are made because of a hierarchical relationship between donor and recipient' (1988*a*: 241). In her later summary article, however, using almost the same words, she goes one step further, a step which seems to me to be more than a slip of the pen and one which is pregnant with consequence:

> Although there are hundreds of named prestations given in order to remove inauspiciousness or to maintain a mutuality among 'one's own' people in Pahansu, there are *no* situations in which a prestation is made precisely because of a hierarchical relationship. (Raheja 1989: 92; my emphasis)

The question of whether there are 'few' or 'no' situations in which such hierarchy is manifested is obviously crucial.

Raheja's configuration A is quite different from the other two configurations in that it refers to a hypothetical context rather than to actual practice. It offers a justification for the Brāhmaṇ's superiority, but one which is continually contradicted by everyday events. It is because configuration A is effectively a fictional ordering of castes that it conjures up hypothetical instances of 'hierarchy' between them. And because it is fictitious, it also ignores other relations—primarily those between kin and affines. As her own ethnography makes clear, however, the disjunction between caste and kinship is very difficult to maintain consistently.[26]

The Limits of Transcendence

Faced with the problem of contradictory evidence, Dumont simply says that the facts are not important. It is no small irony that empiricists like Parry, Fuller, and even Raheja, though she to a much lesser extent, in effect do the same. When Parry, for example, writes that the Mahābrāhmaṇ, though in many respects treated like an Untouchable, is 'after all a Brahman', he is effectively denying the validity of his own observations, indeed of observation in general. The ideal Brāhmaṇ to whom he is

[26] The institution of hypergamy, discussed in the following chapter, illustrates the continuity between caste and kinship more clearly still.

ultimately referring cannot possibly belong to the observable world. Heesterman admits as much when he says that the 'axial breakthrough' which liberated the *brāhmaṇ* from the agonistic exchange of life for death 'posited the ideal of an absolute transcendent order that is, as a matter of principle, incapable of worldly realization' (Heesterman 1985: 157).

The Brāhmaṇ is only supreme, then, provided that he disappears in a cloud of transcendent ethereality. But such vanishing tricks are by no means easy to achieve; in fact, it is not difficult to argue that they are impossible. Perfect renunciation can only ever remain an ideal, and an ordering of castes along a sliding scale of renunciation, such as that suggested at the beginning of this chapter, can only ever be a schema which is incapable of worldly realization. As Fuller's study in particular shows, Brāhmaṇs are themselves hotly divided over the desirability of transcendence. Priests claim superiority over non-priestly Brāhmaṇs and vice versa; renouncers claim superiority over priests and vice versa. Yet Fuller, like Heesterman and Parry, seems inclined to argue that in the end, a sliding renunciatory scale is the best way of ordering Brāhmaṇ castes and, by implication, of relating non-Brāhmaṇ castes to them since the Brāhmaṇ is alleged to be the pivot of the system.

There is no doubt that the appeal of an ideal, a transcendent authority, is seductive. But one is continually obliged to recognize that those who aspire to transcendence are always, inevitably, brought back down to earth by the need to engage in relations with others. Why then should so many authorities revert to an explanation of Brahmanical pre-eminence in terms of transcendent authority? This is puzzling when the same authorities continually point out that this transcendence is forever being compromised.

One suggested answer to this puzzle is that British administrators understood 'the caste system' to be a religious rather than a political phenomenon,[27] and since Brāhmaṇs provided the priests, they were obviously the highest caste. Once this idea became codified and enshrined in census reports, caste became a hierarchical ladder based on the polar opposition between Brāhmaṇs (the most pure) and Untouchables (the most polluted). Colonial administrators can be excused for making such a mistake. After

[27] See e.g. Cohn (1987) and Fuller (1977). The impossibility of divorcing religion from politics in the explanation of caste is discussed in Chs. 6 and 7.

all, their predominant concern was with stable and profitable government. If they interpreted caste in a way which suited their aims, by divorcing what they saw as religious matters from wider politico-economic concerns, this is hardly surprising.

What is more puzzling is that modern scholars should so often concur with the colonial interpretation of caste when their own evidence contradicts it repeatedly. Why should they claim that the Brāhmaṇ stands supreme when, time after time, his status is shown to be at best intensely ambivalent, at worst vilely degrading? It is obviously inadequate to say that they were simply misled by their European forefathers. Nor, I believe, is it reasonable to tar them with the same brush of vested interest by simply branding them as Orientalists—those whose representation of the East as religion-ridden provides intellectual justification for Western political domination.[28]

A more persuasive reason for the near unanimous defence of the Brāhmaṇ's supremacy lies in the fact that authorities on Hinduism have, more often than not, illegitimately fused two very different concepts—*jāti* and *varṇa*—or caste (Brāhmaṇ) and function (*brāhmaṇ*).[29] Here they have indeed made the same mistake as colonial administrators. However, while the confusion made little difference to the way in which the British governed India, it made, and continues to make, a huge difference to the way in which the mechanics of caste are understood. The overwhelming conclusion has been that the status of Brāhmaṇs as a whole derives from a particular function. Some have claimed that the 'true' function is to be a priest; others argue that it is to be a renouncer. But whichever function is adduced as the ideal one, the assumption is that all Brāhmaṇs are superior to other castes because of their alleged association with the ideal.

There are several reasons why such an assumption is untenable. In the first place, there is no agreement as to what the ideal *brāhmaṇ* should be. These disagreements are not confined to modern Western interpreters of Hinduism; Indians themselves have been arguing about this question since time immemorial.

[28] See Ch. 1, 'Is Caste an Orientalist Construct?'

[29] I am not, of course, suggesting that these authorities are unaware of the difference, only that they tend to assume that there is some kind of *automatic* correspondence between them—see e.g. Table 1 in Ch. 5 below which is reproduced from Parry (1979).

Secondly, even if everyone agreed what the ideal *brāhmaṇ* should look like, Brāhmaṇs are fragmented into innumerable different castes which endlessly contest each others' status to the extent that some deny the Brāhmaṇhood of others.

In many cases, such castes are associated with particular ritual functions; in a great many others, Brāhmaṇ castes are not associated with any ritual profession at all, but with secular occupations such as landowning, government service, or some other livelihood. If most Brāhmaṇs cannot demonstrate any association with the ideal *brāhmaṇ*, whoever he may be, how can one assume that the connection is there at all? This would be a very peculiar form of reasoning. And yet it is precisely this kind of reasoning which appears again and again in the accounts to which I have referred in this chapter.

The question is: do these accounts lend themselves to any more convincing interpretation? I believe that they do but in order to embrace it, it is necessary to abandon the first assumption on which most theories of caste are based. This assumption, once again, is that Brāhmaṇs are the highest caste.

We have seen that when Brāhmaṇs are performing the function which is often taken to be specifically theirs—namely, to be *purohit*s to *jajmān*s of other castes—their role is primarily to remove the inauspiciousness, evil, and sin of their patrons.[30] The evidence for this, provided by the authorities cited in this chapter and by the sources they in turn rely on, can hardly fail to impress. If this is indeed the case, it seems rather peculiar to suggest that such Brāhmaṇs are 'higher' than their patrons. Turning Brāhmaṇs into the highest caste because of their association with either priesthood or purity amounts to a fantastic distortion of the evidence.

The relationship between patron and priest is charged with all kinds of difficult tensions and is best characterized as ambiguous or equivocal rather than in terms of higher and lower or superior and inferior.[31] But it is this relationship, I would argue, which provides the key to caste ideology. The really fundamental

[30] In fact, the role of *purohit* is not unique to Brāhmaṇs. Members of other castes are also frequently called upon in this capacity—see Raheja (1988*a*: 26). The point is discussed again in Ch. 6 below.

[31] This ambiguity is brilliantly illustrated in Veena Das's (1977) *Structure and Cognition*.

opposition in all the various representations of caste ideology is not between priests and untouchables, but between priests and kings.

Seen this way, Raheja's use of the distinction between impurity and inauspiciousness is something of a red herring.[32] Both in her interpretation of inauspiciousness and in Dumont's of impurity, the underlying problem is to demarcate the function and status of the king (or patron) from that of the priest (or 'other'). From the patron's point of view, a vessel is required to take away the accumulated sin, evil, and death which is the inevitable result of creating order out of disorder (both natural and social). Normally this is seen as the function of a 'priest' as we conventionally understand this term in English. But in fact, as Raheja demonstrates, any 'other' will do—including affines or 'anyone who happens to pass by a crossroads'.

From the point of view of the priest or the 'other' who functions as a surrogate priest, it is the patron who generates evil in the first place through his attempts to create order out of disorder; the priest or surrogate should therefore try to distance himself from his patron as far as possible. But to do so completely and remain 'in the world' is ultimately impossible. As Heesterman and others make clear, a great deal of Brahmanical metaphysics is given over to precisely this insoluble problem.[33]

[32] This is not to deny that the distinction is made indigenously nor, *pace* Raheja, that inauspiciousness requires an agent to remove it while impurity simply goes away of its own accord after a certain period of time or is removed by the afflicted individual himself or herself, typically through washing. On the difficulties of separating impurity from inauspiciousness, see Parry (1991).

[33] See Heesterman (1985).

5
Caste and Kinship

Hypergamy

IF there is fundamental disagreement about the ideological underpinnings of caste, there is greater agreement on the proposition that caste is inextricably tied to kinship. In the words of Pauline Kolenda: 'The constant feature in caste is its kinship or descent-group structure' (1978: 4). In the world of caste, virtually every aspect of behaviour is regulated by kin—not only major decisions such as marriage, occupation, and place of residence, but everyday activities such as what one eats and who with, or the forms of address one employs for different categories of people.

There is a huge and complex literature on the relationship between caste and kinship and it is no easy task to summarize or synthesize its findings. Rather than attempt a comprehensive review of the literature, I will first focus on one text which addresses most of the relevant issues, Jonathan P. Parry's (1979) *Caste and Kinship in Kangra*. To some extent, this choice is arbitrary. One might equally choose any one of a number of other excellent ethnographies, one's choice perhaps depending on a particular interest in one region or other of the sub-continent. However, Parry's book is a classic of the genre, it provides the kind of literature review which space precludes here, and it also offers a detailed examination of hypergamy (i.e. marrying women 'up'), a practice which throws considerable light on the workings of caste.[1] In the second section of this chapter I will contrast hypergamy with the isogamous pattern (where marriage is between those of equal status).

Parry's ethnography is set in the Kangra hills of north-west India. The central theme of his book is that 'the caste is ordered internally by the same principles which govern relations between

[1] One further reason for considering this book is that it allows one to see the derivation of some of Parry's later ideas which were discussed in the previous chapter. I do not intend to examine every issue which Parry raises; in particular, questions relating to household composition and partition and to the nature of kinship terminology will not be analysed here.

castes' (1979: 6). The greater part of his work examines the internal structure of the Rājput 'caste', a grouping which is frequently viewed as homogeneous from the outside but which is, in fact, endlessly fragmented internally into sub-groups which are hierarchically ranked in much the same manner that 'castes' are. These groups are either united or divided according to whether they admit marriage alliances with each other. Marriage is ideally hypergamous in Kangra; that is, as far as possible, daughters are married up into families of higher status.

In Kangra each caste is divided into a number of named exogamous patriclans which may be dispersed over a wide area. The clans of each of the highest castes are ranked on a hierarchical scale. Marriage is patrilocal and status within this intra-caste hierarchy is expressed by hypergamy: clans of lower status giving daughters in marriage to those immediately above them. Clans of approximately equal status form a single *biradari*, and those girls who are not given to grooms of superior *biradari* are exchanged on a symmetrical basis within the *biradari*. I aim to show that the relationship between one *biradari* and another within the caste is in many respects analogous to the relationship between one caste and another. That is, each *biradari* is associated with a distinctive style of life and a distinctive set of customs, and interactions between *biradaris* are again ordered by a set of transactional rules governing the exchange of food, hookahs, greetings and—of course—women. (ibid.: 4)

To begin with, then, there are three different levels of social organization: the exogamous clan, the *birādari* which groups together a number of clans, and the caste which groups together a number of *birādari*s.[2] In fact, there are a number of other divisions and sub-divisions to which Parry draws our attention, but one may begin with these three.

Much of Parry's discussion concerns the limits within which hypergamy is possible, and this raises a number of interesting questions. He mentions that the caste below the Rājputs are isogamous (ibid.: 228), so why are the high castes hypergamous but not others? What defines status in these contexts? Is it possible to marry up from one caste into another (and not just from one *birādari* into another of the same caste)? If so, under what conditions does this take place? Given that caste is more often

[2] For the sake of consistency I have included diacritics except where I am directly quoting; these are omitted from the transliterations of all words in Parry's book.

than not perceived as a rather static form of social organization in which only marriage between status equals is permissible, what are the consequences for this of pervasive hypergamy? Why is hypergamy found in some parts of the sub-continent but not others where caste organization is also reported? Indeed, why is hypergamy found at all?

This last, and most embracing, question is one which Parry himself does not attempt to tackle: 'Throughout the analysis I treat the prevalence of hypergamy in India, and the general disapproval of hypogamy, as a cultural given, and make no systematic attempt to answer the (perhaps unanswerable) question "why hypergamy?" ' (ibid.: 198). In the second section of this chapter I will offer a tentative hypothesis on this question.

Parry describes Kangra as 'a remittance economy backed up by subsistence agriculture' (ibid.: 45). Those at the bottom of the economic ladder are squeezed both ways. The majority of households 'have very small holdings or no land at all' (ibid.: 39), a fact which pushes them to seek wage labour of some kind. On the other hand, wages are often so low that 'few can afford to support their families from their salaries alone. To make ends meet, a cash income must usually be backed up by participation, in some form or other, in the subsistence sector of the economy' (ibid.: 44). The implications of being welded to subsistence agriculture in this way are not merely economic. The reluctance to abandon one's attachment to the land, however meagre the returns, often appears to be less a matter of economic security than of clinging to one's village identity: 'the local community only maintains itself as a community to the extent that it retains its peasant basis' (ibid.: 45).

All arable land has long since been cultivated. Parry describes pressure on the land as 'terrific' (ibid.: 35) and says that there are many more would-be tenants than there is land to go round (ibid.: 48). This has not always been the case, however. Throughout the nineteenth century, the demand for tenants generally outstripped supply. This was particularly so in the pre-British period when the combined demands of state and landlord made tenancy a very unattractive proposition. As much as three-quarters of the crop was sometimes taken while the tenant still had to meet all production costs from his remaining share. Parry attributes the reversal in the demand for tenancies to two factors: 'growth in population, and the almost total exhaustion of the supply of cultivable waste' (ibid.).

According to Parry, there has probably been very little change in the distribution of lands since the end of the nineteenth century. At that time, Rājputs and Brāhmaṇs, who today account for 30.8 per cent and 13.4 per cent of the district's population respectively, owned 76 per cent of the total cultivated land. A further 13 per cent was in the hands of Girth cultivators who today make up 15 per cent of the population of the district. However, while Rājputs collectively owned 58 per cent of the land, they are generally not—'today at least'—the largest landowners in the sub-division of Palampur where Parry's most intensive research took place. In Palampar, 'Of the 58 holdings of over 10 standard acres, 18 belong to Brahman landlords from Palam, 25 to the trading-caste families who had profited so enormously as money-lenders in the period following the first British Settlement, and only 9 to the Rajputs' (ibid.: 56). This would seem to indicate one major change in landholding patterns though there is unfortunately little further discussion of the position of these trading-caste families.

Parry prefers instead to concentrate on the dominance of the Rājputs and Brāhmaṇs: 'Broadly speaking, the high castes control most of the land, and the majority of low-caste people are either tenants or landless labourers' (ibid.: 55). In the area of his fieldwork, he reports that 'it is the Rajputs who combine most of the elements of dominance though it is, *of course*, the Brahmans who stand unambiguously at the top of the hierarchy' (ibid.: 57–8; emphasis added).[3] The dominant caste Rājputs tend to monopolize the more prestigious and rewarding jobs outside the district. With their long martial tradition, they are immediately advantaged in the military which is the single largest employer. Parry reports that the martial ethic, with which Rājputs are associated, 'permeates the whole of Kangra society' (ibid.: 41).

Whether at home or outside, only a small proportion of men pursue what Parry calls their 'caste-specific occupation' (ibid.: 58). The vast majority either work outside or in agriculture while the remainder of those in the village work in 'the traditional caste-free occupations as, for example, teachers, tailors, masons, village

[3] I have italicized 'of course' here to draw attention to the way in which informants' assertions of the superiority of Brāhmaṇs is taken as unassailable; the previous chapter has illustrated the perils of following such a course.

watchmen, forest guards or *vaids* (Ayurvedic doctors)' (ibid.: 58–9).

This is actually a very misleading way of putting it. It is not so much that everyone has (or ever had) a caste-specific occupation in the first instance. Rather, everyone belongs to kin groups whose traditional function it is (or was) to provide certain functionaries for certain occasions. However, most members of most groups generally are (and always have been) in occupations such as agriculture and administration which do not of themselves identify one's caste.

In Table 1 I reproduce Parry's table of the Kangra caste hierarchy. I have made two amendments to his original. The first is to put the *varṇa* in italics to draw attention to the fact that this

TABLE 1. *The Kangra caste hierarchy (adapted from Parry 1979; 110, Table 14; italics and emphasis mine)*

Caste	*Varṇa*
1 Brahman—Landowners and priests	Brahman (*brāhmaṇ*)
2 Bhojki—Temple priests	
3 Rajput—Landowners and warriors	Kshatriya (*kṣatriya*)
4 Mahajan—Trader	Vaishya (*vaiśya*)
5 Turkhan—Carpenter: Lohar—Blacksmith: Sonyar—Goldsmith: Nai—Barber: Kumhar—Potter: Girth—Cultivator	Most people would say that all these castes are Shudras (*śūdra*). **But on occasion, castes of categories 5, 6, and 7 will claim to be either Kshatriya *(kṣatriya)* or Brahman *(brāhmaṇ)***
6 Koli—Cultivator	
7 Jogi—Beggar and ascetic	
8 Jullaha—weaver	
9 Sanhai—Musician	
10 Dumna—Basket-maker	
11 Chamar—Tanner	
12 Bhangi—Sweeper	

refers to a function and not to the name of a group which is defined by kinship. The second is to put in bold Parry's own comment to the effect that there is no consensus regarding the placement of some castes in the *varṇa* hierarchy.

Once we broach the nature of the precise rankings of Kangra's castes, we enter a minefield of contradictory information, so much so that Parry himself warns us that 'it cannot simply be assumed that all the castes in any local area belong to the kind of linear hierarchy suggested by my tables' (ibid.: 102–3). He draws our attention to three fairly numerous Muslim castes and a group of transhumant shepherds and asserts that 'it does not occur to [the villagers] to rank these castes in relation to village castes' (ibid.: 103). But even if one leaves these non-Hindu groups aside for the time being, the problems of ranking are still not easily resolved.

The difficulties can best be approached by following Parry and concentrating on the Brāhmaṇs and Rājputs. Both Rājputs and Brāhmaṇs are internally stratified and 'the clans of each caste are grouped into four hypergamously ranked categories or *biradaris*' (ibid.: 104). However, it is not the case that all of the Brāhmaṇs automatically have higher status than all the Rājputs: the higher Rājputs often appear to assert their superiority over the majority of Brāhmaṇs.

> The theory is that the two lowest of the Rajput *biradaris* take boiled food from all four 'pure' Brahman *biradaris*; and this is in fact what actually happens. But second-grade Rajputs claim that they are prepared to accept boiled food only from first- or second-grade Brahmans, who traditionally do not plough. The aristocratic Rajputs are fussier still and theoretically refuse boiled food from all but the highest *biradari*, who are the only people they will employ as ritual cooks . . . All this poses some difficult problems for an interactional analysis. By refusing to accept [boiled food], or to smoke with any but the highest-status Brahmans, the aristocratic Rajputs might appear to be asserting the inferiority of most Brahmans. (ibid.: 105–6)

Parry gets out of this difficulty by turning away from actual interactions and back to informants' statements about what is supposed to be the case. In this case, informants are 'clear and precise' (ibid.: 106) about the way in which any two pairs should be ranked:

> For them it is self-evident that all Brahmans, Temple priests and Funeral priests are superior to all Rajputs no matter how aristocratic . . . When

asked to decide, for example, whether the Temple priests rank higher or lower than the Rajputs, my informants would first identify them with the *varna* category to which they belong, and then derive their rank from the status of the category as a whole. (ibid.: 106–7)

The logic behind this reasoning is straightforward: 'Brahmans are Brahmans and as such superior to everybody else' (ibid.: 107). It does not really matter then that on certain occasions some Rājputs treat some Brāhmaṇs as if they were of lower caste because all Brāhmaṇs can arrogate to themselves the status of the highest representatives of the *brāhmaṇ varṇa*. This is even the case for the Funeral priests: 'On this argument, then, the fact that the Charaj Funeral priests are treated much like untouchables in their interactions . . . is quite irrelevant' (ibid.).

Parry seems to find this reasoning relatively unproblematic, reporting that: 'Much the same process is repeated at other levels of the hierarchy' (ibid.). However, he points out that in certain circumstances it was the *rāja* rather than the Brāhmaṇ who stood at the apex of the caste system and who adjudicated on the caste status of others:

The Sanskrit texts give the raja wide powers to legislate on caste matters, and to prevent—as Kautilya puts it—'the confusion of castes and duties'. Evidence from many parts of the sub-continent suggests that the king did in practice use his powers to manipulate the caste hierarchy, and to legitimize a change in caste status . . . In the Kangra region the intervention of the local rajas in caste organization seems to have been commonplace. (ibid.: 120)

Moreover, the fact that the British usurped the power of the *rāja*s did not put an end to this practice, though their presence may have modified it. Parry reports that appeals by the Kolis to improve their status were made 'to an external authority: first to the rajas and subsequently to the British courts' (ibid.). He quotes Lyall at the end of the nineteenth century as saying that ' "at the present time the power of admitting back into caste fellowship persons under a ban for some grave act of defilement is a source of income to the *jagirdar* Rajas" ' (ibid.).[4] And he adds that although the

[4] Lyall (1889: 70). The *jāgirdār rāja*s were those who were allotted a piece of land (*jāgir*) in recompense for their services. It should be noted that Parry later adds the following: 'Although the Raja of Kangra continued to legitimate reforms in the caste hierarchy right up until the beginning of this century, the evidence would suggest that he had long since ceased to be capable of imposing his will'

rājas had been reduced to the position of petty *jāgirdārs* by the British, their erstwhile subjects continued to honour them as if they were still kings—for example, by presenting them with gifts at the annual *seri* festival when the crops were harvested. 'Long after their administrative and judicial authority had all but disappeared, the rajas continued to wield a certain authority in matters of caste precedence' (ibid.: 13).

In the following chapter I will examine the position of the king in the caste hierarchy. First, however, an added complication has to be considered. We have seen that Kangra Brāhmaṇs and Rājputs are each divided into four, hypergamously ranked *birādaris*. At all levels of the caste hierarchy, Parry informs us, 'the *biradari* is equated with the group which exchanges women on a reciprocal basis' (ibid.: 200–1). In practice, however, the Kangra *birādari* is no less subject to the pervasive intrusion of hypergamy than any other level of social organization. This seems to be particularly marked among the Rājputs:

> But although the Kangra theory is that each *biradari* consists of a series of clans which are of equal status and which engage in the symmetrical exchange of women, there is in practice a tendency towards hypergamy and differentiation of status within the Rajput *biradari*, a tendency which becomes increasingly marked as one moves up the ladder . . . within the first and second [*birādaris*] it is possible to identify various informal and hotly disputed gradations of status. (ibid.: 201)

Thus while people tend to conceive of the *birādari* as being the 'real' unit of exchange of women, in practice each *birādari* is fragmented, and this fragmentation is potentially infinite. It is simply not possible for a group as large as a *birādari* to follow a unified strategy of hypergamy by allying itself in a systematic fashion to a *birādari* of higher status: 'A concerted strategy of social climbing does not seem to be a practical proposition for a group any larger than a sub-clan, and is often pursued by a segment of a sub-clan' (ibid.: 204).

In fact, Parry concludes, there are no 'real' units which exchange women at all even though people normally talk as if

(1979: 263). This he adduces to the fact that these *rājas* lost all real power to the Sikhs in the early 19th century. Unfortunately, there is no further exploration of the continued *de jure* regulation of caste afffairs by the *rājas* in spite of their *de facto* loss of power.

marriages were transactions between groups. It is rather that marriage itself creates the inequality between the wife-giving and wife-taking groups.[5] So it is not so much that all the members of one group rank higher than all of those in another, but that those who take wives from others without exchanging their own women in return are considered superior.

Parry takes hypergamy to be the 'normal' state of affairs among Kangra Rājputs, particularly among the more aristocratic lineages. These latter only resort to egalitarian endogamous marriage circles when put under considerable pressure—as the British did in order to eliminate some of the more unpleasant consequences of hypergamy such as female infanticide. There are at least two other consequences of such high-caste hypergamy. One is an escalation in the size of dowries, a by-product of the competition for the most desirable, artistocratic grooms. The second is the geographical extension of marriage ties given both that it will often prove difficult to find spouses of acceptable status locally and that marriage alliances in other areas can also prove useful politically.[6]

Parry notes that girls tend to move westwards since the higher-status Rājputs are thought of as belonging to particular localities to the west of Kangra. This desire springs from the fact that to the west lie 'more fertile and prosperous areas with easier access to the plains' (ibid.: 220). It seems reasonable to suppose that the more highly desired localities are former centres of (royal) power.[7] The more barren and inaccessible land to the east is, by contrast, associated with a lack of civilization and the absence of the martial *kṣatriya* tradition which is often taken to be the hallmark of the 'true' Rājput.

The fact that pervasive hypergamy sends women up the marriage ladder tends to create a shortage of brides among the lower Rājput *birādari*s. Men in these groups have therefore been obliged to seek wives elsewhere and, as Parry puts it, 'to transgress the ideal of caste endogamy by contracting unions with women of the cultivating and artisan castes below them' (ibid.: 229). This leads Parry into a consideration of the relationship between caste

[5] A similar point has been made by Vatuk (1975) and others since.

[6] Parry also writes that 'since the mere existence of wife-takers is galling to the self-esteem of a Rajput royal clan, the desire to be separated from them by as large a distance as possible is perhaps understandable' (1979: 219).

[7] See Galey (1989).

exclusiveness and endogamy. Drawing on comparative material, he concludes that

> endogamy is not, as Dumont (1964) points out, the ultimate principle, but is rather entailed by the demands of status. Where caste affiliation is purely patrilineal (e.g. Barth 1959, 1960; Stirrat 1975), the endogamous requirement is dispensed with altogether. (ibid.: 230)

He notes, however, that in spite of their own patrilineal bias, 'endogamy continues to stand as an ideal for the Kangra Rajputs' (ibid.).

Like the question of the relationship between caste and occupation, that concerning the relationship between caste and endogamy has been subject to a great deal of ambivalence. In spite of his own insistence that 'breaches of caste endogamy are not quite such a radical solution to the problem of the shortage of women at the bottom of the hierarchy as they might at first sight appear' (ibid.: 234), Parry himself is sometimes inclined to fudge the issue. In order to demonstrate the difficulties of adjudicating on who is entitled to Rājput status, he quotes an official report from 1926:

> It is not easy to indicate the line which separates the Rajput from the class immediately below them, known in the hills by the appellation Thakur and Rathi. The Mian [i.e. the most aristocratic lineages] would restrict the term Rajput to those of royal descent: while the Rathi naturally seeks a broader definition, so as to include his own pretensions. The limit here given on the authority of Mr. Barnes is probably just; and those who are legitimately entitled to rank as Rajputs who are themselves the members of the royal clan, or are connected in marriage with them. (District Gazetteer 1926: 166, quoted in Parry 1979; 232)

Following Dumont, Parry argues that the idea that there are some who are 'legitimately entitled' to be called Rājput and others who are mere pretenders is a 'substantialist fallacy'. The whole point is that the system is 'segmentary'—by which he means lacking in precise boundaries, or that the way in which boundaries are drawn varies according to context.

To put fixed limits around categories such as Rājput, to suggest that there is some ultimately unambiguous criterion for deciding who is a 'real' caste member and who is not, is to introduce a rigidity which the evidence simply does not sustain:

. . . to avoid the kind of 'substantialist fallacy' the British authorities committed when they tried to define a precise boundary between the two categories [Rājput and Rathi], we need to remember that the people themselves think in segmentary terms, and that neither in language nor in other symbolic aspects of behaviour do they appear to signal an absolute discontinuity between groups at different levels of segmentation. (ibid.: 233)

One should, however, note Parry's choice of vocabulary very carefully. Where the 1926 District Gazetteer refers to Rājputs and Rathis as 'classes', Parry prefers the term 'categories'. On the one hand, this allows him to lambast British census-makers for being too punctilious in the manner they drew up divisions between groups. Effectively he argues that they became victims of their own administrative need to have a *Who's Who* of India once and for all time.[8] On the other hand, however, Parry does not in any way suggest that divisions between castes disappear altogether. While he may have some reservations about the overdetermination of the census reports and even about the rigidity implied in his own tables, he is nevertheless clear that Brāhmaṇs, Rājputs, Kolis, and Chamars are different castes. Moreover, the index of caste membership remains, by and large, intermarriage with others of the same caste.

The result, then, is that some castes (or all?) are internally divided and these divisions are ordered in much the same way that castes themselves are. Some castes (or all?) are also subject to infiltration from outside through the mechanism of hypergamy so that the boundary between one caste and another is sometimes (often, always?) blurred. There is a difficulty here in that Parry's work focuses on the Rājputs and it is not always clear whether the same applies to all other castes as to them. Brāhmaṇs, for example, are also internally divided into different *birādaris* which are hierarchically ranked but it is not clear whether non-Brāhmaṇs are able to contract hypergamous unions with them or whether, indeed, they would aspire to.

The position for other castes is even less clear. Are they also endlessly fragmented along the Rājput model? Do hypergamous marriages take place among these castes in the same way as between the lowest ranking Rājputs and the cultivating and artisan castes immediately below them? While Parry claims that the

[8] See also Ch. 7.

Kangra ideal for all castes is hypergamy, he describes the lower castes as isogamous, implying that *in practice* hypergamy does not occur among them, or at least not with significant frequency. However, for all castes one might still ask: is hypergamy normal or exceptional? When can the rule of (or preference for) endogamy be breached and when can it not be?

Dumont's answer to these last two questions is that hypergamy and endogamy are not necessarily mutually antagonistic. As has been made clear earlier, his argument is that one ought to concentrate on the relations between castes, the structural features of caste systems, rather than on the substantialist nature of castes themselves. But the underlying hierarchical opposition of purity/impurity does not of itself make any recommendation in favour of either isogamy or hypergamy; both strategies can be seen as consonant with it. For Dumont, 'endogamy is not only not attached *ne varietur* to a fixed level of segmentation, but also is more an implication of hierarchy than an independent principle' (Dumont 1980: 125). This allows him to maintain that there is nothing odd or exceptional about hypergamy; it simply shifts the level of acceptable marriage partners to a different level of segmentation: 'Not only does it [hypergamy] "temper" the endogamy of the caste segment and transfer strict endogamy to a higher level (caste), but in certain cases (Rajput) it even produces a breakdown of endogamy at the group's lower limit' (ibid.: 124). Hypergamy stretches the limit of the endogamous group because a certain difference in status between marriage partners is tolerated: 'This fact probably accounts for the existence of extremely large endogamous units, for example in the Gangetic plain, which would be inconceivable in the south' (ibid.: 117). Isogamy, on the other hand, is accompanied by 'a high degree of fissiparity of groups within the caste' (ibid.: 116): in other words, it leads to small, introverted, and tightly regulated groups.

Unlike Dumont, who sees endogamy as being entailed by hierarchy, many others have seen endogamy to be the very essence of caste, the crucial characteristic which sets it off from other forms of social organization. In a recent theoretical book on the origins of caste, for example, Morton Klass has written that South Asian society

> has from the time of the earliest external observation been characterized by some kind of a rule, or set of rules, limiting marriage—which has been

required to take place *within* certain categories of relationship, and not between members of certain separated categories. (Klass 1980: 29)

Klass takes issue with others who have argued that it is the *jāti* (whether this refers to caste or sub-caste) which is the effective endogamous unit, preferring instead 'the much more accurate and meaningful term, *marriage circle*' (ibid.: 93; emphasis in original).

Klass's argument is a kind of uneasy alliance between inference and observation which is very common among Indianists. For all his self-congratulation on having finally discovered the true nature of caste, Klass's theory is as defective as those which he criticizes, and for much the same reasons. According to him.

the system is characterized by a rule of endogamy and so somewhere within the system there must be a unit capable of enforcing such a rule—and these are the 'smallest endogamous units.' Further, the field anthropologist observes the unit in action as soon as he or she reaches the South Asian countryside. (ibid.: 94)

In other words, his theory hangs on the 'As everybody knows . . .' kind of argument that also lies behind the alleged supremacy of the Brāhmaṇ. In Klass's case everybody is supposed to know that castes are composed of endogamous groups, marriage-circles which he gives the corporatist label of *Verband*. But if Parry's argument about hypergamy is correct, then the observation made by Klass and others is illusory and Klass is guilty of precisely the same substantialist fallacy as the British census administrators. One might also question his argument that endogamy *must* exist because 'the system' demands it: 'the rule of endogamy is necessary for the maintenance of the total *caste system*' (Klass 1980: 133; emphasis in original). But why should the caste system be maintained? The reification implies an unwarranted teleology.

For Klass, endogamy is the rule and the marriage-circle is its concrete manifestation. Where hypergamy exists, it is an anomaly, 'a special exception to what everyone knows to be the rule' (ibid.: 98). But everyone does not know this and some have been arguing a different tack for a long time. Blunt, for example, said of Uttar Pradesh that 'amongst all Hindus there is probably a tendency towards hypergamy' (quoted in Dumont 1980: 370, fn. 54b). Parry comes to much the same conclusion, arguing that it is hypergamy which is the rule and a strict endogamy which is the exception.

In Kangra, attempts by the lowest Rājput *birādari* to subvert the hypergamous system and to improve their own status by merging with the *birādari* above were repulsed. For a short time, this resulted in *birādari*s turning in on themselves and forming close-knit endogamous units. But the prior hypergamous pattern soon re-established itself. Parry infers that

> the Kangra facts suggest that it is short-lived (and possibly recurring) periods of *birādari* endogamy which appear to be the 'pathological' development, and that it is hypergamy which is the norm. The whole ideology stresses the asymmetrical status of affines . . . (Parry 1979: 267)

Drawing on comparisons with Leach's classic study (1954) of the oscillation between hierarchical and egalitarian political systems in highland Burma, Parry's conclusion is that *birādari* endogamy is inherently unstable: 'endogamy poses its own structural problems which push the system back in the direction of anisogamy' (Parry 1979: 269).

This conclusion has to be tempered in two respects, however. In the first place, it is only the higher castes (i.e. Brāhmaṇs and Rājputs) which are hypergamous while the castes below them are isogamous. Secondly, hypergamy only takes place within certain limits, between groups which are not too far separated in status: wife-takers no less than wife-givers will always try to secure as prestigious a marriage alliance as possible. Parry relates this to the ideology of *dān*, of which the gift of the virgin bride *kanyā dān* (particularly associated with hypergamy) is a sub-category:[9]

> On an ideological level, the notion of *dan* puts all the stress on the merit and prestige to be derived from giving to superiors. Just as the *purohit* may not accept *dan* from the lowest castes, so the wife-takers may not accept brides from people who are substantially inferior to themselves. But provided that the recipient stays within the prescribed limits the acceptance of *dan* does not appear to be considered demeaning (ibid.: 283)

There is a difficulty here, however, because it is not entirely clear what 'the prescribed limits' are, or how they are arrived at. When Parry refers to 'brides from people who are substantially inferior to themselves', he appears to refer to a concept of inferiority based primarily on politico-economic criteria—aristocratic or royal pedigree. This not only puts in question his own interpretation of

[9] See Ch. 4 for the ambiguities surrounding the concept of *dān* (*dāna*).

the parallel between *kanyā dān* and ritual gifts of *dān* to a *purohit*; it also undermines the very basis of Dumont's theory of caste (which Parry seems to endorse) where politico-economic concerns are encompassed by ritual notions of purity.

If, as Parry and Blunt suggest, hypergamy is built into the way in which caste systems operate, this obviously poses problems for a ritual ordering of castes in which Brāhmaṇs are at the top. The aim of hypergamy is to ally oneself with the most aristocratic, 'kingly' caste possible. Hypergamous marriages into Brāhmaṇ castes are rarely reported and I doubt whether there is any significant degree of intermarriage between those Brāhmaṇs who provide *purohit*s to Rājput patrons and those Brāhmaṇs who provide temple priests or funeral priests. In what sense, then, are Brāhmaṇs the highest caste if there is no aspiration for social mobility into this group?

The remainder of this chapter will explore whether there is a connection between the two qualifications to Parry's 'hypergamy is the norm' hypothesis—namely, the facts that only high castes are hypergamous and that hypergamy is only acceptable within certain limits. I will argue that Kangra illustrates how caste systems work in general, that because of certain underlying political and economic constraints, some groups tend to be pushed in the direction of hypergamy while others are constrained to follow a strategy of isogamy.

The general problem is to demonstrate what those constraints are, and unfortunately Parry's study is limited in this respect because the only detailed ethnography is on the hypergamous Rājputs; the internal workings of the isogamous groups are not discussed in any depth. In the following section I will try to redress the balance by examining a case study of a group of people among whom isogamy is the explicit and pervasive norm. It is also very interesting that these people are, in many respects, the equivalent of the Rājputs in their own milieu.

Isogamy

The Kathmandu Valley in Nepal is the homeland of a complex ethnic group called the Newars. It is dominated by the three medieval towns of Kathmandu, Patan, and Bhaktapur, each of which was, until 1768, the centre of a small kingdom. In 1768–9, the 'Valley' was conquered by the king of Gorkha, then a small principality, some eighty kilometers to the west. The conquering Gorkhālis were Hindus though their expansionism was only made possible by the military support of non-Hindu hill tribes. By the end of the eighteenth century they had forged the boundaries of modern Nepal and they have remained the dominant political force ever since. The present king is a direct descendant of the eighteenth-century king of Gorkha who unified Nepal.

Both because of its exceptionally fertile base, and because the Kathmandu Valley lay on one of the main trade routes between India and Tibet, the local economy was able to sustain a complex, urban society from a very early period. Even those settlements which are predominantly inhabited by peasants are densely populated and have a strong urban character to their architecture. Apart from the three royal cities, there are also many other small Newar towns in and near the Valley and this urban legacy provided the Newars with a wealth of experience in administration and trade. From the late eighteenth century onwards, many emigrated from the Valley to provide the administrative and commercial manpower in the centres established by the new state, and still today they are prominent in urban settlements throughout Nepal.

At the time of the Valley's conquest, each Newar settlement had its own complex network of castes and these have been preserved, more or less intact, down to the present day. Indeed the Gorkhāli conquest probably had the effect of making these local caste systems more rigid in much the same way that resulted from British rule in India. Where the British attempted to pigeonhole castes and tribes once and for all by means of the census reports, the Gorkhālis did the same in Nepal with the introduction of a Legal Code, called the *Muluki Ain*, the first edition of which appeared in 1854.[10]

In this code all of the new state's tribes and ethnic groups were treated as castes and strict rules were promulgated concerning relations between them. This was irrespective of whether or not they had observed Hindu concepts of commensality and connubium—and such ideas were foreign to the vast majority of Nepal's mountain peoples. The Legal Code also paid little attention to whether vanquished groups had maintained their own

[10] See Höfer (1979).

caste system prior to conquest, as the Newars had. The fact that the inhabitants of the Kathmandu Valley had enjoyed a complex, caste-based civilization for centuries gave the urban Newars slightly higher status than the rustic, mountain tribals, but they were still regarded as distinctly lower than the Gorkhālis.

The Legal Code of 1854 did, however, give some minimal recognition to the Newars' internal caste differences. The Rājopādhyāya Brāhmaṇs, for example, were allocated a special position in recognition of their priestly services. The nobility are referred to as *tharghar ra asal śreṣṭh*—'well-bred, good-quality Śreṣṭhas'. Śreṣṭha appears to refer to all 'high' Newar patron castes—the equivalent of the Chetri among the Gorkhālis or the Rājput of northern India.

As with the Rājputs, however, it is extremely hazardous to describe the Śreṣṭhas as a single caste. They are an aggregation of lineages rather than a homogeneous group. Whatever unity Śreṣṭhas are observed to have (or to have had in the past) derives from the fact that their traditional function is to patronize other groups. From the outside, this function of patronage imbues all Śreṣṭhas with a collectively high status. For non-Śreṣṭhas, Śreṣṭhas are those lineages which are owed respect because it is primarily they who command the services of others.

Newars often say that nowadays anyone can call himself a Śreṣṭha. But this does not mean that everyone who calls himself a Śreṣṭha is regarded as such. There is continual dispute about whether particular families, or particular lineages, merit the status of Śreṣṭha at all, and among those that do, what 'quality' of Śreṣṭha they are—aristocratic, *nouveau-arrivé*, commoner, degraded, or pretender from a lower caste. From the inside, Śreṣṭhas are endlessly fragmented.

There are two main bases on which claims to Śreṣṭha status in general, and to membership of a particular sub-division, are made. The first is genealogy—kinship and marriage connections; the second is economic standing. These two are always woven together and it is frequently impossible to decide where the basis of any claim 'really' lies. Thus a certain family will claim aristocratic status and point to its marriage alliances with other prestigious families. But others will assert that this family has only been able to make these alliances because of its wealth and that 'in fact' they have much lower origins.

Since there has been no Newar court for over two hundred years, there is no final internal authority to adjudicate on the relative merits of one claim over another. In general, the post-1769 Gorkhāli regime has been indifferent to the internal wrangling over status among Newars. In cases where disputes were so acrimonious that they became socially disruptive and were brought before the courts, their legal 'resolution' has not automatically settled the affair for the parties concerned.[11] In short, one may say that while every household (defined as those who share a common kitchen) belongs to a particular lineage and, by virtue of this, claims a certain status, the claim may either be generally accepted, generally rejected, or be the source of much contention.

Śreṣṭhas have a number of ways of referring to the different status groups within them. The most common adjectives in use in the cities are *chatharīya* (literally 'six clan') and *pāñctharīya* ('five clan'). Śreṣṭhas from other settlements are commonly referred to by their place of origin—e.g. Thimi Śreṣṭha or Dhulikhel Śreṣṭha, the implication being that these groups are different from, and inferior to, the Śreṣṭhas of the cities. The name Śreṣṭha without any qualifying adjective is sometimes construed as referring to those who are neither *chatharīya* nor *pāñctharīya* but this depends completely on context. Thus some with the surname Śreṣṭha may say that in fact they are *chatharīya* and will not marry others who call themselves Śreṣṭha because the latter are of lower status. By and large, people say that these different status groups do not intermarry: the problem is that it is not always possible to say unambiguously which group any particular household or lineage belongs to.

The *chatharīya* lineages are generally identified as descendants of the aristocracy who ruled the Valley before its conquest in 1769. The *pāñctharīya* Śreṣṭhas, by contrast, are those lineages which are not able to demonstrate aristocratic origins or which are believed to be the descendants of cross-caste unions between *chatharīya* men and lower-caste women. Rosser (1966: 102) points out that the use of these terms is not consistent. While people use the term *chatharīya* 'commonly and openly to describe themselves', the word *pāñctharīya* is somewhat derogatory and is normally used only in reference to others. Indeed when people use it with

[11] Outside commentators have also been divided about such disputes—see e.g. Rosser (1966) and Greenwold (1975).

reference to themselves, it 'usually means that they actually belong to the grades lower than the Panchthare but are claiming this higher position' (ibid.). In other words, it appears that such people are not quite sure what the rules of self-identification are, and this is what gives them away. As for the 'Śreṣṭhas' who come below them, they are, says Rosser, 'barely distinguishable if at all from the topmost grade of Jyapus [the Farmer caste]' (ibid.). To make matters more complicated still, there are yet other adjectives, such as 'half-Śreṣṭha' or 'half-caste Śreṣṭha', which are used to make further distinctions.[12]

One might think that it should be relatively straightforward identifying the Newar *chatharīya* lineages—those which can demonstrate their genealogy back to the Newar aristocracy of the eighteenth century. In fact, however, the demonstration of *chatharīya* status is anything but straightforward. For example, one household or lineage may insist that they are *chatharīya* because their family surname proves it: this is often asserted by people with names such as Pradhān (first minister), Amātya (minister), Rājbhaṇḍāri (royal storekeeper), and a number of others suggesting an association with the Newar palaces. However, it is well known that many people have adopted such family names regardless of their origins and this leads to a great deal of claim and counter-claim. It is common for two groups to say of each other: 'We are the "real" Pradhāns (or whoever) while they are simply pretenders'.

In other cases it might be generally believed that a certain family are indeed of noble origins but that they have become degraded in some way—typically through marriage with a lower-caste group. The 'degradation' may also be by association: thus if one member of a lineage marries unacceptably, this may downgrade the entire lineage in the eyes of others. It is equally possible that the other members of the lineage will try to avert this by dissociating themselves from the offending family, and thus effectively outcasting them.

The difficulty here is that any evaluation of the status of others is subject to a certain amount of self-interest. For example, one will not want to question the status of those with whom one has marriage connections since this will automatically prejudice one's

[12] Rosser himself does not employ diacritics; I have included them here for the sake of consistency with general usage.

own standing. Moreover, the degree of relational proximity required to cause loss of status is a subject of interminable dispute. Every lineage has some skeleton in the cupboard and given the close-knit, highly concentrated nature of Newar society, skeletons are difficult to conceal.

All this means that virtually no household's claims to pure *chatharīya* status are beyond dispute. A household which claims this status will point to its alliances with other 'noble' households and conveniently forget the less prestigious marriages. Similarly, a household which has been previously regarded as *pāñcharīya* may, through a rise in its fortunes, be able to arrange a marriage with a household regarded as *chatharīya* and then itself claim to have had this status all along. But in the eyes of others the very same alliance may be seen as degrading the *chatharīya* household rather than enhancing the status of the *pāñctharīya* household. What is claimed as an indisputable pedigree from one point of view will be seen as so much pretension from another.

Another possibility is that the fortunes of a particular household may rise or fall from one generation to the next and not necessarily in tandem with others of the same lineage. Thus a group of brothers may find themselves considerably poorer than their father once his property is divided among them, and they may then be unable to attract the same high-status marriage partners as others in the lineage. Or the reverse: through success in trade, for example, a previously unconnected household might find itself able to attract marriage partners who would not have considered such an alliance before.

Does this mean that hypergamy (or hypogamy) is easy or frequent? The short answer to this is no. In spite of the ambiguities involved in status evaluation, few people are at all confused about who they can or should marry. The general principle is that one should, as far as possible, marry one's status equals. Pervasive isogamy depends, however, on being sure of who one's marriage partners are. In a sense the only way to be absolutely sure about this is to marry into those lineages one has always married into. The result of this, as Dumont has point out, is the formation of a 'marriage alliance' which endures from one generation to the next.[13] This pattern is particularly associated with South India and with a rigid application of rules governing purity and impurity. It

[13] See Dumont (1957).

ensures the creation of small, endogamous marriage-circles each extremely jealous of its own status and intensely suspicious of attempts by outsiders to infiltrate.

The general suspicion attaching to all alliances among Newars means that extreme care is taken before embarking on them. The most obvious reason for this pervasive suspicion is the exclusion of Newars from political power for the last two hundred years. Deprived of the fundamental basis of their status, the erstwhile aristocratic Newar lineages made a virtue out of necessity by turning in on themselves in an attempt to preserve what prestige they could. Hypergamy is always the attempt by relatively powerful groups to consolidate their power, to legitimize it by marrying into groups whose status is beyond question.[14] In the case of the Newars, newly acquired wealth could not be translated into political power (in the sense of governmental power) because Newars as a whole were excluded from this arena.

In the tightly structured world of the Kathmandu Valley, it is almost impossible to 'beat the system', to subvert the ideal of isogamy by concealing one's true origins. It is nearly always possible to ascertain anyone's ancestry very easily and in those cases where it is not possible, there is extreme reluctance to negotiate a marriage. Failure to elucidate origins is construed as a sign that the household under investigation must have something to hide. This raises an obvious question: who exactly make up the group which has the capacity to oblige individuals to conform? Disapproval, of itself, would hardly be sufficient; it must be strong enough to bite, to prevent people from breaking the rule of isogamy rather than simply admonish them for doing so.

The shading off of the various divisions of Śreṣṭhas into one another shows that there are no corporate marriage-circles with this capability—no *Verband*, as Klass would have it. There is,

[14] The same is true of hypogamy: the cultural emphasis on hypergamy in the Indian sub-continent is probably associated with extreme political instability and a consequent prestige attached to (male) martial ethics such that grooms from militarily powerful households were particularly desirable: 'in most of western Asia and India, women are regarded as an appropriate form of tribute from the weak man, who seeks protection, to the strong, who gives it' (Barth 1960: 135). However, there is some evidence to suggest that in Newar society (where there is a marked absence of a martial tradition), hypergamy is more highly disapproved of than hypogamy. This is because a low-status wife is a potential source of pollution for all the members of the household if she cooks for them; a low-status husband, by contrast, only threatens the purity of his wife.

however, another set of institutions among Newars where corporate identity is more manifest: generically these institutions are referred to as *guthi*s. Newars operate a variation on the South Indian practice of isogamy. Rather than ensuring endogamy by placing a premium on the direct repetition of alliances, they restrict their marriages to other lineages in the locality whose status they can be more or less sure of. The *guthi*s, which are local, socio-religious associations with an exclusive membership, underpin this system. There are two principal kinds of *guthi*—the *dyaḥ pūjā guthi* and the *sī guthi*. The *dyaḥ pūjā guthi* brings together all the households in a lineage to worship the ancestral deities called *digu dyaḥ*. The *sī guthi* groups together a number of households in a locality for the purpose of ensuring that death ritual is properly carried out.[15]

Worship of the ancestral deity by the *dyaḥ pūjā guthi* normally takes place once annually and its observance is regarded as extremely important by all Newars. Those who worship together always belong to the same patrilineage, which often has a name or a nickname. While the *pūjā* has sometimes been called a kind of ancestor worship,[16] it is more accurate to describe it as the worship of gods who symbolize the lineage. Should a lineage split, each segment forms a new *dyaḥ pūjā guthi*. Splits may occur for a number of reasons, the most common being quarrels and the movement of lineage members to another settlement.

The *sī guthi* is a rather different kind of association. The name comes from the Newari *siye* ('to die') and the primary function of these groups is to ensure that funerals are promptly and correctly carried out. Members of a *sī guthi* always belong to the same caste. To be excluded from such an association is tantamount to being casteless, which is an option that few Newars are prepared to consider. To be casteless means to be without potential marriage partners, and while this may not matter to those who are already married, it is obviously of prime concern to their children. This is the ultimate force in the obligation to conform to the demands of both the lineage and death *guthi*s. Not to do so is to jeopardize the future of one's offspring.

[15] On *guthi* organization, see Quigley (1985). A collection of essays which highlights the similarities and differences in institutions among various Newar castes is in preparation—D. N. Gellner and Quigley (eds., 1995).

[16] See G. S. Nepali (1965: 194).

The hallmark of the *guthi*s is the exclusion of outsiders. Newars as a whole are acutely conscious of their ethnic separateness from other groups in Nepal. While Newars themselves often stress cultural differences such as language, ritual, art, and architecture, what underlines their separateness at base is their autonomous caste system, bounded from the outside by the Legal Code of the Gorkhālis. More accurately, one should talk of Newar caste system*s* since the idea of Newars as a social and cultural unity really only derives from the period following on the Gorkhāli conquest. Before then the Valley was interminably divided into different political units and the persistence of local caste systems today is an index of the division.

Competing claims to Śreṣṭha caste status are one consequence of the cultural unification imposed on the indigenous inhabitants of the Kathmandu Valley. Newars have always been divided into those who employ Brāhmaṇ domestic priests and those who use Buddhist domestic priests.[17] Nevertheless, Newar Buddhists no less than Hindus are organized along caste lines, a reflection of the political ascendancy of Hindu kings in the Valley throughout the centuries. The Gorkhālis, however, saw themselves as more orthodox Hindus and effected a policy of vigorous Hinduization in their attempts to create a unified Hindu kingdom of Nepal. This was perhaps particularly marked during the hundred-year oligarchy of the Rāṇas from approximately 1850 to 1950.[18] The Rāṇas tolerated no cultural opposition in the political centre and their policy of Hinduization (of which the 1854 Legal Code was an early concrete manifestation) had serious implications for Newar Buddhists. During the period of Rāna hegemony,

> Toute manifestation culturelle est interdite . . . Les Bouddhistes Néwar, désignés comme les dépositaires de l'ancienne culture 'népalaise', sont les plus particulièrement visés; les Rana les forceront à respecter les lois hindoues et à plier à l'autorité des brahmanes. (Toffin 1977: 14)

[17] The extent to which this distinction can be used to label Newars as either Buddhist or Hindu is discussed by D. N. Gellner (1992) and, more briefly, by Locke (1989).

[18] The Rāṇas were one of the most powerful Chetri families in the Gorkhāli court. After massacring most of their fellow aristocracy in 1846, they assumed control of all important political positions and reduced the king to the status of a puppet figurehead for over a century. The best short introduction to Nepal is Gaborieau (1978).

The effect of this subjugation was to make it politically much more attractive for Newars to assert their own Hindu identity. Śreṣṭhas, being the dominant patron caste among Hindu Newars, were the obvious choice for emulation:

> The Ranas utilized the ideology of caste to validate and reinforce their own political authority and to ensure the political stability of an absolute and autocratic despotism . . . This determined Hinduism had the effect of notably raising the prestige (and of course the tangible rewards) of the Hindu Newars in particular the Shrestha merchants and of depressing the status of Newar Buddhism, particularly the Gubhaju priests. These Gubhaju family priests found themselves increasingly deserted by their jajmans for their more favoured and influential Brahman competitors. (Rosser 1966: 82)

Śreṣṭhas did not, then, simply benefit from the intangible kudos of being Hindu. Some of them were also granted access to government positions as a means both of profiting from their experience in this domain and simultaneously defusing a united Newar opposition:

> During the Rana period, government positions were monopolised by some two hundred 'client families—mostly Kathmandu-based Brahmans and Ksatriyas but with a few Newari Shresthas included. These three high-caste groups still provide 80–90 per cent of the bureaucracy. (Rose and Fisher 1970: 70)

By adopting the name Śreṣṭha or a high-sounding Śreṣṭha caste name such as Pradhān, a political claim is made, identifying oneself with those who are dominant.

There is also the fact that the traditional occupations of many Śreṣṭhas were trade and administration and this has brought them to settlements throughout Nepal, particularly in the last two hundred years. But many others who also emigrated from the Valley took to calling themselves Śreṣṭha whatever their caste origins were. As some of the descendants of these people have returned to the Valley, the result has been to fuel suspicion about who the 'real' Śreṣṭhas are. The system of *guthi*s is a means of coping with this problem of identification.

Isogamy among the Newars involves a kind of circular logic which has as its consequence that the territorial expansion of affinal ties is inhibited: 'Acceptable affines are those of the same caste status: those of the same caste status are people with whom we have married before.' But the direct repetition of marriage alliances is precluded because this would be considered a kind of incest: all the members of one's mother's natal lineage are regarded as kin. However, by marrying into the other lineages of one's *sī guthi* and with their affines, one is relatively assured of finding a spouse who will be acceptable to everyone who matters. The end result is to set up a territorially limited marriage-circle—those who belong to *guthi*s which are seen to perform their rituals in the locality. This pronounced preference for local endogamy has been reported in every ethnography on Newars.[19]

Hierarchy and Endogamy

As already pointed out, Dumont has stated that endogamy is not an independent principle but is entailed by the demands of hierarchy. This is true but it does not explain why some groups are rather more markedly endogamous than others. What is missing in Dumont is a consideration of the political nature of caste hierarchy, the fact that some groups have access to power while others are denied it.[20]

In a stimulating essay which might serve as a bridge between the respective ethnographies of the Śreṣṭhas and the Rājputs, Richard Fox shows clear linkages between caste, kinship, and territory in north India. Looking at the early formation of small-scale 'urban-like' locales, he draws on Sjoberg's (1960) hypothesis that the pre-industrial city depended on a well-established political apparatus and was not simply a commercial centre. He then argues that the groups which stimulated urban development at the local level in north India were 'locally dominant "stratified lineages" claiming Rajput, Bhuinhar, or other Kṣatriya identification' (Fox 1970: 171).

These 'rurban' settlements were lineage centres which reproduced the political, economic, and ritual functions of the state-level pre-industrial cities on a smaller scale. They depended on retainers and specialist services and attracted people 'escaping the uncertainties of the rural areas or the exactions of unscrupulous state

[19] See D. N. Gellner and D. Quigley (eds., 1995) for a comprehensive bibliography.

[20] The volumes edited by R. Guha in the series *Subaltern Studies* attempt to redress this fault.

revenue authorities' (ibid.: 179). These settlements were also fortresses, and 'When no more room existed at the fort, the raja or chaudhuri settled a cadet line in the villages (usually nearby), so that they could pose no threat to his command. Often these junior lines began their own urban-like centres' (ibid.: 176). One has here the beginnings of a theory of hypergamy—a mechanism by which less prestigious Rājput lineages could increase their status as the settlements over which they presided grew in power. This is the obvious explanation for the expansionist nature of hypergamous alliances and for the fact, reported by Parry and others, that such alliances were preferably made to the west with territories which were more fertile and prosperous. Galey reports that James Tod, the Political Agent for the Western Rajput States from 1818,

> was able to show with precision the way direct management and control was kept under the supervision of the royal and most senior branch of the clan, while indirect control was distributed among junior branches, other politically allied clans and officials holding titles over land in exchange for services, all embodying at their level the power held in court by the king. (Galey 1989: 136)

For the north Indian castes below the Rājputs, and for the Śreṣṭhas of the Kathmandu Valley since the Gorkhāli conquest, the option of hypergamous alliances has not been available. In the case of the landless north Indian castes, they had nothing to bargain with. In the case of the Newars, an outside politically dominant force unsurped their power and denied them the opportunity of marriage alliances with the new élite. Isogamy can be seen as an attempt by the powerless to come to terms with their situation: unable for one reason or another to enter the ranks of the powerful, the one thing they can do is prevent those who are even less powerful from entering their ranks. Strict control over affiliation by kinship or marriage is the solution to this.

One might add a supplementary hypothesis here, though it is one which requires considerable research before it can be substantiated. The pre-modern history of south India is, for the most part, one of the encapsulation of one Hindu kingdom by another.[21] If the example of the Kathmandu Valley is typical of such situations, one might conjecture that the absorption of one or more caste systems into another which is more powerful simul-

[21] See e.g. Stein (1980) and Basham (1975).

taneously leads to a proliferation of castes and to a rigidity of the boundaries between them. Whether or not it will prove possible to show that there is a general tendency of this kind, one thing is clear: hypergamy and isogamy are two sides of the same hierarchical coin. Both are attempts to maximize one's status given the political constraints of a society where power ultimately derives from control over land.

The final chapter will relate the sociology of caste to the more general sociology of complex agrarian society. First, however, it is necessary to examine in greater detail the institution which lies at the heart of caste organization: kingship.

6

Caste and Kingship: Hocart's Theory

Kings and Priests

ARTHUR MAURICE HOCART, who died in 1939, is probably much better known to students of the Pacific and of kingship than to students of South Asia and caste. Before the First World War he conducted research with W. H. R. Rivers, principally in Fiji, Tonga, and Samoa, and he was, for a time, headmaster of the local school in Lau, Fiji. After the war, however, he became Archaeological Commissioner in Ceylon (Sri Lanka) and it is during this time that his ideas on caste crystallized, although his first article on the subject did not appear until 1935.[1] Hocart's book on caste, the last of his major works, has an authoritative though provocative style and was first published in French in 1938. An English edition entitled *Caste: A Comparative Study* was brought out in 1950.

Although Hocart's explanation of caste is somewhat short on historical and ethnographic detail, the theory allows one to consider the historical factors which have shaped the structure of caste-organized communities in a way which Dumont's theory does not. Hocart's theory has not been altogether ignored by post-war students of Hinduism though recent interest in his ideas has focused more on his views on traditional kingship.[2] In fact Hocart's theory of caste *is* a theory of kingship but this equivalence has not always been made clear. On the contrary, the tendency has been to obscure it because the recently rediscovered interest in

This chapter is substantially the same as an article published in *The Eastern Anthropologist* (1991); it is a more critical version of an earlier article published in *Pacific Viewpoint* (1988*a*).

[1] See Rodney Needham's introduction to Hocart (1970) for a discussion of his life and work. Needham's other work on Hocart includes an edited collection of his essays (1987) which contains a significant excerpt from his book on caste and bibliographic references. Schnepel (1988) provides an excellent discussion of Hocart's central concerns with kingship and ritual.

[2] Examples which spring to mind are Toffin's work on royal rituals in the Kathmandu Valley (1979; 1984; 1986), Inden's (1986; 1990) attack on 'orientalist' accounts of India, the historical research of Stein (1980) and Dirks (1987; 1989) on South India, and Galey's (1989) reconsideration of Indian kingship.

Indian kingship has not generally aimed at endorsing Hocart's theory of caste. It is more an expression of dissatisfaction with the European preoccupation with concepts of purity and pollution and an attempt to shift the focus of debate about the nature of Indian social organization away from ideology and towards an understanding of political institutions.

Hocart believed that caste formations were widespread throughout the ancient world and were certainly not confined to Hindu India. While the main essay of his book discusses India and Ceylon, over fifty pages are devoted to a comparison with the social organization of South Pacific islands, principally Fiji, while a brief sweep is made over Persia, Egypt, and Ancient Greece and Rome. Comparison is at the heart of Hocart's method and it is no accident that the sub-title of the English edition is 'A Comparative Study'. There are strong resonances with his two books on kingship, and striking parallels between his consideration of the relationship between kinship and early state formation and that found in Fustel de Coulanges' *The Ancient City*.

One of Hocart's main aims was to challenge certain conventional European notions about caste—for example that members of any caste always follow a particular occupation. His attack on European misconceptions led him to assert that 'We must search for [the principle of caste] not in our minds, but in the minds of those people who practise the caste system, who have daily experience of it, and are thus most likely to have a feeling for what is essential in it' (Hocart 1950: 3). Such an approach is, of course, often the beginning of the slippery road to relativism. Like Dumont, Hocart is inclined to present caste ideology as a sufficient explanation of the problem and, like Dumont, this leads him into certain intractable difficulties.

There are several implications in Hocart's theory of caste and some of these are more fully drawn out by him than others. I will first present his theory, more or less in the original words, bringing out the implications as I see them. I will briefly describe the extent to which Hocart elaborated on these implications and suggest that some of them must be made rather more explicit in order to appreciate fully the significance of his approach.

Hocart's theory of caste revolves around four concepts: kinship, domination, ritual, and decay (or pollution). While he writes with persuasive elegance, there is a danger in reproducing his argument in his own words because at first sight the flamboyant style makes it appear rather exotic. He summarizes his theory of caste in the following way:

> The conclusion we have arrived at on modern evidence is that the caste system is a sacrificial organization, that the aristocracy are feudal lords constantly involved in rites for which they require vassals or serfs, because some of these services involve pollution from which the lord must remain free . . . Castes are merely families to whom various offices in the ritual are assigned by heredity. (ibid.: 17, 20)

This is the theory, no more and no less, but this formulation is obviously too compact to be clear. In particular, his definition of the caste system as a sacrificial organization is puzzling. Initially one is tempted to treat this as some kind of metaphor but Hocart makes it very plain, through continual repetition, that this statement is to be taken literally, not symbolically: 'The organization is sacrificial and therefore it is entered through the sacrifice' (ibid.: 71); 'The farmers . . . feed the sacrifice from their lands and cattle' (ibid.: 40); 'the basis [of the caste system] is twofold: descent and sacrifice. Of the two, sacrifice is the essential one . . .' (ibid.: 56).

This emphasis on sacrifice derives in the first place from Hocart's assertion that the Vedic theory of the four *varṇa*s accurately reflects the nature of Hindu society. It will be remembered that the Vedic concept of *varṇa* is tied to a sacrificial theory of human society.[3] However odd this preoccupation with sacrificial ritual may appear to modern man, Hocart believes that it should not be summarily dismissed as 'a pure figment, the invention of priests for their own glorification' (ibid.: 24)—the generic view which he scornfully attributed to nineteenth- and early twentieth-century scholars of Hinduism. Nor is it simply an elaborate piece of doctrinal wishful thinking about the *ideal* condition of the universe; it is also a commentary or reflection on the *actual* social world. According to Hocart, the Vedic theory of the *varṇa*s is neither priestly mysticism nor a deliberate attempt to obscure the 'true' nature of social divisions. The true nature of these divisions is what the texts say it is.

But why should these texts be so concerned with sacrifice? Hocart gives two clues. The first concerns the personnel involved:

[3] See Ch. 1 for a brief description of the *varṇa* theory.

> . . . the worthy or excellent castes are those which alone are admitted to share in the sacrifice, with whom alone the gods hold converse . . . the ritual books are not concerned with religion in general and the rites of all classes, but mainly with the state sacrifices, such as the king's consecration, the priest's installation, and so forth. (ibid.: 18)

The second clue to the preoccupation with sacrifice concerns the purpose of these rituals:

> The main object of these sacrifices was the pursuit of immortality, not immortality as we understand it, but freedom from premature death and the diseases that cause it and the renewal of this vigorous life hereafter. It is a very concrete and immediate immortality. It is to be secured by becoming a god and ascending to the world of the gods . . . the process is:
>
> sacrifice = gods;
> sacrificer becomes = sacrifice;
> sacrificer becomes = gods. (ibid.)

Hocart believed that this Vedic theory, in which each of the *varṇa*s is allocated a specific function in the continual re-ordering of the universe through the repetition of the primeval sacrifice, explains quite adequately the observable organization of *jāti*s today: 'the alleged inconsistencies are misunderstandings on our part . . . India has not changed as much as is often supposed' (ibid.: 23).

This rather understates the claim being advanced: for Hocart, the essential principles of caste have not changed in over 2,000 years—an extremely bold claim. What appears even bolder is his assertion that it is the '*kshatriya* caste' which is the apex of the system, an assertion which is made without the slightest hint of self-consciousness. He seems innocently unaware of the fact that putting the king above the priest is a startling reversal of the usual assumption that Brāhmaṇs are 'the first caste'.

Hocart's assertion must be read very carefully because it is he who invokes the epithet 'the first caste' for the kings, not the texts which he relies on. The references which he makes to these texts (the *Satapatha Brāhmaṇa*) are simply to the effect that the function of the king is to be the patron (*yajamāna*) of the state sacrifice. Hocart interprets this sacrificial function as being the pivot on which the caste system turns. Kings are 'the first caste' because their function is the crucial one—to command the sacrifices which regenerate the cosmic order, and thus guarantee the well-being of the community.

In making the king the pivot of the caste system, Hocart hoped to counter the commonly held idea that the principal function of the *kṣatriya* is to be a warrior. For Hocart it is not fighting which is the crucial attribute of the *kṣatriya*, but kingship; physical dominance had to be legitimated through ritual.[4] He makes it clear that his interpretation does not derive simply from textual exegesis but also from actual practice: 'kings not of *kshatriya* descent sooner or later forge themselves a *kshatriya* pedigree. Kings should properly come from that caste. We can therefore speak of this caste as the royal one or the nobility' (ibid.: 34). This assimilation of the nobility to royalty is crucial. Whenever Hocart says 'kings', this should be interpreted loosely in the sense of rulers—those who are politically dominant over others.

In fact, for Hocart, the royal attribute—'*kshatra* which we can render approximately by the Roman *imperium*' (ibid.: 37)—is reproduced throughout society. Even families with relatively little power may still be in a position to command yet other families to serve them in some capacity. Whenever Hocart refers to kingship and nobility, one must understand these as relative, never absolute, terms:

> The king's state is reproduced in miniature by his vassals: a farmer has his court, consisting of the personages most essential to the ritual, and so present even in the smallest community, the barber, the washerman, the drummers and so forth. (ibid.: 68)

Those who are less powerful may not always be so. In time they may come to challenge the position of the nobility or even the king: 'in ancient days low caste men, washermen and others, not uncommonly became kings' (ibid.: 3).

For Hocart the position of all others depends on their relation to the *kṣatriya*, the caste which provides the king and the nobility:

> The question which we (unfortunately) translate 'What is his caste?' means simply: 'What is his birth, lineage?' . . . The term *jāti* has much wider and looser a meaning than we have put upon the Portuguese creation 'caste'. It does not refer to any particular kind of division or grouping, but simply to hereditary status. (ibid.: 32–3)

[4] 'We can perhaps best sum up the first caste as the one that provides the king. It is equally so in the earliest texts and in late inscriptions' (ibid.: 34). See Hocart's book for the sources he relied on.

Caste is a question of pedigree—of kinship affiliation to noble lineages. Put another way, it is the purity of kingship (or nobility) which is the central axiom of caste (and not the purity of priesthood). What is at stake is the purity of those whom others emulate.

From the point of view of the ideology of caste, every function is a ritual function, a moral duty: '. . . every occupation is a priesthood . . . The craftsman is, as it were, the man who has the ear of the deity presiding over some particular activity' (ibid.: 16). Again, this must not be taken too narrowly. It is not just crafts as we understand the term which are peculiarly ritual occupations. *Every* occupation is a priesthood, including those which appear to us as devoid of ritual content (for example, ruling and farming) and those which are represented as ritually defiling (such as being a washerman or a barber).

Each of the four 'castes' has a specific ritual function. That of the king is to offer up sacrifices—not to perform them himself, but to command others and to bear the expense. This role sets him apart from the rest of society: 'The sacrificer is much more than a worshipper, as we understand the term. He represents a god or gods, more particularly Indra . . .' (ibid.: 35). This assimilation of the king with the gods means that '[T]he temple and the palace are indistinguishable' (ibid.: 68). The priest is the servant of the king: 'The *second* caste supplies the priests, brahmans, who perform the rituals for the king *or for whatever great man is offering the sacrifice*' (ibid.: 37, emphasis added).

The third caste, in the earliest texts referred to as the *viś* (later *vaiśya*), 'are the support on which the monarch and the priesthood rest and their duty is to feed the sacrifice from their lands and cattle' (ibid.: 40). Hocart generally refers to this caste as 'the farmers' but he makes it clear that producing agricultural wealth is not their only function. They are also responsible for the defence of the kingdom: 'the farmers are the king's mainstay in battle. They are just as military then as the nobles' (ibid.: 40).

It is significant that Hocart does not refer to the *śūdra* as the fourth caste but simply as 'low castes' or, more revealingly still, as serfs. He notes that they are excluded from the sacrifice, an indication that they are different in kind from the three 'worthy or excellent castes' (ibid.: 18). Like everyone else in society, however, the *śūdra* should be regarded as priests of a kind: 'The barber and the washerman, like the drummers, are not so much technicians as priests of a low grade, performing rites which the high-caste priest will not touch. The brahman, priest of the immortal gods, can have nothing to do with death' (ibid.: 11). *Śūdra* castes, therefore, are those which deal with death.

Low as these serfs are, they must be distinguished from those who stand outside society altogether: 'we must not confuse the serfs with the outcastes. The so-called serfs are quite honourable people who owe service to the king or feudal lord. We can perhaps describe them as retainers' (ibid.: 42). What constitutes an outcaste is not being *lower* than the *śūdra* but being outside society altogether, beyond the pale: 'all those who stand outside the communion, members of nations that worship other gods, represent the demons' (ibid.: 36). Whether these outsiders are kings, priests, or commoners, those who belong to other communions are outcastes. The communion that Hocart speaks of is the kingdom; it is a political as much as a ritual unit.

The sacrificial character of the caste system means that birth is not a sufficient condition of caste membership: 'initiation is indispensable' (ibid.: 71). This is especially so for the high castes: 'A nobleman's, a priest's and a farmer's rank thus still depends not only on birth, but on initiation' (ibid.: 56). What is more, initiation can override kinship in certain circumstances. In Sri Lanka, Hocart reports, priests are recruited from the Farmer caste who 'have usurped in the ritual the place held by the brahmans when priesthood was hereditary' (ibid.: 26). So not only is birth insufficient to establish caste membership; it may not even be necessary for the performance of particular ritual functions which are traditionally regarded as the preserve of certain castes: 'descent is merely a qualification which may at times be dispensed with' (ibid.: 56). Initiation, on the other hand, cannot be dispensed with.

To pursue the question of the connections between caste, kinship, and function, Hocart notes that 'Not all washermen wash, nor because you see a person washing are you safe in concluding that he is a washerman by caste' (ibid.: 2). And what goes for Washermen goes for other castes too. Carpenters by caste are not necessarily woodworkers, Farmers by caste may not necessarily be cultivators, Goldsmiths and Potters may have no idea how to work gold or clay, and so on. Though Hocart himself does not say so, this also of course means that Brāhmaṇs need not be *brāhmaṇs* (i.e. priests). However, Hocart gets into difficulty here. In his book on caste, he does not use the upper case to distinguish the caste (Farmer) from the occupation (farmer). The distinction is, however, made in *Kings and Councillors* where he writes: 'in India a fisherman is always a Mr. Fisher, but a Mr. Fisher is not always a fisherman: he may be a lawyer, a shopkeeper, a cook, anything that is not above or below the rank of the Fishers' (Hocart 1970: 120). While the second half of this sentence is true, the first is not, for if a cook can be a Mr Fisher, a fisherman can be a Mr Cook!

There is one final element of Hocart's theory:

> Royalty and priesthood form a pair . . . This pairing is conceived of as man and wife . . . Man and wife are heaven and earth, so are king and priest. The royal gods are celestial, more especially solar. The priestly gods are their [earthly] counterparts. (1950: 38)

Hocart insists that the demonstration of the underlying logic of caste which, among other things, explains this pairing of the priest and king, can only be made through comparison with other societies. His own view is that the main principles of caste are best preserved in Fiji, a country which is remarkable for the following reason: 'The whole organisation of society in Fiji is based on ritual' (ibid.: 79). The various offices which exist 'are purely ceremonial. They all form part of the king's state, and the king's state is an organisation for prosperity by the due observance of traditional rules' (ibid.: 97).

This is really the crux of Hocart's argument. Caste is fundamentally about kingship and ritual and these, in turn, are necessarily inseparable. He finishes his book with a flourish which, depending on one's mood, can seem either breathtaking or vacuous. Caste society, says Hocart, is like this:

> It is a society headed by a king who is responsible for the life of the people and of the things on which the life of the people depends: crops, cattle, fish, sunshine, the world. In this task he requires the assistance of various chieftains who are in charge of the various departments. (ibid.: 150)

This is the theory: there are kings and chiefs. Some of these chiefs are more rewardingly perceived as priests while others are aspirant kings or minor kings themselves. Priests, too, in so far as they may act as patrons of other priests, replicate the role of kingship on a lesser scale.

There is just one other aspect of Hocart's theory which remains to be brought out: '. . . the system', he says, 'is certainly more rigid than it used to be' (ibid.: 55). He offers no explanation of how, why, or when this rigidity set in.

Problems with Hocart's Theory

Needless to say, Hocart's vision of Hindu society, which ties caste inextricably to kingship, represents a radical alternative to Dumont's picture. In Dumont's eyes empirical matters ought not to be allowed to distract one too much from the underlying ideological structure and the actual organization of political units is an empirical consideration. Unity, Dumont believes, is only to be found in the internal structure of people's ideas, not in externally observable facts.

But how, if at all, does Hocart's theory account for empirically observed phenomena, and can it explain the way in which caste works any better or is it simply a contrary interpretation of Hindu ideology? In order to answer this, it is perhaps advisable first to effect a kind of translation of Hocart's theory which cuts away everything which might seem mysterious—notions such as sacrifice, kings who become gods, washermen who are not washermen, and so forth.

Stated more plainly still, and without the use of contentious adjectives such as 'sacrificial' and 'feudal', Hocart's theory can, I believe, be translated as follows:

There are two kinds of families: those who rule and those who are ruled. It is the ritual task of the ruled to keep their rulers free from pollution and the ritual task of the rulers to ensure that they do.

This can be reduced still further to one 'simple' principle:

Those who rule must be pure.

This is the rationale behind the repetition of sacrificial ritual. For Hocart, the myths which state that the castes are born of the sacrifice 'do not record an event that took place in the distant past, but a process which was continually re-enacted, the ennobling of the sons of noble houses' (ibid.: 56–7).

The vagueness of the terms—particularly 'kinds of families', 'rulers', and 'pure'—sins against anthropological convention which has long endeavoured to make such concepts more precise. My retention of the imprecision which characterizes Hocart's approach is deliberate and is central to the adaptation of his theory of caste which I wish to present. In order to arrive at this adaptation, however, it is necessary to introduce a certain amount of information which Hocart himself does not provide.

To begin, three general observations may be made—two about pre-colonial India, the other about post-colonial India. The first observation about pre-colonial India is this:

> The first crucial fact to be noted is that throughout pre-British India there was a surplus of land and a shortage of cultivators and labourers . . . the cultivators' ultimate sanction against oppressive rulers was flight to unoccupied land, of which there was plenty. (Fuller 1977: 96)[5]

There was, then, no shortage of virgin land on which to settle—and it is known that flight to new territory was a common strategy in the medieval period for those who wished to escape the tax-collecting demands of over-zealous kings.[6] The second observation concerns the chronic instability of pre-modern India:

> Few areas of the world's surface have seen more bloodshed and rapine, more external aggression and internecine strife, more movement and intermixture of peoples, more coming and goings of policies, religions, creeds and customs, than the Indian subcontinent. (Stevenson 1970: 25)[7]

The observation about post-colonial India concerns the relationship between Brāhmaṇ castes and the new political rulers. One of the consequences of the British administration was that European ideas about the separation of church and state were imported. The British dismantled the old *rāj* or, to be exact, they replaced the old plurality of *rāja*s and *rājya*s (kings and kingdoms) with a new unitary state. But they did not attempt to dismantle what they perceived to be Hindu religion. On the contrary, they effectively abdicated any responsibility for social issues which appeared to

[5] Fuller draws particularly on Habib (1963), Srinivas (1975), Baden-Powell (1892), and Embree (1969).

[6] See e.g. Stein (1968).

[7] Here I would endorse Baechler's argument that caste is essentially a solution to the problem of political instability in the sub-continent (Baechler 1988: 9). However, the author's characterization of caste is seriously limited by his failure to consider modern anthropological research on the subject—see my (1989) review.

them to be primarily religious.[8] They refused, for example, to intervene in caste disputes, or to adjudicate on the relative position of castes, in the mistaken belief that these functions were the preserve of Brāhmaṇ priests.

In fact, these duties had traditionally been the prerogative of the king.[9] Indeed they were the principal functions of the king since his role was not simply to rule, but to rule *well*. To be king was to be the representative of the gods on earth, to ensure justice, prosperity, and order for all within the kingdom:

> One of the fundamental requirements of Indic kingship was that the king be a munificent provider of fertile lands for Brahmans who would study and chant the vedas, perform sacrifices and provide ritual services for the king so as to ensure and protect his prosperity and that of his kingdom; for temples which were the centres of worship and for festivals such as Dasara which renewed the sovereignty of the king and regenerated the kingdom; and for *cattiram*s (*chatram*s, also called *choultrie*s, which were feeding, sometimes lodging, houses for pilgrims) which provided sustenance and shelter for itinerant Brahmans and pilgrims. (Dirks 1989: 66)

In other words, the king was responsible for everything that went on within the kingdom and for making sure that it flourished.

In the new colonial regime, the resolution of 'moral' questions such as the order of caste precedence fell less to priests, as the British fondly imagined, than it did to the bureaucrats who administered the *rāj*. It was primarily the responsibility of civil servants to decide who was who in the census-derived pecking order of the new imperial regime. These bureaucrats were, for the most part, Brāhmaṇs by caste. They were Brāhmaṇs because this was one of the principal traditional functions of Brāhmaṇs—not simply to be priests in the narrow sense of the term (i.e. ritual practitioners), but to be, in the fullest sense, 'king's councillors'—as Hocart put it in another book (1970).

[8] I am grateful to Peter Webster for reminding me that the abolition of *sati*, the practice whereby widows immolated themselves on their husband's funeral pyre, demonstrated that the British were not prepared to accommodate themselves to all customary ritual practices without reservation. Even with respect to *sati*, however, some very interesting soul-searching went on as to whether or not it should be prohibited—see the fascinating article by Stutchbury (1982).

[9] Of the Kandyan Sinhalese, Yalman writes: 'At times the king might lower the caste rank of an entire community (Ryan 1953: 217). One reason why caste status is today a matter for dispute is that the central government no longer lays down caste precedence' (Yalman 1960: 81).

The civil servants of the new *rāj* were Brāhmaṇs by caste, just as they had been in the many old *rājyas*, because Brāhmaṇs had always provided the majority of scribes and literati—the heart of the administration. The function of the Brāhmaṇ castes in traditional Indian kingdoms was not merely to be masters of ritual, but also to be masters of written texts. There was, of course, as in many other parts of the world, a historical connection between the two functions. But that is a separate issue which cannot be broached here.[10]

What European colonials did was to accept without question that the only possible interpretation of the *varṇa* system was one which placed priests at the top of a hierarchy. Once Hindu kings had disappeared, there seemed to be no other conceivable way of making the correspondence between the *varṇas* and the local hierarchies of *jātis*. If *varṇa* ideology was to be applied at all to the contemporary Indian world of caste, it seemed that the only legitimate way of doing so was to make Brāhmaṇ castes supreme just as the *brāhmaṇ varṇa* was assumed to be supreme.

By and large, academic interpretations of caste have continued to depend on the same assumption. Dumont's explanation is a systematic attempt to build a theory upon it by openly introducing a disjunction between status and power (which many others introduce surreptitiously). The irony of this position is that while the disjunction of status and power is supposed to refer to traditional Hindu kingdoms, it really only applies to the post-traditional situation when Hindu kings had been replaced by a secular British administration:

> However much Dumont's theory is predicated on an a priori separation of what he describes as the domains of religion and politics, with the former encompassing the latter, he was almost certainly influenced by an ethnographic reality in which kingship played only a very small, residual role. (Dirks 1989: 71)[11]

The great merit of Dumont's theory is that he forces us to examine where this apparent disjunction comes from. Most others have

[10] See Jack Goody's *The Logic of Writing and the Organization of Society* (1986) for a far-ranging comparative view of this question.

[11] See also Fuller (1977: 113): 'I would suggest that it is the very differentiation of the caste system from the wider politico-economic system of land control, which resulted from British rule and which is reflected in the materials on which he draws, which makes Dumont's thesis concerning the separation of power from status plausible.'

regarded the supremacy of the Brāhmaṇ's status as something which can be so taken for granted that it does not require any explanation.

There is, however, an alternative explanation of the Brāhmaṇ's status. For Hocart, as was made clear, the priest is the instrument of a powerful man, a *yajamāna* (*jajmān*, patron), the archetype of whom is the king. What made the Brāhmaṇs into 'the first caste' subsequent to British rule was precisely that they were no longer seen by the general populace as instruments of the ruler—whether as priests or scribes—but as rulers themselves. They were quite correctly seen by all, natives and British alike, to be an integral part of the British *rāj*. Indeed in a sense Brāhmaṇs were now seen to *be* the *rāj* because the British had handed over to them what had traditionally been regarded as the primary responsibility of the Hindu king—to regulate the moral order of the world through the allocation of particular ritual duties to particular kinship groups (*jāti*).

After independence, the new administration did not, of course, attempt to revert to the pre-colonial patrimonial mini-states where the traditional relationship between king and priest had been clear. The process of centralization had gone too far and was by then irreversible. But this does not mean that the relationship between priest and patron in modern India or Nepal is not essentially as it has always been. The old *rāja*s may have disappeared but locally dominant landholding castes remain, and it is these which continue to be the main supply source of patrons of ritual specialists: 'Strong contemporary evidence and a massive number of facts illustrate today the presence of kingship despite its disappearance from the political scene' (Galey 1989: 129).

Nor has the kinship foundation on which caste is based been fundamentally dismantled, as any good ethnography will testify. The twin pillars of caste organization—kinship (either unilineal or bilateral endogamous) and an inegalitarian agrarian economy—continue to stand firm in many, perhaps most, areas of the subcontinent.

This brings us to the way in which caste is actually organized today. As mentioned earlier, there are four key ingredients in Hocart's interpretation of caste: kinship, domination, ritual, and decay (pollution). In order to understand the ideological representations of caste, it is essential not to unpack these ideas. From the Hindu's point of view, it is not a particular form of kinship which is at issue, but simply kinship—whether or not one is connected to others through blood and marriage. Nor do Hindus generally associate caste with any particular institutionalized form of domination, although everyone will agree that caste society is always hierarchical in a politico-economic sense as well as a ritual sense. Wherever there is caste, there is an unequal distribution of resources resulting in some people being more powerful than others. Similarly, everyone knows that caste distinctions are connected with ritual and pollution even if it is not always clear which rituals are crucial or what exactly is implied by pollution.

In the final analysis, these four elements can be reduced to two—kinship and domination—which, for the sake of elegance and conformity with Hocart's theory, we can call kinship and kingship. They can be reduced to two because ritual and pollution can both be seen as expressions of kinship, as explained below. Kingship, on the other hand, is an elementary denial of kinship, an assertion that not all men are brothers, that kinship does not have the power to operate throughout social life. There can only be kings when others are not kings.

Castes are simply groups of intermarrying lineages each of which is trying to present itself in the best possible light. For all practical purposes, as Hocart says, the question 'What is your caste (*jāti*)?' means simply 'What is your lineage?' To call oneself a Brāhmaṇ is not necessarily to say anything about one's occupation, or to say anything about the profession of one's relatives, present or past. It is simply a claim to high status based on kinship association with others who enjoy high status. These others may include civil servants, army personnel, engineers, taxi drivers, university professors, farmers, or whatever.

By calling oneself a Brāhmaṇ, one indicates both the families with whom one's own relatives have traditionally married and those with whom they have not married. But those claiming Brāhmaṇ status need not be priests or related to priests and there may be no proof that they ever were. Moreover, the fact that one proclaims oneself a Brāhmaṇ does not mean that one can marry all other people who call themselves Brāhmaṇṣ. Throughout the subcontinent there are thousands of groups claiming Brāhmaṇ identity and the question of their status relative to each other is one of continual negotiation and re-negotiation. In most cases, of course, the question never arises since the groups concerned live too far apart to have any contact with one another. Where it does arise, and particularly in the case of marriage alliances, each proposal of marriage is subject to the test of pedigree. And pedigree in India, as everywhere else, is a very fickle business.

When the argument is made, as it commonly is,[12] that it was the Brāhmaṇs who gave a unity to Indian civilization, this is to turn the truth on its head. Brāhmaṇs have no unity whatsoever: there are so many kin-groups claiming Brāhmaṇ status but they do not generally agree on their equality with one another. Quite the contrary: they are in interminable dispute as to their relative status and manifest this, as other 'castes' do, through restrictive marriage strategies and exclusive ritual and commensal associations. This exclusiveness is aimed just as much at other groups claiming Brāhmaṇ status as it is at those claiming membership of other castes.

The gloss 'sub-caste' for *jāti* is extremely misleading in this regard since it implies that sub-castes somehow join together to make up castes. The fact that two *jāti*s (i.e. sets of intermarrying lineages) claim equality of status with each other, perhaps even calling themselves by the same name, does not necessarily mean that they ever consider themselves a unit or are prepared to marry or eat with each other. Their only unity derives from an outside perception that they are more like each other than they are like other groups.

This, in itself, is not an illusion. Any group always occupies a particular structural position in any caste hierarchy which both relates it to, and differentiates it from, other groups. It is not unreasonable to assume that Potters in one's own caste hierarchy are similar to Potters in another even though these two groups may not actually maintain any relations with each other, or perform the same ritual functions in their respective communities.

The constant preoccupation with ritual and pollution is an expression of strategies of differentiation and assimilation. Hocart does not explain why there should be a constant need to re-enact the ritual drama of sacrificial purification except by saying that it is a question of 'the ennobling of the sons of noble houses' (p. 57). This argument has to be generalized somewhat, principally because of another observation of his which has already been

[12] See e.g. Hall (1986: ch. 3).

referred to: 'The king's state is reproduced in miniature by his vassals: a farmer has his court, consisting of the personages most essential to the ritual, and so present even in the smallest community . . .' (ibid.: 68). In other words, the structure of kingship is reproduced at all levels of society. The pervasiveness of notions of pollution and separation derives from the need to make kinship boundaries unambiguous as a way of creating stability in this political climate.

In traditional India, everyone claims the prerogatives of kingship, every peasant has his court. The attempt to maintain a hierarchical centralized society, one in which there is a single unambiguous king, is continually militated against.[13] Kingship—the elementary denial of kinship—can only ever be made palatable through ritual, but the reason that ritually marked divisions are as pervasive in caste India as they are in nineteenth-century Bali[14] stems from the political failure of kingship. The reproduction of the structure of kingship at all levels of society was a function of general political instability.

Constant internecine conflict and the always available option of moving to another kingdom, another administration, or to virgin territory, turned pre-colonial India into a collection of fragile patrimonial states, endlessly crumbling and being rebuilt.[15] On the other hand, there was little alternative but to strive for centralization. A retreat to tribalism was an option available only to those in the most inhospitable or inaccessible places. And most of India has never been that inaccessible.

Caste results when kingship attempts to assert itself against kinship but ultimately fails because the conditions do not allow for stable kingdoms. Put another way, caste results when the retention of power and the imposition of stability through kingship are continually under threat and there is no option but to fall back on

[13] This is the reason for the proliferation of superlative adjectives which differentiate great kings from little ones and them from lesser still. The present title of the King of Nepal is Śrī Pāñc Mahārājādhirāj—lit. 'Five times glorious, Great King of Kings'.

[14] Geertz's (1980) work on the theatre state in Bali is a brilliant illustration of the way in which politically weak kingdoms attempted to compensate for their ineffectiveness through extravagant displays of ritual.

[15] The fluid nature of political boundaries and the inherently relative character of sovereignty and centralization are captured in Stein's discussion of the 'segmentary state' (Stein 1980: 23, chs. VII, VIII). See also Galey's portrayal of Hindu kingship (Galey 1989: 166).

kinship. The organization of *jāti*s ('castes', lineages) into a coherent whole depends on making kinship boundaries unambiguous and is an attempt to counteract the fluidity of political boundaries.

Geertz's idea of the exemplary royal centre has relevance here.[16] It is not, however, necessary to take too literally Geertz's statement on nineteenth-century Bali that 'Power served pomp, not pomp power' (1980: 13), or Galey's very similar epithet on Hindu kingship that 'we are not dealing with the religion of politics but with the politics of religion' (1989: 132). It is a sociological truism that all authority requires ritual just as the performance of ritual always requires persons of authority, and it is meaningless to present these as mutually antagonistic theses.[17]

Galey's argument—that one ought to distinguish lords, who represent the royal function by virtue of their ritual connection with temples and gods, from chiefs who merely exercise local dominance without ritual legitimation (ibid.: 163)—seems to me to misrepresent the segmentary nature of caste. As both Hocart and Raheja point out, even lowly castes such as Farmers and Washermen attempt to replicate kingship by employing their own ritual specialists. That dominant castes (chiefs) do so is axiomatic. In practice, however, there is no such thing as dominance *tout court*, or at least not for long. Every group attempts to institutionalize its position through ritual control over others. Temple ritual is one means to this end but it is only one among others.

Galey explicitly pushes Hocart's idealism to its limits. Where Hocart sees the *kṣatriya* as a king rather than a warrior, Galey sees power deriving from authority rather than the reverse, as the conventional sociological wisdom would have it:

[16] This idea has been taken up by D. N. Gellner (1983) for the Kathmandu Valley kingdoms in Nepal, Dirks (1987; 1989) for South India, and Galey (1989) in his reappraisal of Indian kingship which draws particularly on his research in Tehri-Garhwal, North India. As Dirks also points out (1987: 402–3), Tambiah's concept of the 'pulsating galactic polity', based on the Indo-Tibetan *maṇḍala* design, is also useful here. However, any such tidy representation as '[t]he galactic duplication of ranked territorial domains of authority arranged in concentric circles surrounding a dominant center' (Tambiah 1976: 123) is likely to over-emphasize the degree of effective centralization.

[17] The question raised by Geertz of whether power is offered up from the bottom rather than imposed down from the top is much more interesting and problematic.

> Power is not here an essence but an attribute of authority, received and exercised mainly through ritual legitimacies. Kingship could thus be recreated through different investiture ceremonies for it is not every chief that has power but only those into which the ritual has put power (Hocart, 1954, p. 30) . . . it is not so much the king who has this ritual access but the royal function . . . we would gain little in dealing with Indian kingship from a political point of view. It is a ritual organisation which, along with priesthood and the gods, orders the world in a continuous series of transformations. (Galey 1989: 130–1, 184)

The problem with this perspective is that it ignores the brute fact that not anyone could instigate an investiture ceremony. Without actual dominance, there would be nothing to legitimate.

The Ideologies of Caste

The most elementary difference between Hocart's vision of caste and Dumont's lies in their opposition of the relative positions of the king and priest. But perhaps more important than the difference between them is their agreement on the pairing of priest and king—at once separate but joined. At one level, the respective judgements of Hocart and Dumont on the nature of this pairing stem from their interpretation of what Hindu ideology is saying. But these interpretations in turn derive from fundamentally opposed theoretical premises about the nature of sociological comparison and the relationship of ideas to social structure.

Dumont (and Pocock) gave Hocart's book a certain amount of prominence by considering it alongside the work of Bouglé in the second issue of the journal *Contributions to Indian Sociology*, which they then jointly 'edited'.[18] Their first objection to Hocart is that he adopted a comparative perspective. This prevented him, they argue, both from seeing the uniqueness of India and from understanding the systemic nature of caste. Not only do they ignore the comparative sections of his essay; they make a virtue out of this, speculating that Hocart's comparative bent prevented him from making 'the fundamental observation upon which the caste system is organized' (Dumont and Pocock 1958: 63). For Hocart, they observe:

[18] In fact Dumont and Pocock contributed most of the articles to the early issues themselves.

caste in India is only one variety of a widely spread *genus* and he offers the definition that 'castes are merely families to whom various offices in the ritual are assigned by heredity' (p. 20). We would draw attention to the fact that here Hocart is defining *castes*, that is to say the units of the system seen as individuals. He is not attempting to define the system as Bouglé did. We do not rule out the possibilities of comparison between castes thus seen and similar groupings in, say, Fiji but this must take place at a level in which we are not at present interested. At the moment we are concerned with the light which Hocart threw upon the caste system as a unique phenomenon in India. To move from this level to that of comparison is inevitably to violate that uniqueness, to isolate the parts from the whole and to see the castes as abstracted groups. (ibid.: 45–6)

There are two counter-objections to these criticisms. To say that Hocart focused on the nature of the individual castes at the expense of the underlying logic of the system is a gross misrepresentation, and the very quote which Dumont and Pocock choose makes this clear. The expression 'offices in the ritual', ritual which has as its purpose to remove the pollution of lords or kings, makes the structure of the relations between castes crystal clear. The criticism that Hocart was misled by his enthusiasm for broad comparative sweeps is somewhat odd given Dumont's similar inclinations. It is not that Dumont is against comparison as such; quite the contrary, his whole approach depends on it. What he is against is the attempt by Hocart (and others) to use comparison to show similarities between caste in India and other institutions elsewhere. For Dumont, comparison demonstrates that India is unique.

Given Dumont's refusal in the 1958 *Contributions* article to have any truck with Hocart's comparative perspective, it is noteworthy that in *Homo Hierarchicus* this is the feature to which he pays most attention. This is particularly interesting because here Dumont speculates on the possible origins of caste. Pre-Aryan India, he says, 'would have had a system similar to that in Fiji, as Hocart suggested' (Dumont 1980: 365, fn. 32h) but post-Vedic India, the period of caste society, looks quite different for the following reason:

above all one must bear in mind the correlation between two phenomena: (1) the replacement of the king by the priest on the topmost rung of the status ladder; (2) the introduction of the opposition between pure and impure, with the innovation it entails. The opposition represents a ritualistic point of view: it originated historically in Vedic ritual and spread to the whole of social life . . . (ibid.)

The long footnote from which this quote is taken is one of the best summaries by Dumont of his own overall position on the nature of caste and its probable origins. What makes India unique, and therefore defies the attempt to find a comparable form of social organization elsewhere, is the introduction of the disjunction between status and power which puts the priest above the king. This disjunction, 'which was after all Indo-European, led to the transformation of the "Hocartian" system into a caste system' (ibid.: 213). Hocart did, then, have a 'system' after all.

Dumont and Pocock applaud Hocart for the importance he attached to religious values. By placing the king at the pivot of the caste system, however, they argue that he unwittingly inverted the ultimate values of the ideology.

It is very remarkable that Hocart who has stressed the pre-eminence of religious values in this system should formally present it as an articulation around the centre of power, which, in relation to the values of this system appears as negative. Once the scale has been readjusted Hocart's demonstration of the relation between this aspect of the *varṇa* scheme and the local hierarchy of *jāti* is one of the most important parts of his work. (Dumont and Pocock 1958: 56)

Here, of course, they equate power with force, not authority.[19] On the other hand, they also remark that Hocart's elevation of the *kṣatriya* to the status of a divine king 'is no less "ideal" than that of the ancient texts which resolve the conflict [between priest and king] in favour of the Brahman' (ibid.: 58). This is perfectly true and is, I believe, the major weakness in Hocart's theory. Like Dumont, Hocart often seems to take ideology as a sufficient blueprint for social organization and to believe that the elucidation of the beliefs surrounding caste in itself provides a satisfactory sociological explanation of caste systems.

Unlike Dumont, however, Hocart repeatedly undermines his insistence on fidelity to native interpretation by his equal insistence on comparison with similar institutions in other societies. The difficulty here is that since other societies (or indeed other groups within the same society) may have a different ideological

[19] On Dumont's ambivalence concerning the concept of power, see my discussion in Ch. 3.

explanation for the same institution, sociological explanation must somehow go beyond any particular system of beliefs. Had Hocart consistently adopted an idealist explanation, his argument would have had no greater cogency than Dumont's. It is perhaps ironic that the strength of Hocart's approach is his failure to put forward a consistently idealist theory, one which explains caste solely in terms of the ideas those who practise it profess to believe. The weakness of Dumont's approach is that he consistently does precisely that (though of course he also interprets the ideology very differently).

The fact is that whatever caste ideology is, and the versions of Hocart and Dumont are far from being the only ones available,[20] ideologies can never satisfactorily explain the social organization which produces them. The task of the sociologist (anthropologist, historian) is to examine the articulation between the conditions which give rise to various systems of belief and the beliefs themselves.

The merit of Hocart's theory is that in spite of its idealist bent, ultimately it explains caste organization not simply in terms of ideas, but in terms of other institutions—namely 'families' and (ritual) kingship. We know of course that neither kingship nor corporate kinship groups of themselves lead to caste organization. What is crucial is their combination and the fact that neither is able to submerge the other. These two institutions are also fundamental in Dumont's theory of caste but this is obscured by his making the system revolve around a particular ideological interpretation rather than around empirically observable phenomena.

One further objection of Dumont and Pocock to Hocart's theory derives from what they see as an inconsistency in his method between the study of living societies and his concern with 'historical developments (known or hypothesized) and with identifications' (ibid.: 59). Specifically they single out his discussion of the relationship between *varṇa* and *jāti*:

> His discussion of the supposed break down of a *varṇa* society which involved changes of occupation and status would, taken by itself, lead us back to that chaos of caste dictionaries and census reports from which Hocart had earlier lead us away. His discussion concludes with a glaring inconsistency . . . 'Even the brahmins have failed to keep out aboriginal

[20] An explanation which sees caste as a form of exploitation is an obvious alternative.

blood, as can readily be seen by the black skin and thick lips and noses of some of the southern ones.' (p. 46). It is scarcely credible that the same person wrote this who earlier (p. 29 et seq.) dealt so magisterially with the race theory of caste . . . (ibid.: 59)

This is indeed a very unfortunate inconsistency in Hocart's book, though I am not convinced that the origin which Dumont and Pocock attribute to it is the most profitable way of seeing Hocart's train of thought.

Dumont and Pocock derive this inconsistency from what they see as Hocart's failure to come to terms with the relational nature of Hindu thought and his tendency to substitute relations with identities.

We may take as an example his account of the relation between kings and priests and what he conceives to be their divine counterparts. He opens his brief discussion with the statement: 'Royalty and priesthood form a pair. As usual the world of gods reflects the world of men and *vice versa*.' But immediately he passes from speaking of reflection to speak of 'impersonation' and finally of 'identity': 'the identity of priest and priestly god is carried out in detail', and earlier 'the king and the other worthy people *stand for* the gods' (pp. 35–6 our italics): compared with 'The king *is* Indra. He *is* also Varuna'. (ibid.: 60)

The editors of *Contributions* prefer instead to follow Dumézil, the comparative historian of Indo-European ideologies, and anthropologists such as Evans-Pritchard, arguing that if one concentrates upon the structure of systems of thought, their relational nature will become apparent. It is, of course, impossible to know what Hocart would have made of 'structuralist' analyses of belief systems but I would suggest that he is not as far removed from them as these two critics claim.

Hocart's 'confusion' (as Dumont and Pocock call it) between relation and identity seems to me deliberate. During a royal ritual, the question of whether the king is *like* a god or actually *is* a god is often not distinguished in Hindu thought.[21] To quote a more recent authority on this subject:

One might say, from this point of view, that Hindu ritual (e.g. vedic sacrifice, or a coronation; see Inden [1978]) converts *symbols*, arbitrary signs (e.g. a sacrificial horse), into *icons* where the signifier (the horse) is *like* what it signifies (the universe) and finally into *indexes*, where the

[21] See also Stein (1980: 278) and Hopkins (1931: 313).

signifier is *part* of what it signifies; the horse is the Universe is Prajāpati, so that in sacrificing and partaking of it one is sacrificing and partaking of the Universe itself . . . (Ramanujan 1989: 50)

In trying to get inside the minds of those who practise sacrificial ritual, Hocart seems to me more faithful to their representation than the more academic rationalization of Dumont and Pocock. This does not undermine Hocart's analysis of caste *systems* (as opposed to caste ideology) in terms of relations. The difference between Hocart and Dumont (or Bouglé) is not that the one thought in terms of units and the others in terms of relations. What is at stake is the nature of the relations which they respectively see as providing the logic of the system, or systems, in question.

There is, however, confusion in Hocart's account of the relation between *varṇa* and *jāti*. This stems from his apparent belief that there was an original situation when Indian society was clearly divided into four groups: he writes, for example, of the composition of these groups being 'no longer as clear cut as it once was' (Hocart 1950: 33). But the idea that this situation ever existed is entirely implausible. In suggesting otherwise, Hocart is guilty of precisely the same mistake as those who explained caste in terms of race (as Dumont and Pocock point out) or those who explained it in terms of occupations.

There is another aberration in Hocart's book which Dumont does not pick up, surprisingly because it accords well with his own position. Towards the end of his essay on India Hocart writes: 'The great master of ritual we call a priest, and he is so high that he becomes higher than the king, so his line ranks above all others, farmers, artisans and the rest' (ibid.: 68). There is no explanation of how this is compatible with the statement quoted earlier that 'The second caste supplies the priests, brahmans, who perform the rituals for the king or for whatever great man is offering the sacrifice' (ibid.: 37).

One might also point out a certain *naïveté* in Hocart's characterization of kingship. While he is correct to insist that it is more accurate to regard the *kṣatriya* as a king or noble rather than a warrior, he goes too far in asserting that 'Fighting is not a primary attribute, but only a derivative' (ibid.: 36). After all, kingship in India, as everywhere else, depended on actual dominance. As Dirks writes (1989: 66): 'The underlying political base of any little kingdom in the old regime was its military capacity.' It is no accident that the post-colonial legatees of kingship are referred to as the dominant caste, those who exercise control over the land.

The only way in which both the institution of caste and its ideological representations can be understood is by seeing them against the political realities they faced. Dumont's insistence on the connection between hierarchy and holism in traditional India can be defended but the reason which he gives for this connection should be dismissed. It is not that Hindus are any more addicted to hierarchical social life than anyone else in the world but, paradoxically, because stable hierarchy in traditional India was intensely problematic.

Recent ethnographic and historical research suggests that Hocart's thesis on the political *and* (not 'or') ritual centrality of kingship is more illuminating.

> The priority of *dharma*, which might be seen to be a primitive feature to critics dazzled by the achievements of the secular state since the Reformation, was only a part of the teaching of moral teachers; and that brings us to the real nature of *rājadharma*, the teachers of which (all of them brahmins) regarded kingship as a practical *and* religious necessity, for they feared nothing more than chaos. (Derrett 1976*a*: 606)[22]

King and priest each play a particular role in coping with instability (ibid.: 607) but ultimately it is kingship, not priesthood, which provides the orientation to the whole simply because the king is responsible for providing overall order: 'sovereignty is considered both as an element of the totality and the totality itself' (Galey 1989: 170).

Indigenous representations of caste cannot simply be ignored or taken for granted.[23] One of the conditions for the survival of caste is that those who practise it must be acutely aware of what is involved: caste requires a high degree of intellectual participation. Any adequate explanation of caste must, at some stage, show what exactly those who practise it *are* aware of—namely, domination and kinship. This is precisely what Hocart does show and what

[22] '*Rājadharma* is "the way a king should comport himself in order to be righteous" ' (Derrett 1976*a*: 606).

[23] Two recent examples of analyses of Hindu society which have basically ignored caste ideology are Baechler (1988) and Hall (1986)—notwithstanding the latter's deference to Durkheim. Hall's model of traditional India is discussed in the following chapter.

Dumont obscures by representing the underlying ideology as something other than it is. What is more, in Hocart's interpretation, the preoccupation with purity and pollution seems perfectly sensible; it is a means of defending boundaries between differentially powerful kinship groups. By contrast, the views attributed by Dumont to Hindus often seem extremely odd and mysterious—in particular, the idea that a complex society has an overarching value which gives primacy to the purity of the priest and derives all other values from this.

Dumont's statement that Hocart generalized 'by insisting on the magico-religious aspect of any craft' (1980: 337, fn. 41b) puts things the wrong way round. That the universe keeps going is magical and everyone must play some part in this. It is not that every craft has a magico-religious aspect; rather it is that everyone must be given a magico-religious function as their part in the overall ordering of the cosmos. The potter is simply someone who makes pots. The Potter, however, is someone who comes from a kinship group whose duty it is to supply personnel to perform a particular ritual function, that is, a function which is necessary to ensure continuing order within the kingdom.

Which functions are performed by which groups is something that is ordained by the king or dominant caste. The ritual function of the Potter need not have anything to do with making pots though one assumes that the supply of pots was an integral feature of many rituals. Equally, the Potter could be someone who carries the palanquin bearing a deity during a village festival or someone who has a particular role to play during a death ritual. In the same way, the Brāhmaṇ may perform functions which are generally seen as auspicious, such as marriage rituals, or functions which are generally seen as inauspicious, such as removing death impurity. But equally the Brāhmaṇ may not be a religious specialist at all; he may be the patron of such specialists and in this way be assimilated to the *kṣatriya varṇa*. There is no *necessary* connection between being a Brāhmaṇ and being a *brāhmaṇ*, or between any *jāti* and any *varṇa*.

There is general agreement that the *varṇa*s must be kept apart because the functions they represent are so different in kind that to confuse them would be to imperil both the social order and the very safety of the universe. In Hocart's interpretation, what is absolutely paramount is that the king (the *kṣatriya*) must be kept separate from everyone else. The king's purity at the moment of sacrifice guarantees that the world will be a safe and abundant place to live in.[24] The sacrifice is an act of appeasement: through the ritual the king becomes one with nature and the gods who continually threaten man's harmonious existence with disease and drought, death and decay. (The gods and nature are sometimes conflated, sometimes distinguished.)

The primary function of the king is to provide order. Through the sacrifice, which he commands, he continually regenerates the order of the universe; he controls the gods and natural forces which are otherwise uncontrollable. Ritual is essentially a question of order; order is essentially a question of ritual. He who controls the order controls the ritual; he who controls the ritual controls the order. 'The temple and the palace are indistinguishable, for the king represents the gods' (Hocart 1950: 68). What is interesting here is that while the king is venerated as a god, he is simultaneously made the scapegoat of society's ills. In a way, the king's position is every bit as perilous as that of the *brāhmaṇ*, indeed more so because it is he who is ultimately responsible for order and well-being.[25]

The function of *brāhmaṇ* and *śūdra* alike is to ensure that the rulers are kept pure—free from the dangerous and polluting forces of nature—particularly at the moment of sacrifice when order is ritually re-established. The function of the *vaiśya* is also to patronize priests but, unlike the *kṣatriya*, his powers of patronage do not come from physical dominance and so he cannot be responsible for providing overall order. This explains the residual nature of the *vaiśya* category and the fact that upwardly mobile groups normally seek *kṣatriya* identification.

[24] 'Above all the sovereign is indeed responsible for rainfall . . . The monarch is always pure lest his business be impeded' (Gonda 1966: 7, 16). 'The rāja looks after the spiritual needs of the kingdom by exercising his special priestly functions, without which fertility and security will be endangered' (Derrett 1976*b*: 57).

[25] I have not attempted to explore the extensive literature on divine kingship and its perils since this would require at least another book. However, one might be tempted to begin by following Hocart to Fiji, as Sahlins has done: 'Sovereignty never shakes the ambiguities of its locus. For the Fijian ruler, all this might be present at the moment of his installation, when Society took some pains to protect itself against the State . . . Hocart observes that the Fijian chief is ritually reborn on this occasion; that is, as a domestic god. If so, someone must have killed him as a dangerous outsider. He is indeed killed by the indigenous people at the very moment of his consecration . . .' (Sahlins 1985: 94–5).

Patrons may in fact be assimilated to any of the four *varṇa*s since even low castes may employ yet lower groups to remove their pollution. Untouchables are, in a sense, the *śūdra* of the *śūdra*—those who remove pollution from groups who remove the pollution of others.[26] In practice as well as in theory, untouchables are those who lie outside the limits of the kingdom so that death and impurity can be transferred back to where they belong—the uncontrollable forces of nature. To recall Hocart's words: 'all those who stand outside the communion, members of nations that worship other gods, represent the demons' (ibid.: 36).

There is, then, a separation of kingly function and priestly function but the reason for this is precisely the opposite of the one which Dumont gives us. It is not that priests must be kept pure but that kings (patrons) must be kept pure. The priest is essentially a vessel and as such is a liminal, ambivalent character—at once necessary but dangerous.[27] The king cannot be a priest because to do so would be to interiorize his own impurity, and to proclaim that he was sufficient unto himself. One might call the institution of priesthood the original division of labour.

How the division between king and sacrificer initially arose is a fascinating question which requires much more detailed consideration than can be given here. It is Dumont's ill-considered speculation on the origins of this division which is at the heart of his unsatisfactory explanation of caste and one should be careful not to repeat his mistake. Obviously, however, the splitting of functions always has historical origins. In India, the development of an elaborate system whereby different ritual functions were allocated to specialized groups must have been connected with the building of complex, agriculture-based, surplus-producing societies—stable, rather than roving, kingdoms. But the initial division between king and priest came earlier.[28]

If one were to indulge in a little premature speculation, one might conjecture that as kingdoms became more settled, the priests and scribes of the powerful arrogated to themselves an exalted position, in the process passing on their own liminality to less powerful groups. The *brāhmaṇ* becomes a high priest, a manipulator of text and guardian of traditions, and assigns to the

[26] For a very clear illustration of the replication by untouchables of dominant caste structures, see Moffat (1979).

[27] See also Banks (1960: 66 ff.).

[28] See e.g. Thapar (1966: 28 ff.).

śūdra the more dangerous functions which he previously performed and which before him were performed by the king himself. But one sees in the ambiguity surrounding the functions of both kingship and priesthood that such attempts were not entirely successful.

The allocation of specific functions to particular 'families' makes these families in some fundamental way different from each other, as different species (*jāti*) are. Miscegenation is thus impossible because it would threaten the 'natural' order. The problem, of course, is that the unchanging moral order implied by the *varṇa* schema is continually undermined by the instability of kingdoms and by the attempts of servile groups to escape their condition and become themselves the patrons of others.

Idealists like Dumont make the mistake of thinking that purity must be about ultimate values when it is about kinship and power, about making boundaries to include and exclude. His materialist critics make the mistake of thinking that hierarchy must be about material wealth when in fact it is about order. Hocart's sacrificial theory ploughs a furrow between the materialist and idealist conceptions of traditional Indian society. For Hocart, the myths which state that the castes are born of the sacrifice do not belong to some forgotten primeval past, but are an expression of the continual attempts to legitimate the authority of kings when everywhere about this authority is continually challenged.

Simultaneously complex and unstable, in traditional India neither kingship nor kinship has the capacity to organize social life fully. Caste is a means of creating order through their combination where the alternative would be no order at all.

7

The Courts of Kings and Washermen

A Model of Caste Systems

In his (1983) book on nationalism, Ernest Gellner offered a general model of the social structure of complex agrarian societies. This has since been adopted by John Hall (1986) who suggests four basic variations on the general model to cope with the different types of social organization paradigmatically thrown up by the civilizations of imperial China, India, Islam, and Christian Europe respectively. Gellner's general model is reproduced here as Figure 3, and Hall's adaptation of it for the traditional Indian case will be considered in due course.

Gellner argues that agrarian polities can be roughly divided into two poles—local self-governing communities and large empires. A characteristic form, he says, is one which finds the two together: 'a

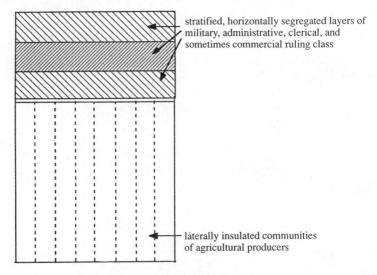

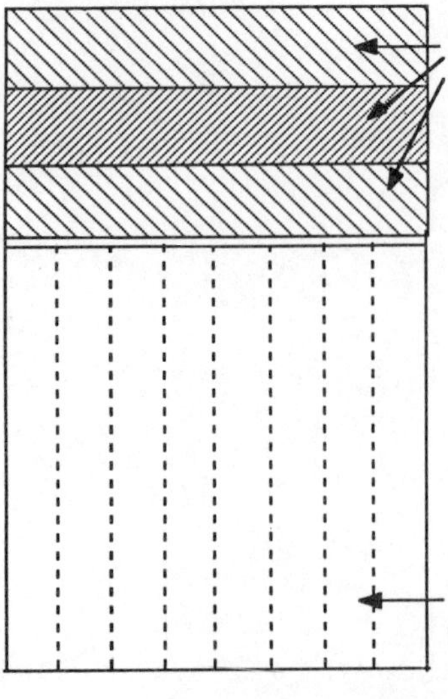

Fig. 3. Gellner's model of the general form of the social structure of agrarian societies (E. Gellner 1983: 9)

central dominant authority co-exists with semi-autonomous local units' (E. Gellner 1983: 13), and his model reproduces this kind of situation.

Gellner's argument about the structure of complex agrarian societies is the converse of his theory of modern, industrial, nationalist societies—'perhaps the central, most important fact about agro-literate society is this: almost everything in it militates against the definition of political units in terms of cultural boundaries' (ibid.: 11). Within these units, rulers and ruled are rigidly separated and culture acts to reinforce this separation:

> both for the ruling stratum as a whole, and for the various sub-strata within it, there is a great stress on cultural differentiation rather than on homogeneity. The more differentiated in style of all kinds the various strata are, the less friction and ambiguity there will be between them. (ibid.: 10)

Typically, the rulers (military, clerical, priestly, commercial) form a small minority of the population. The majority are agricultural producers, peasants, who live in 'laterally insulated communities', separated both from their rulers and from each other.

Peasant populations are notoriously immobile and insular:

> Here, once again, cultural differentiation is very marked, though the reasons are quite different. Small peasant communities generally live inward-turned lives, tied to the locality by economic need if not by political prescription. Even if the population of a given area starts from the same linguistic base-line—which very often is not the case—a kind of culture drift soon engenders dialectal and other differences. No-one, or almost no-one, has an interest in promoting cultural homogeneity at this social level. The state is interested in extracting taxes, maintaining the peace, and not much else, and has no interest in promoting lateral communication between its subject communities. (ibid.)

This characterization of the agro-literate polity assumes a relatively stable underlying structure:[1]

> Thanks to the relative stability of agro-literate societies, sharp separations of the population into estates or castes or millets can be established and maintained without creating intolerable frictions. On the contrary, by

[1] See also Gellner's major statement on the philosophy of history—*Plough, Sword and Book*: 'agrarian society is, all in all, stable. If turbulent, and it often is turbulent, its turbulence leads only to cyclical and not fundamental change' (E. Gellner 1988: 276).

externalizing, making absolute and underwriting inequalities, it fortifies them and makes them palatable, by endowing them with the aura of inevitability, permanence and naturalness. (ibid.: 11)

By contrast, the fluidity and mobility of modern industrial societies makes it extremely difficult to maintain ascribed inequalities.

On the one hand, then, the economic and ideological introversion of peasants means that they can only mobilize politically with the greatest of difficulty. The peasant's universe—of kin and affines, language, religion, and customs—is necessarily circumscribed, for the most part limited to what can be covered in a day or two's walk. After this, he enters territory where there are few or no kinsmen, where the language or dialect becomes incomprehensible, and where the customs, and even gods, may be foreign. On the other hand, peasant communities can, for the same reasons, be relatively easily absorbed into larger political frameworks. Precisely because they offer little potential for resistance, they can be dominated by some outside force which has a centralized administrative machinery at its disposal.

As Gellner points out, literacy is crucial here—'The written word seems to enter history with the accountant and the tax-collector' (ibid.: 8).[2] Literacy makes possible cultural and cognitive centralization and dramatically alters the potential for social organization. The formalization of the written word also introduces a huge gulf between the great tradition of the élites and the cults of the majority who remain illiterate. At first sight, Gellner's characterization of this gulf seems tailor-made for the Indian case—the great tradition of Sanskrit literature and Vedic ritual, and the innumerable little traditions of local cults:

> The tendency of liturgical languages to become distinct from the vernacular is very strong: it is as if literacy alone did not create enough of a barrier between cleric and layman, as if the chasm between them had to be deepened, by making the language not merely recorded in an inaccessible script, but also incomprehensible when articulated. (ibid.: 11)

In the agro-literate world, then, the political integration of diverse peasant and tribal groups does not normally require their cultural assimilation. There is no good reason why the masses should share

[2] See also Goody (1986).

the culture of those who dominate them, and in fact the cleavages which literacy introduces militate against cultural homogeneity.

There is also a pronounced political attractiveness in maintaining this state of affairs. Centralized agrarian polities require regional satellites to facilitate both the smooth collection of taxes and the maintenance of order. But if the rulers in the centre are to retain control over their representatives in the satellites, they must ensure that the latter remain dependent on them and do not use their local power to assert their independence. And they must ensure that the peasants do not unite in opposition either to their local rulers or to the centre. One extremely useful strategy for effecting this is the well-proven colonial policy of divide and rule, but if Gellner's model of the structure of complex agrarian societies is generally applicable, it is often unnecessary to employ such a strategy deliberately.

Since peasants are generally ideologically fissiparous anyway, they have neither the inclination nor the opportunity to present a political threat to those who dominate them. And as long as they remain ideologically divorced from their local rulers, the latter have little guarantee of their support should they wish to stage a revolt against the centre. This raises a very interesting question: under what conditions is a unifying culture not only able to develop among previously fissiparous peasant communities, but actively encouraged? Under what conditions are peasants not only constrained to share their grain with their rulers, but also to partake in their rituals and adopt their beliefs?

In the modern, nationalist world, Gellner argues, ethnicity (shared culture) becomes a pervasive political medium as a result of uneven industrialization. The structure of industrial society requires that everyone, or nearly everyone, be literate in a common language: 'A high culture pervades the whole of society, defines it, and needs to be sustained by the polity. *That* is the secret of nationalism' (ibid.: 18; emphasis in original).

The secret of caste is also to be found in the relationship between polity and culture. There are, however, two essential differences between caste-organized polities and national polities. The first is that caste depends on the relative failure of centralization and the parallel persistence of kinship in shaping social institutions. The second is the expression of common culture through ritual rather than through the written word. One way to develop this argument is by comparing Gellner's general model of complex agrarian society with Hall's adaptation of it for the traditional Indian case, which is reproduced here as Figure 4.[3]

With regard to the relationship between ethnicity and political organization, there is a striking difference between Hall's model of traditional India and Gellner's general picture of agro-literate societies. For Hall, the chronic political instability of pre-colonial India was compensated for by the unifying nature of Brahmanical ideology and ritual, and he offers a 'reasoned speculation' on the Brāhmaṇs' hold over society.[4]

The Aryans felt threatened by the native population, larger in sheer numbers and probably of a different racial composition. It is quite possible that their desire to distinguish themselves was met by the Brahmans who captured and enshrined *the Aryan ethnic inheritance* in emerging caste-type organization. The Brahmans provided rituals which enabled the community to survive. (Hall 1986: 62–3; my emphasis)

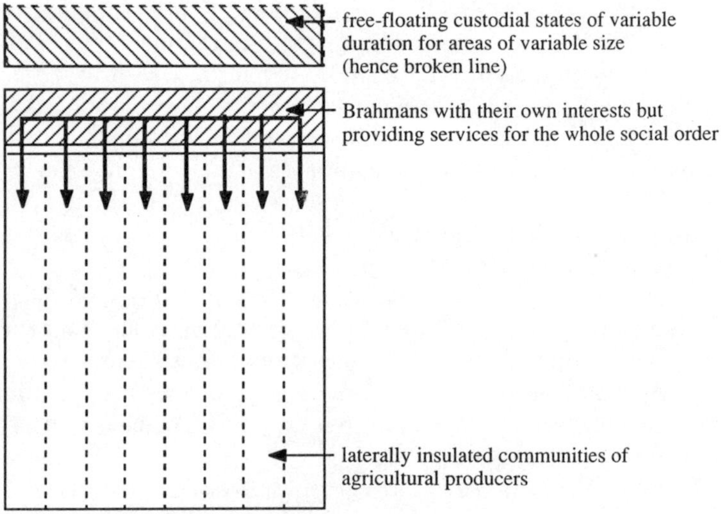

FIG. 4. Hall's model of 'The land of the Brahmans' (1986: 71)

[3] Hall is not an authority on India and his argument contains a number of misunderstandings, some of which are outlined below. His main merit is in the *attempt* to undertake the kind of broad comparative analysis which most others have avoided since Weber's *The Religion of India*.

[4] Hall derives this hypothesis from Mann (1986).

On two further occasions, Hall refers to the Brāhmaṇs' 'ability to capture the ethnic heritage of the Aryans'. This is intriguing because Gellner's model is intended to demonstrate the structural constraints in agro-literate societies which inhibit the possibility of a unifying culture being harnessed to political ends. Hall's argument also deserves consideration because it once again makes Brāhmaṇs the driving force behind caste.

Hall draws an important distinction between Brahmanical *claims* to power which appear in the earliest Vedic texts and the actual success of those claims which is only witnessed much later. Classical Hindu social organization, he argues, only emerged when Brahmanism beat off the challenges to its hegemony which developed in the soteriological (i.e. salvation-oriented) forms of Buddhism and Jainism. It was able to achieve this success for two reasons. On the one hand, Brahmanism proved capable of integrating a great many cults and (often contradictory) beliefs. It is this integrated, neo-Brahmanism which became known as Hinduism: 'The secret of this religion lies in its capacity to tolerate differences rather than any desire or ability to organise or police belief' (ibid.: 72–3).

Even more important, however, was the sociological function performed by the revitalized Brāhmaṇ:

> The greatest achievement of neo-Brahmanism lay, however, in its capacity to organise social relationships. The Brahmans extended and regularised the services they performed on every occasion of the life-cycle and their presence became firmly anchored in the locality . . . The *Laws of Manu*, finally codified in the early Christian era, demonstrate that the Brahmans provided *law*, perhaps the most crucial of all social services. These laws sought to organise every aspect of social life: distinctions were drawn at every point between different caste obligations and privileges, whilst the very minutiae of social life, including, as the *Kama Sutra* demonstrates, the sexual act itself, became the subject of regulation. The Brahman was sometimes the last resort in terms of conflict between and within castes. However, the great effectiveness of the system lay ultimately in the fact that coercion was managed by the castes themselves. (ibid.: 73; emphasis in original)

There are a number of problems with this argument, but it is best to begin with the central thesis that Brāhmaṇs supplied services for the whole society and in this way ensured a stability which political systems did not, and could not, provide.

Both in theory and in practice, Brāhmaṇs do not normally work for the community at large, or at least not in the sense that Hall means. The majority of Brāhmaṇs are not, and have probably never been, ritual specialists; they are simply landowners or engaged in some other, non-religious occupation. Like members of other castes, they may be the patrons of such specialists but then the relationship will be between one household and another. Conversely, those Brāhmaṇs who do function as priests most often work for particular patrons and normally only for high-caste patrons; the priests of low castes come from other low castes. Temple priests might be said to provide services for the community as a whole but even here certain groups were traditionally excluded from temple worship because their presence was considered polluting. Moreover, the 'Brāhmaṇhood' of temple priests is frequently questioned, as Fuller points out,[5] precisely because their services are not exclusive to high-status groups.

The second problem with Hall's characterization concerns the picture of Brāhmaṇs as law-givers. In the first place, the eclectic nature of Hinduism means that there has never been either a single body of laws (no unifying dogma), or a single body of Brāhmaṇs.[6] As Chapter 4 attempted to show, Brāhmaṇs are intensely divided both doctrinally and sociologically. The fact that some Brāhmaṇs and some laws sought to organize every aspect of social life does not mean that they managed to do so. Some Westerners today may read sex manuals in search of models to enhance their erotic technique, but this option has never been open to the illiterate peasants who have always formed the majority of India's population. What one can say is that the relationships between priests and kings or dominant castes have always been emulated by less powerful groups in the society. In general, however, the peasant is not modelling his behaviour on the priest, but on the priest's patron.

The idea that Brāhmaṇs were the final arbiter on caste matters is also highly questionable. The British, and the Muslims before them, may have believed this to be the case but the reason for this is precisely that they themselves usurped the final authority of the Hindu kings, as Hutton noted some time ago:

It is probable that the powers of the secular ruler in caste questions have

[5] See Ch. 4. [6] See Derrett (1973*b*: 4, 42)

been allowed to lapse in many states, and Ibbetson attributes this to the Mughal conquest which he regards as having deprived the Hindus of their natural leaders, the Rajputs, and so strengthened caste rather than otherwise, by leaving matters in the hands of the Brahmans and of caste councils acting under their influence. In the marginal areas and in remoter fastnesses of hills and forests the older order held good, and the Rajput princes in the Kangra hills classified Brahmans, promoted from one caste to another, and readmitted expelled persons to caste partially at any rate for money payments. (Hutton 1963: 95)

Moreover, the fact that disputes about status ultimately reverted to the court drew both the Mughals and the British into the web of caste, whatever their explicit aspirations to hand such questions over to Brāhmaṇs:

So clearly has the principle that the secular power is the final arbiter of caste been accepted in the past, that the Mughal rulers of Bengal and their British successors have in turn found themselves in the position of judges of such matters. (ibid.: 96)[7]

Hutton's characterization of traditional Indian kings as 'secular' must, however, be challenged. He is not, of course, alone in making this characterization. The secularization of the Hindu king is the converse of the assumption that 'Brāhmaṇs are the highest caste' and it is not only Dumont's theory of caste which depends on this assumption. So too does the position of the majority of his critics, including that of a comparative sociologist such as Hall, in spite of the latter's bold claim that his model 'sins against caste ideology by placing the political realm above the religious order' (Hall 1986: 71).

In fact, Hall's model does not so much sin against caste ideology as against one particular interpretation of it—the interpretation which sees the central axis of caste as being the opposition between Brāhmaṇs and Untouchables. Even then, Hall himself at times succumbs to this interpretation, particularly in his acceptance of the idea of the secular king: 'There is no conception of kings as providers of services for the society. Their duty in life is simply to

[7] One further revealing remark from Hutton concerns the way in which some castes chose to present themselves in successive censuses. A number, he says, 'who claimed to be some special sort of Kshatriya or Vaishya at the 1921 census claimed to be some peculiar kind of Brahman in 1931' (1963: 113). This again suggests that it was the British who elevated Brāhmaṇ castes unambiguously above the erstwhile 'kingly' castes and that it was indeed the ruler who was 'the final arbiter of caste'.

fight, and they have no other secular duty than that of protecting the social order. This is a *custodial* state'[8] (ibid.: 78; emphasis in original). Such a model of Hindu kingship is repeatedly challenged both in Sanskrit texts and by historical and ethnographic evidence. That kings were not simply fighters, that they provided services to the community in the form of gifts and patronage, and that this was expected, even demanded, of them is convincingly demonstrated by Raheja's penetrating appraisal:

> far from being simply a matter of secular power and force, the role of the king is ritually central to the life of the kingdom . . . Kings are enjoined, in the textual traditions, to give gifts if they wish to enjoy sovereignty;[9] and to give is seen as an inherent part of the royal code-for-conduct, *rājadharma*.[10] Gifting is also taken to be a powerful ritual means of constituting relations of incorporation, authority, and power in the realm.[11] (Raheja 1988*b*: 514–15)

The argument against the secularization of the king is neatly captured in Dirks's pithy aphorism: 'ritual and political forms were fundamentally the same' (Dirks 1987: 5).[12]

The most intractable difficulties with Western interpretations of caste stem from the attribution of secularism to an arena which has always been, and continues to be, heavily ritualized. The fact that the functions of king and priest were long ago separated does not mean that the king thereby became a secular figure. It simply means that the priest was given one function to perform in the ritual and the king another. The primary function of the king (or dominant caste) is to command the rituals which ensure both

[8] The idea is taken from Stein whose characterization is, in fact, broader: 'Medieval Indian states . . . were custodial, tributary, locally based, and oriented to local networks. By "custodial" is meant that the state did not arrogate to itself and attempt to monopolize the coercive functions and authority of other, essentially nonpolitical institutions in the society. Notably, the Indian ruler tended to leave to kinship, occupational, and religious groups the authority for social control of its members; he tended to leave to various territorial associations—villages and circles of villages—the same authority with respect to their constituent groups' (Stein 1975: 76).

[9] Gonda (1966: 62; 1965: 198–228).

[10] Price (1979).

[11] Appadurai (1978; 1981), Breckenridge (1978), Burghart (1987), Dirks (1976; 1987).

[12] 'There is not the least doubt that the king, as actual ruler, was a surrogate for various deities, and needed to function, periodically, as a ritual agent of the people in relation to nature; and apart from that, he must take steps to see that no ritual performances on the part of the public are neglected, lest the rains fail' (Derrett 1976*a*: 605). See also Stein (1980: 24).

cosmic and social stability; this is no more a secular function than the priest's actual performance of the ritual. If anything, it underlines the ritual centrality of the king because the priest is often made to appear as a kind of technician.

No doubt the relativism of Hindu religion, as Hall calls it, did foster weak polities. But the fact that 'a single community of equal individuals was not even aimed at' (Hall 1986: 77) does not at all imply that a sense of community was generally lacking. On the contrary, every ethnography stresses the importance of local affiliations. Caste ritual not only establishes divisions between different groups in the same locality; it differentiates one locality from another.[13]

There are two problems in applying Gellner's model to the sociology of caste. The first is that his model applies to a situation where centralized and uncentralized communities pull against one another (while at the same time forming a symbiotic relationship). In the caste situation, however, the main tension is between communities *all* of which are attempting to centralize. Paradigmatically the degree of centralization achieved is relatively weak, but there is no choice about centralization itself.

Uncentralized (tribal) communities may still be found in peripheral, not easily accessible, zones—mountain, jungle, or desert, for example—which are difficult to centralize to any significant degree without the apparatus available to the modern, industrial state. Pilgrimage sites also frequently operate outside the contours of 'normal' political organization and may indeed provide neutral zones between one polity and another. But the main political threat to caste-organized kingdoms comes neither from tribes nor from pilgrimage centres, but from other caste-organized kingdoms.

The second problem with Gellner's model is that it tends to reinforce the idea of a linear hierarchy. While caste is indisputably hierarchical in that there is markedly unequal access to both resources and status, the hierarchy is not linear. It is frequently impossible to evaluate the status of one caste relative to another even when there is no difficulty in judging either of them in relation to a third.

[13] For a particularly impressive example of the use of ritual to demarcate a territory, see the articles by Levy (1987), and Gutschow and Bāsukala (1987) on the Navadurgā of Bhaktapur, an ancient royal city in the Kathmandu Valley, Nepal.

There is, however, an alternative way of representing Gellner's model which allows one to appreciate more immediately the structure of caste-organized societies. To do this, it is necessary to put the élites not at the top, but in the centre. I have also schematized the relations between the élites in order to represent the possibility that they are not necessarily antagonistic but may act in coalition. The 'lateral insulation' of uncentralized peasant communities is retained and in such a way as to mirror their territorial separation both from the centre and from each other. This model is produced here as Figure 5.

The general form of the social structure of caste-organized societies is, however, quite different. While communities of agricultural producers by and large remain laterally insulated from each other, they do not remain insulated from élites: this would be a contradiction in terms. Every caste-organized community reproduces an élite structure within itself and this is replicated at all levels of society: each group attempts to emulate the king's

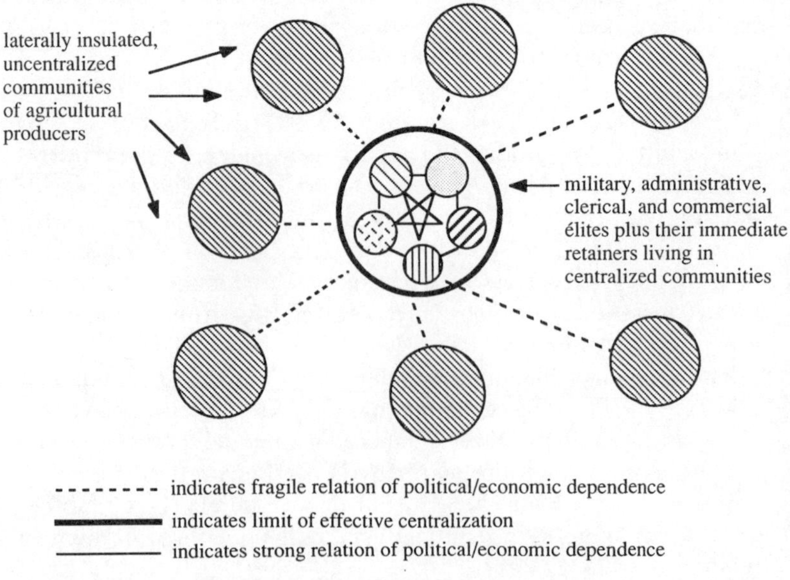

FIG. 5. General form of the social structure of complex agrarian societies which are divided between centralized and uncentralized communities (adapted from E. Gellner 1983: 9, fig. 1)

court by attaching retainers to itself.[14] It is difficult to depict this in a two-dimensional figure because of the number of cross-cutting ties, but an image can be built up by comparing how the structure appears from a number of different viewpoints. From the perspective of the king or dominant caste, the structure appears as shown in Figure 6.

The ruling group will generally have ritual connections with all others in the kingdom or community though there may be exceptions. Groups such as merchants or property-owning sects may well be able to set up independent, and to some extent competing, networks of patronage. This does not mean that such groups are, in reality, politically or economically independent. The fact that they are able to operate at all will depend on a

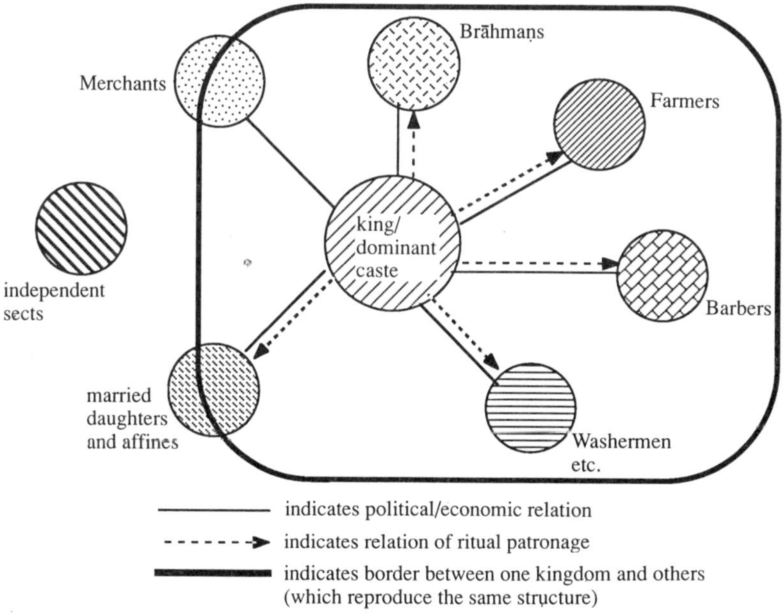

FIG. 6. Social structure from the viewpoint of the king or dominant caste

[14] What Stein writes of South India is generally applicable to all Hindu areas of the sub-continent: 'the principal custodians of the Sanskritic learned tradition in South India lived in rural settlements with peasants' (Stein 1980: 6).

stability which they themselves will rarely be in a position to create.

Figure 6 also shows that women may be exchanged in marriage with members of other kingdoms. This is particularly common where hypergamy is prevalent: as noted in Chapter 5, hypergamy is a form of tribute and is thus a means of forming political alliances.

From the perspective of a merchant caste which is separate from

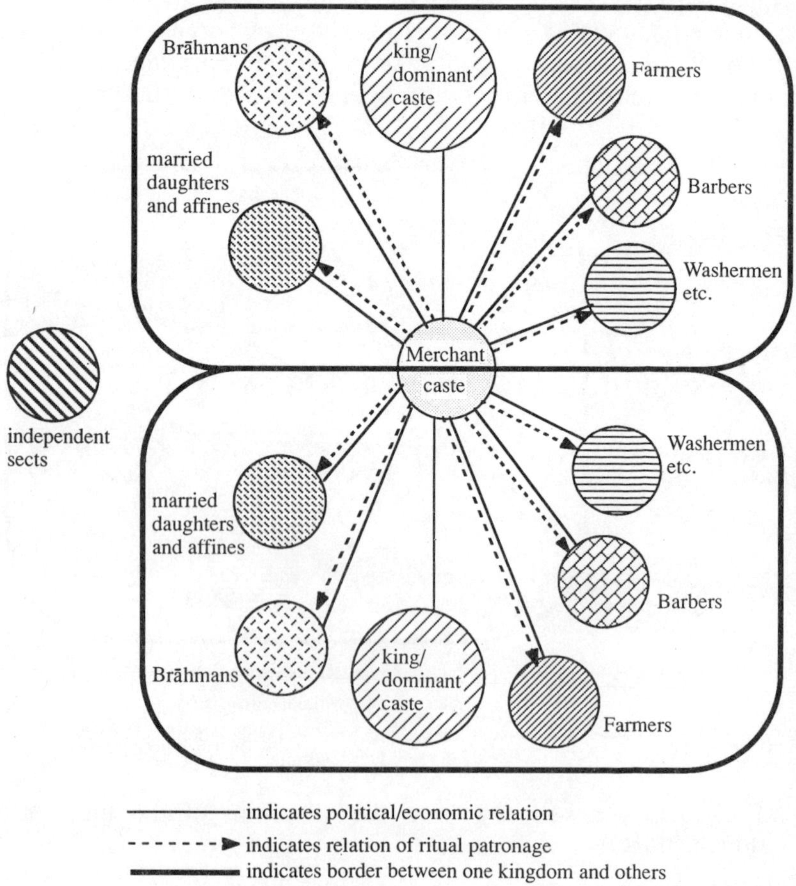

FIG. 7. Social structure from the viewpoint of a non-dominant Merchant caste

the dominant landowners, the configuration of castes might appear as represented in Figure 7. (It is also entirely possible that merchants are themselves the dominant landowning caste.) Intrinsically there is nothing to prevent merchants from being connected, both ritually and economically, to castes of more than one kingdom (or the sphere defined by the dominant caste). Frequently, merchants do in fact operate across political boundaries. In modern times, of course, the borders between 'caste kingdoms' are very fluid and often, where there are no ethnic divisions, the boundaries of the past may not be discernible at all.

It is not only dominant castes and merchants who act as the patrons of ritual specialists. To a greater or lesser extent, depending on their resources, members of *all* castes fulfil this role. Those who cannot find other castes to perform ritual duties for them will use their married daughters and affines as substitutes.[15] From this point of view, the social structure may look very much the same to a Brāhmaṇ as it does to a member of a 'low' caste. The ambiguities of the patron–priest relationship allow the Brāhmaṇ to claim superiority, but they also permit 'low' castes to claim that they are 'really' members of the *kṣatriya* or *brāhmaṇ varṇa*s (as Parry points out in his table of castes in Chadhiar, Kangra District).[16]

From the viewpoint of those castes which supply ritual specialists, the configuration can be schematized as shown in Figure 8. Such castes simultaneously provide services for others and get others to provide services for them. The Barber might well employ another Barber as his priest. The Washerman might employ some kind of Brāhmaṇ. If kings and peasants can have their courts, so too can Washermen and Barbers.

More often than not, the ritual specialists employed by such castes will come from the same kingdom (or sphere defined by the dominant caste) but they need not and, on particular occasions, specialists from outside may be employed. They are also very likely to give and receive women across political boundaries for the simple reason that such castes are generally small in number in any one locality.

What all of these schemas have left out are those who stand outside the immediate field of vision. Outsiders must, however, be

[15] See the discussion of Raheja in Ch. 4; this is one of the most interesting continuities between caste and kinship.

[16] See Ch. 5, pp. 91–2.

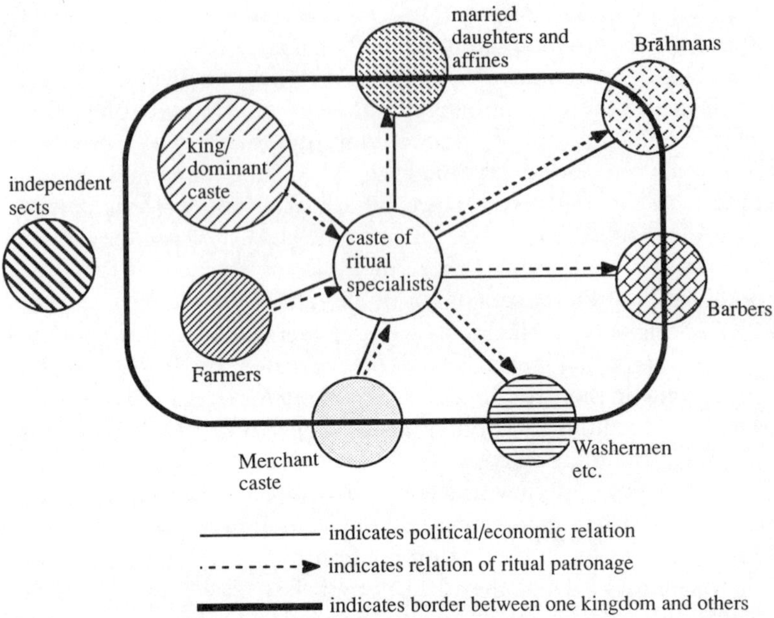

FIG. 8. Social structure from the viewpoint of castes which supply ritual specialists

included in the configuration in order to appreciate fully how caste works. One reason for this is that untouchability is often defined with reference to the outside, the dangerous unknown or the barbarian *mleccha*. Untouchable castes normally live outside the ritually defined boundaries of the community and the idea seems to be that impurity should be returned to where it properly belongs—to the uncontrollable forces of nature. In a way, Untouchables are seen as not quite fully human and so must be excluded from society proper. Hall puts it the wrong way round when he states that 'these casteless people brought pollution and were the fundamental justification for the caste system' (Hall 1986: 61). Rather, the creation of an ordered community entails the existence of those who do not belong.

If Untouchables stand both literally and symbolically on the margins of society, they also form a kind of buffer zone between one community and another. Historically, however, the real threat to order came not from the lowest castes or outcastes, both of whom were generally landless and consequently bereft of power; it came from those, both within and without, who had expansionist designs and the resources to further them. The other side of the coin of generalized instability was generalized predacity.[17]

The early formation of caste-organized communities always has certain elements in common. A group of people gain control over a locality by settling the land and seek to consolidate their dominance by attaching others to them. However, their political hold is weak (*a*) because these others often have the option of moving elsewhere, (*b*) because they compete among themselves for power and status, and (*c*) because their communities are continually subject to being overrun from outside. Allegiances and divisions are expressed through kinship and ritual because they are the most stable media available.

As in pre-colonial Indonesia, the political horizon of traditional India was 'an expanding cloud of localized, fragile, loosely interrelated petty principalities' (Geertz 1980: 4). Had Geertz not been misled by Dumont's conception of Hindu kingship, he might well have concluded that his portrayal of nineteenth-century Bali could be seen as a microcosm of pre-colonial India.[18] In India, argues Geertz,

> the king was what Louis Dumont has called a 'conventional' rather than a 'magico-religious' figure—a ruler 'dispossessed of religious functions proper,' whose priests ritually connected him to the other world as his ministers administratively connected him to this one. (ibid.: 126)

But we have seen that this was not the case. Geertz's characterization of Bali, though intended to be contrastive, in fact perfectly captures the essence of traditional Indian kingship: 'the king, no mere ecclesiarch, was the numinous center of the world, and priests were the emblems, ingredients, and effectors of his sanctity . . . priests were part of the king's regalia' (ibid.).

It is unfortunate, as Dirks has remarked, that Geertz tends to let his enthusiasm for abstraction run riot: 'As Geertz so rightly insists, the symbolic aspects of power are not, as the saying goes, "merely" symbolic. However, Geertz himself sometimes seems to

[17] See also Stein (1982: 20).

[18] The relevance of Geertz's study for Hindu South Asia was first drawn to my attention by David N. Gellner's (1983) review of *Negara*. Since then, Dirks (1987) has argued in the same vein.

be suggesting that power, certainly state power, is "only" symbolic' (Dirks 1987: 402). Challenging the Western view which sees power in terms of domination, Geertz claims that classical Bali offered an alternative conception of politics as 'a structure of thought . . . a constellation of enshrined ideas' (Geertz 1980: 135). Invoking Wittgenstein, he argues that 'such an assertion involves no commitment to idealism, to a subjectivist conception of social reality . . . Ideas are not, and have not been for some time, unobservable mental stuff. They are envehicled meanings . . .' (ibid.).

It is indeed the case that a position which holds that ideas are constitutive of social action need not be idealist in the sense of proposing that societies are *only* the product of ideas. But this is precisely what Geertz does tend to argue when he pronounces on the *essence* of Balinese political life: 'The dramas of the theatre state, mimetic of themselves, were, in the end, neither illusions nor lies, neither sleight of hand nor make believe. They were what there was' (ibid.: 136). That there was, of course, a great deal more to politics than ritual drama is made extremely clear by Geertz's own historical ethnography which shows a plethora of cross-cutting ties based on locality, kinship, title groups, membership of irrigation societies and of temple congregations. Ritual and drama were not simply self-generating, 'mimetic of themselves'; they were a product of the fragmentary nature of allegiances. The 'exemplary center' and its aspirant replicas provided some centralizing order where otherwise there would have been none. Effectively this is Geertz's own scenario but he tends to obscure it in the more pithy distillations of his argument.

The Explanation of Caste

If ever there was a Pandora's box, caste is it. Immediately one is drawn into every sphere of anthropological concern: ritual, kinship, politics and economics, ethnographic and historical analysis, the nature of comparison and the difficulties which arise when trying to understand another society whether through indigenous or imported concepts. The central problem facing any explanation of caste is that, in the end, one is not confronting one question but several, and any form of reductionism is bound to fail.

That caste cannot be reduced to politics or economics is obvious to all except the most entrenched of materialists. According to them, caste divisions mirror underlying inequalities of wealth and power while obscuring this fact through a kind of ideological smokescreen, divisions based on material factors being substituted by divisions based on religious purity. The irony of this view is that it tends to conceive of the order of castes in precisely the same way as the idealists do, with Brāhmaṇs at the top and Untouchables at the bottom.

In order to account for the fact that there is no clear fit between ritual status and economic strength, the materialists are forced to admit the very disjunction of status and power which they want to dispose of. The only strategy open to them is to argue that this disjunction is an ideological fabrication—a religious conspiracy to hide the truth. The trouble with economic determinists, as Levinson has argued, is that they like to have it both ways: 'if an ideology fits and reflects an economic order it is claimed that this proves the dominance of the latter, while if it fails to fit, the notion of mystification can be invoked to prove the same thing' (Levinson 1982: 98).[19] All caste systems exhibit what has become known, somewhat misleadingly, as a 'rigidity of the poles'. By this is meant that the status of certain castes is very inflexible. The reason for a caste's high or low ritual status cannot simply be a question of its economic position. If it were, then caste status and economic strength would always coincide and quite clearly they do not.

One cannot talk about the connection between caste and dominance without introducing the concept of ritual authority. Similarly, one cannot talk about caste in terms of a distributive system (the *jajmānī* system) without introducing the ritual umbrella within which this distribution takes place. But this does not mean that caste can be reduced to ideology or ritual either—not only because the phenomenon is interpreted locally in a number of conflicting ways,[20] but because none of these interpretations explains all of the facts as they present themselves to us. What we

[19] The models of caste developed by Levinson from studies of language usage are very similar to the general model proposed here.

[20] See also Burghart's (1978) argument that the various indigenous interpretations of caste uphold the supremacy of the renouncer, the priest, or the king depending on the predilections of the commentator.

are obliged to explain is the articulation of the various ideological positions with each other and with all of the other known facts.

Dumont's mistake is to believe that because there is no *automatic* connection between ritual status and economic and political strength, there is no connection at all. For him, caste ideology is somehow self-generating without regard to the vagaries of the real world. His claim is that the opposition of pure (represented by Brāhmaṇs) and impure (represented by Untouchables) is the expression of a pure form of hierarchy which comes about *because of* the disjunction of ideology (status) from power. But, as we have seen, Brāhmaṇs and Untouchables are often not seen as belonging to opposite ends of the spectrum, 'poles apart'. On the contrary, they are often assimilated.

For Dumont, the ritual positions of Brāhmans and Untouchables are fundamentally defined in opposition to each other. But this view obfuscates more than it reveals. Ultimately, and this is a matter of both fact *and* ideology, the positions of Brāhmaṇs and Untouchables depend on their respective relations with the dominant caste. Any opposition which is perceived between Brāhmaṇs and Untouchables is derivative of these relations; it is not primary. That the status of castes depends on material factors is itself true. Castes are either dominant or non-dominant and this depends firstly on access to certain resources—primarily land, but also trade. The position of non-dominant castes also depends, however, on the nature of the relation they have with the dominant groups and the relative importance of the roles they play in legitimating dominance (or kingship) and thereby promoting order. Some roles are more highly valued than others—typically those which require specialized training in literacy or ritual techniques—but this is for reasons which have little to do with economics *per se*.

The status of Brāhmaṇs is particularly indicative of the inadequacy of reductionism. The economic position of Brāhmaṇs tells us firstly whether they are a dominant or non-dominant caste. If the former, then we cannot be sure if they owe their high status to their wealth and political power or to their alleged ritual superiority. If they are a non-dominant caste, and some of their members perform ritual services for others, they may be seen both as exemplars of purity and/or as vessels of impurity, but their economic position does not tell us which of these interpretations is to be preferred. Both interpretations can only be understood *in relation to* their economic dependency, but neither can be *reduced* to that dependency.

Notions of purity and impurity are extremely pervasive in Indian social and religious life; this is not Dumont's invention.[21] Hindus continually resort to this idiom to explain social divisions and cultural practices and it would be absurd to have a theory of caste which could not cope with this fact.[22] Dumont is also undoubtedly correct to insist on the structuralist (i.e. relational) nature of caste systems. However, his own structural analysis breaks down because he denies the relational nature of ideology to reality. In the end, Dumont makes precisely the same mistake he chastises others for—namely, of reducing the whole to one of its parts, in his case to hierarchy (or status). But this is simply the way that ideologies, systems of values, represent the world. If anthropology does the same, the comparative perspective is lost. Effectively Dumont renounces the sociological, holistic perspective—which is, of course, the very last thing he aspires to do.

Perhaps the strongest case against reductionist explanations of caste (whether materialist or idealist) is provided by the fact that caste affiliations are expressed in terms of the presence or absence of kinship. Economic and political fortunes can, and do, change. The actual ritual functions which particular castes are called upon to perform also can, and do, change. Kinship identities are, however, much less malleable and at any particular time will appear to be almost completely unmalleable. This, combined with the fact that any group's position is defined in relation to control over land, accounts for the apparent inflexibility of caste systems in the synchronic snapshots provided by the censuses and by those ethnographies which lack a historical dimension.

In its irreducibility, caste shares something else with kinship. Of itself, kinship has no logic; anything is possible, including incest or fratricide. In order to account for the rules and taboos which make up kinship systems, one has to introduce concepts other than consanguinity and affinity—notions such as power, hierarchy, order, reciprocity. Intrinsically, there is nothing whatsoever to

[21] One of the best treatments of this issue remains Stevenson (1954) in spite of his misleading distinction between ritual status and secular status.

[22] The materialist thesis cannot begin to explain why the idiom chosen is in terms of purity and impurity; it simply says that it is a distortion of the truth.

prevent one from denying any social relationship with one's genealogical brother, or from calling others 'brother' when there is no genealogical connection. The concept of brotherhood depends on recognizing and respecting certain factors which are extrinsic to biological kinship. Similarly with 'casteness' or '*jāti*ness'. Of course, some will wish to attribute caste fellowship (or brotherhood) where others wish to deny it: in a way, the whole question of caste identity, as of kinship, is a never-ending dispute between self-perceptions and the perceptions of others. Both points of view are equally self-interested; neither can be taken as definitive.

The essential difference between caste and class is not that the latter is a system of social stratification and the former is not.[23] Both systems are manifestly hierarchical. The difference lies in the extension of kinship ties into the political arena. Caste works through the idiom of kinship because this is the only means of providing order in an otherwise unstable political climate. In class societies, the state provides most order and opposes the extension of kinship beyond what is minimally necessary.

In caste-organized societies, the constraints of kinship and political centralization are each limited by the pull of the other. Ineffective centralization encourages the formation of corporate kinship groups, but the unremitting drive towards centralization inhibits those groups from becoming too strong. The prevalence of hypergamy is the best illustration of this: those who aspire to power seek alliances with the already powerful, in the process weakening their erstwhile kinship bonds.

The constraints imposed on caste by culture are weaker, or more generous, still than those imposed by either kinship or politics. The most distinctive characteristic of caste is not, as the majority of commentators would have it, that it is culturally *specific* by being tied to Hindu India. The really outstanding characteristic is that caste is culturally blind—it does not respect ethnic or religious divisions but absorbs all in its path. To say that caste is a product of Hinduism is to look at things the wrong way round. Hinduism is a product of caste organization; just as caste is a fragmentary phenomenon, so too is the complex of beliefs we refer to as Hinduism. Hinduism is a hotch-potch of different beliefs many of which contradict one another. There are, for example, pious Hindus who oppose caste, and while the majority

[23] See Dumont (1980: 247 ff.).

may endorse it, there are, as I have tried to show, many disagreements about what is being endorsed.[24]

The most striking fact about the Sanskritic tradition is that it has never been unified by any event, text, or person. The idea that the *varṇa* system provides some kind of cultural unity is impossible to sustain because there is a great deal of disagreement about how the *varṇa*s should be interpreted. European interpretations have normally taken as axiomatic that the four *varṇa*s should be presented in the order *brāhmaṇ, kṣatriya, vaiśya, śūdra*—and that each successive category is inferior to, less pure than, the preceding category. I would argue that this view is at best of very limited utility and at worst completely misleading. It both conceals the ideological disputes about the *varṇa* system within the Indian tradition and ignores their one fundamental point of agreement.[25] The essential quality of the *varṇa*s is not that they are arranged in a linear hierarchy, pure over impure, but simply that they must be kept separate. Impurity and danger derive from the mixing together of things which should be kept separate.

From an outsider's point of view it may seem implausible that, in systems as complicated as caste systems are, one opposition can provide the idiom for all social relations. In fact this is relatively easily explained: purity and impurity are empty boxes which can be filled in a variety of ways. Concepts of purity and impurity are universally employed as means of differentiation or classification; there is nothing unique to Hinduism about this. In a sense, then, the argument that caste divisions can be reduced to the opposition of pure and impure is a vacuous claim because all systems of classification operate on a similar opposition. In order to compare and contrast one system of classification with another, it is necessary to introduce other variables. The idea of purity, pure and simple, explains nothing.

The second main problem with using the *varṇa* model as an explanatory framework for actual caste systems is that the earliest theories of the *varṇa*s make no prescriptions about hereditary

[24] One question which has particularly vexed modern Hindus is whether it is possible to endorse caste without endorsing untouchability.

[25] 'The statement that there are four *varṇas* and that the brahmin *varṇa* is the most superior was not uncontradicted in ancient India, either in practice or in theory. But, even in theory, that superiority was not a *spiritual* superiority; it was the result of a mature rationalization of a set of ritual facts which could conveniently be summarized in this way' (Derrett 1976*a*: 602).

status. The commonly held assumption that any *jāti* can be automatically mapped on to a particular *varṇa* is therefore extremely problematic. In order to retain the correspondence, it is necessary to make a careful distinction between *occupations* and *ritual functions*. The clue to caste organization does not lie in the hereditary transfer of occupations, as is often supposed, but in the hereditary transfer of ritual functions which connect different groups to the palace or dominant caste. The attribution of inherent ritual properties to particular populations is an attempt to perpetuate a contingent power structure. This is, of course, a very widespread phenomenon and not at all limited to caste-organized societies.

The ambiguities inherent in the *varṇa* system do not mean that it is redundant as far as the sociological explanation of caste is concerned because it reminds us that we are dealing with forms of organization which fundamentally concern the ritualization of social relations. To this day, the theory of the *varṇa*s is found in all of the different representations of caste ideology. In a crucial sense, Hindus see castes as being who they are and where they are because of their position in relation to the continuing rituals which are necessary for the ordering of society and the universe itself. The *varṇa* schema provides a model of the basic functions which are necessary for the correct performance of these rituals.

Caste requires the existence of kings and priests; it does not require that these priests be Brāhmaṇs, and even in parts of South Asia where caste organization is found, Brāhmaṇs are sometimes absent.[26] The question of whether caste is a structural or cultural phenomenon can be answered by saying that it is necessarily both.[27] Caste is a form of political structure where kinship and kingship pull against one another and priests are the mediators of the tension. The various ideological representations of caste are all, in some way, trying to come to terms with this structure but all of them do so by excluding certain facts from consideration.

This does not mean that the anthropology of Hinduism 'refuses to take seriously the beliefs of its objects'.[28] What it means is that the problem which we, as comparativists, are trying to explain is

[26] See e.g. Greenwold (1974); Barth (1960).
[27] On this question, see Leach (1960) and Dumont (1967).
[28] Pinney (1988: 147), discussed above in Ch. 1, pp. 14–15.

not the same as the one which Hindus are trying to explain. In giving no particular set of beliefs *a priori* primacy over any other, all beliefs are, in a sense, taken equally seriously because they all provide clues for our understanding of how a society works.

The explanation of caste, like the explanation of any sociological phenomenon, makes it impossible to avoid using a substantialist shorthand. Sooner or later one must refer to actual social groups which have to be given some kind of label—'ethnic group', 'caste', 'sub-caste', 'effective caste group', 'lineage', and so on. But the fact that one has no option but to employ some such labels does not mean that one is blind to the fact that the boundaries of all of these groups are often fuzzy, arbitrary, or contextual:

> Castes are not homogeneous status groups hierarchized from the outside, an ordered series of pigeonholes. This is a substantialist fallacy . . . The caste itself is more or less 'stratified' to the extent that its lower fringes may be shadowy. (Dumont 1964: 83)

To this one should either add 'and also the upper fringes', or do away with the words 'upper' and 'lower' altogether. The essential point is that both the boundaries between castes and those within them are contextual.

A second reason for using substantialist terminology, for employing the words 'caste', 'sub-caste', and so on as if these do actually designate fixed entities, is that Hindus themselves usually speak in this way. For example, someone may say: 'We will not marry those people because they are Potters; but we can marry these people because they are Farmers, as we are' (remembering, of course, that both Potters and Farmers may in fact be taxi drivers or civil servants). This kind of statement does not preclude the likelihood that neither the speaker in question nor the outsider he or she is explaining things to will be able to draw up a definitive list of those people it is permissible for that speaker to marry. In other words, one has an *idea* that there is a fixed group of people with whom one can marry but in fact it is often impossible to specify precisely who they are.

A third reason for retaining a substantialist terminology is that there are situations in which one does find closed or virtually closed groups referring to themselves and each other as 'castes' (*jāti*). Of course this is popularly thought of, both by Hindus and by non-Hindus, as the way that 'castes' are everywhere. The ideology of caste, which insists on the thoroughgoing pervasiveness of separation, represents *all* social relations in terms of bounded groups. But in fact very strict separation and endogamy only operate in particular circumstances and for particular groups. As a somewhat simplified shorthand, one might say that non-dominant castes are more bounded than dominant castes. Castes which supply services for others are defined by those who patronize them. Dominant castes, however, or those which aspire to dominance, have to define themselves and this is always an inherently fluid business. In any case, caste exclusiveness is always a matter of degree. Castes are always relatively, rather than absolutely, bounded.

In order to account fully for the development of caste, one would have to consider over 4,000 years of Indian history and a quite bewildering array of historical developments, ethnic groups, tribes, groups endorsing caste, schismatic sects, oppositional ideologies, political movements, major and minor conflicts. The list is truly endless. One way to begin explaining caste is to say what it is not—that is, to see it in comparative perspective.

Caste organization is opposed to tribalism: that is, a form of uncentralized social structure which is based on kinship. Historically caste is a phenomenon of the plains, of relatively productive agriculture which makes some degree of centralization not only possible and desirable, but, once it takes off, irreversible. However, caste organization is also opposed to a very effective form of centralization and to universalist creeds, such as Islam, which aspire to it. Caste is a means of regulating localized political units; it is ill-suited to empire building.

Caste is also resistant to any attempt to construct unambiguous league tables (by substantializing castes). This is so for two reasons. Internally, castes are organized on principles of kinship and marriage and these can be manipulated to produce more or less exclusive groups; the boundaries, in other words, are fluid. Externally, the orientation of castes is primarily to the dominant centre, not to each other. Potters and Tailors both know that they are inferior to dominant landholding castes because they have to serve them in various capacities. But if Potters and Tailors have neither economic nor ritual relations with each other, then *ipso facto* it will be impossible to decide who is higher and who is lower. Each can claim superiority by excluding the other from its ritual and kinship networks and by virtue of its relationships with yet other castes.

Finally, one can say that while the ultimate goal espoused by many Hindu thinkers may be transcendence, caste is essentially concerned with relations in this world. As such, whatever its apologists may claim, it is also fundamentally opposed to the renouncer's attempts to deny the constraints of social and political organization altogether.

To return one last time to Dumont, it can be seen that there is a certain amount of agreement between his position and the position, derived from Hocart, which has been adopted here. In particular, two elements of Dumont's theory have been endorsed, though they have been employed to rather different effect:

(1) the centrality of the relationship between priest and king who simultaneously form a pair but must also be absolutely distinguished:

(2) the emphasis on structure and relations rather than on bounded groups and substantial entities.

The Hocartian solution to the problem of caste which is offered here has, I believe, at least three advantages over Dumont's position:

(1) It is consistent—it not only abjures relativism in principle; it does so in practice.

(2) It is a theory which combines history and ethnography to generate hypotheses about events, structures, and processes, hypotheses which are modifiable or refutable as historical or sociological evidence requires.

(3) It is a more encompassing sociological theory—among other things, it offers a unified explanation of why kingship is central to caste organization, why some groups are hypergamous and others isogamous, why some statuses are relatively fixed while others are much more fuzzy, why mobility is not only possible but actually takes place, and why Brāhmaṇs may be regarded both as exemplars of purity and vessels of impurity or inauspiciousness.

Two facts, above all, provide the most revealing clues to the way in which caste works. These are that priests need not be Brāhmaṇs by caste and Brāhmaṇs need not be *brāhmaṇs* by profession. The only pure Brāhmaṇ is the one who does not work for a patron. He may himself be the patron of a priest (in other words, he may be a kind of king), but he must not be the priest of anyone else. With one exception, all priests are impure and some of them are exceptionally impure. The only pure priest is the one who sacrifices for no one but himself and he is, in every sense of the word, a renouncer. Even the renouncer can only achieve a state of absolute purity by *completely* forsaking the social and material world. Perfect renunciation requires extinguishing one's own existence.

The king alone has a path to purity in this world but only at the moment of sacrifice when his impurity is carried away by the officiating priest. And at this moment, the king, too, is no longer in the world. For a fleeting second he is assimilated with the gods; his perfection is established and social and cosmic harmony prevail. Kingship and the kingdom are saved by abstracting them from the living king. The king's divinity is a momentary illusion but the fact that he can re-create this illusion time and again through the agency of his priests (i.e. through other people) means that he is not a mortal like other mortals.

In this sense, kingship is indeed mimetic of itself and everyone aspires to it—the peasant no less than the noble, the Washerman no less than the Brāhmaṇ.[29] In a way one can agree with Dumont that caste is the expression of a pure form of hierarchy, but only because the hierarchy is perpetually threatened with dissolution both internally and externally. By making kingship inviolable or pure, order is continually regenerated. In reality, of course, kingship must be invested in a living king, but ultimately it is kingship which is sovereign, and not the king.[30]

[29] 'The brahmin's abnegation of secular power is a myth. Brahmins took power when they could, and they do still' (Derrett 1976*a*: 603).

[30] 'The dominant idea of the *dharmaśāstra* writers seems to have been that it was not the king who had a divine nature, but the royal function itself . . . The exercise of the royal function is equivalent to the celebration of a sacrifice of long duration (*sattra*), and that is why the king remains pure, whatever acts he is led to commit . . .' (Lingat 1973: 208, 215, quoted in Stein 1980: 279). Similar sentiments on the purity and inviolability of kingship are widespread. Consider Evans-Pritchard's comments on the divine kingship of the Shilluk of Southern Sudan: 'Because of the mystical values associated with the kingship and centred in the person of the king he must keep himself in a state of ritual purity, by performing certain actions and observing certain prescriptions, and in a state of physical perfection . . . a king symbolizes a whole society and must not be identified with any part of it . . . It is the kingship and not the king who is divine' (Evans-Pritchard 1962: 75–6, 84).

Much of the recent anthropology of Hinduism which I have referred to suffers from a kind of intellectual involution which is intriguingly Brahmanical in form. Its practitioners cling on to the flotsam of a theory which their own evidence devastatingly undermines. Unable to visualize a general structure of caste which would displace Dumont's theory, they hang on to it unremittingly even though their own evidence shows again and again that this theory simply does not explain what is known about India. Here, I have argued, the entrenched idea that 'Brāhmaṇs are the highest caste' has done most to hinder an alternative formulation of how caste systems work.

A more convincing alternative is, however, available. One way of putting it is as follows: 'A Brāhmaṇ need not be a *brāhmaṇ*, and a pure Brāhmaṇ must not be a *brāhmaṇ* to anyone but himself.' Fortunately there is another formulation of the underlying idea which gives greater, and more immediate, insight: 'Those who rule must be pure.' Ultimately, however, purity is not to be found in the social world of caste at all, but by transcending that world altogether, by severing all relations. This is an avenue which is available only to perfect kings and perfect renouncers. For those who embrace caste, kingship is by far the more attractive aspiration of the two because it allows the option of remaining in the world.

To rephrase the problem of caste in terms of kingship is to offer a solution of a kind, though only to raise another, equally formidable, problem. In order to confront that problem, it is necessary to put kingship in comparative perspective, to explain it in terms of other institutions, as I have tried to do here with caste. Once again, Hocart's seminal work might be taken as a profitable starting point.

BIBLIOGRAPHY

AHMED, A. S. (1986) *Toward Islamic Anthropology: Definition, Dogma and Directions*. Herndon, VA: International Institute of Islamic Thought.

ALLEN, N. J. (1985) 'Hierarchical Opposition and Some Other Types of Relation', in R. H. Barnes, D. de Coppet and R. J. Parkin (eds.) *Contexts and Levels: Anthropological Essays on Hierarchy*. Oxford: JASO (Occasional Papers No. 4).

APPADURAI, A. (1978) 'Kings, Sects and Temples in South India, 1350–1700 A.D.', in B. Stein (ed.) *South Indian Temples*, 47–73. Delhi: Vikas.

—— (1981) *Worship and Conflict under Colonial Rule*. Cambridge: Cambridge University Press.

BADEN-POWELL, B. H. (1982) *The Land Systems of British India*, 3 vols. Oxford: Clarendon Press.

BAECHLER, J. (1988) *La Solution Indienne: Essai sur les origines du régime des castes*. Paris: Presses Universitaires de France.

BAILEY, F. G. (1957) *Caste and the Economic Frontier: A Village in Highland Orissa*. Manchester: Manchester University Press.

—— (1959) 'For a Sociology of India?' *Contributions to Indian Sociology*, iii: 88–101.

BANKS, M. (1960) 'Caste in Jaffna', in E. R. Leach (ed.) *Aspects of Caste in South India, Ceylon and North-West Pakistan*, 61–77. Cambridge: Cambridge University Press.

BARTH, F. (1959) *Political Leadership among the Swat Pathans*. London: Athlone Press.

—— (1960) 'The System of Social Stratification in Swat, North Pakistan', in E. R. Leach (ed.) *Aspects of Caste in South India, Ceylon and North-West Pakistan*, 113–46. Cambridge: Cambridge University Press.

BASHAM, A. L. (1971) [1954] *The Wonder That Was India: A Survey of the History and Culture of the Indian Sub-Continent before the Coming of the Muslims*. Calcutta: Fontana/Rupa & Co.

—— (1975) 'Medieval Hindu India', in A. L. Basham (ed.) *A Cultural History of India*, 51–9. Oxford: Clarendon Press.

BAYLY, C. A. (1988) *Indian Society and the Making of the British Empire*. Cambridge: Cambridge University Press.

BENNETT, L. (1983) *Dangerous Wives and Sacred Sisters: Social and Symbolic Roles of High-Caste Women in Nepal*. New York: Columbia University Press.

BERREMAN, G. (1979) *Caste and Other Inequities: Essays on Inequality*. Meerut: Folklore Institute.

BLUNT, E. A. H. (1931) *The Caste System of Northern India with Special Reference to the United Provinces of Agra and Oudh*. London: Oxford University Press.

BOUGLÉ, C. (1908) *Essais sur le régime des castes*. Paris: Alcan (English translation with an introduction by D. F. Pocock; Cambridge: Cambridge University Press, 1971).

BRECKENRIDGE, C. (1978) 'From Protector to Litigant: Changing Relations between Hindu Temples and the Rājā of Ramnad', in B. Stein (ed.) *South Indian Temples*, 75–106. Delhi: Vikas.

BURGHART, R. (1978) 'Hierarchical Models of the Hindu Social System'. *Man*, NS 13: 519–36.

—— (1983) 'Renunciation in the Religious Tradition of South Asia'. *Man*, NS (18)4: 635–53.

—— (1987) 'Gifts to the Gods: Power, Property and Ceremonial in Nepal', in D. Cannadine and S. Price (eds.) *Rituals of Royalty: Power and Ceremonial in Traditional Societies*, 237–70. Cambridge: Cambridge University Press.

CLIFFORD, J. and MARCUS, G. E. (1986) *Writing Culture: The Poetics and Politics of Ethnography*. Berkeley: University of California Press.

COHN, B. S. (1970) 'Society and Social Change under the Raj'. *South Asian Review*, 4: 27–49.

—— (1987) *An Anthropologist Among the Historians*. Delhi: Oxford University Press.

CRONE, P. (1989) *Pre-Industrial Societies*. Oxford: Basil Blackwell.

DAS, V. (1977) *Structure and Cognition: Aspects of Hindu Caste and Ritual*. Delhi: Oxford University Press.

DAS, V. and UBEROI, J. S. (1971) 'The Elementary Structure of Caste'. *Contributions to Indian Sociology*, NS 5: 33–43.

DERRETT, J. D. M. (1973*a*) *History of Indian Law (Dharmaśāstra)*. Leiden/Cologne: E. J. Brill.

—— (1973*b*) *Dharmaśāstra and Juridical Literature*. Wiesbaden: Otto Harrassowitz.

—— (1976*a*) 'Rājadharma'. *Journal of Asian Studies*, xxxv(4): 597–609.

—— (1976*b*) [1969] 'Rulers and Ruled in India', in *Essays in Classical and Modern Hindu Law*, 50–79. Leiden: E. J. Brill.

DIRKS, N. B. (1976) 'Political Authority and Structural Change in Early South Indian History'. *The Indian Economic and Social History Review*, 13: 125–57.

—— (1987) *The Hollow Crown: Ethnohistory of an Indian Kingdom*. Cambridge: Cambridge University Press.

—— (1989) 'The Original Caste: Power, History and Hierarchy in South Asia'. *Contributions to Indian Sociology*, NS 23(1): 59–77.

DOUGLAS, M. (1970) *Purity and Danger: An Analysis of Concepts of Pollution and Taboo*. Harmondsworth: Penguin.

DOUGLAS, M. (1972) 'Introduction' to Dumont (1972).

DOWSON, J. (1982) [1879] *A Classical Dictionary of Hindu Mythology and Religion, Geography, History, and Literature*. Calcutta: Rupa & Co.

DUMONT, L. (1957) *Hierarchy and Marriage Alliance in South Indian Kinship*. London: Royal Anthropological Institute (Occasional Papers No. 12).

—— (1962) 'The Conception of Kingship in Ancient India'. *Contributions to Indian Sociology*, vi: 48–77; reprinted in Dumont (1970) and Dumont (1980).

—— (1964) 'Marriage in India: The Present State of the Question: Postscript to Part One. II. Marriage and Status, Nayar and Newar'. *Contributions to Indian Sociology*, vii: 77–98.

—— (1967) 'Caste: A Phenomenon of Social Structure or an Aspect of Indian Culture?', in A. V. S. de Reuck and J. Knight (eds.) *Caste and Race: Comparative Approaches*. London: J. & A. Churchill.

—— (1970) *Religion, Politics and History in India: Collected Papers in Indian Sociology*. Paris: École Pratique des Hautes Études/Mouton & Co.

—— (1972) [1966] *Homo Hierarchicus: The Caste System and its Implications*. London: Paladin.

—— (1977) *From Mandeville to Marx: The Genesis and Triumph of Economic Ideology*. Chicago: University of Chicago Press.

—— (1980) [1966] *Homo Hierarchicus: The Caste System and its Implications*, Complete Revised English Edition. Chicago: University of Chicago Press.

—— (1986) *Essays on Individualism: Modern Ideology in Anthropological Perspective*. Chicago: University of Chicago Press.

DUMONT, L. and POCOCK, D. F. (1958) 'A. M. Hocart on Caste'. *Contributions to Indian Sociology*, ii: 45–63.

DURKHEIM, E. (1915) [1912] *The Elementary Forms of the Religious Life*. London: George Allen & Unwin.

DURKHEIM, E. and MAUSS, M. (1963) [1903] *Primitive Classification*. London: Cohen and West.

EMBREE, A. T. (1969) 'Landholding in India and British Institutions', in R. E. Frykenberg (ed.) *Land Control and Social Structure in Indian History*. Madison: University of Wisconsin Press.

—— (ed.) (1988) *Sources of Indian Tradition*, i: *From the Beginning to 1800*. New York: Columbia University Press.

EVANS-PRITCHARD, E. E. (1940) *The Nuer: A Description of the Modes of Livelihood and Political Institutions of a Nilotic People*. Oxford: Clarendon Press.

—— (1962) 'The Divine Kingship of the Shilluk of the Nilotic Sudan', in E. E. Evans-Pritchard, *Essays in Social Anthropology*. London: Faber and Faber.

FOUCAULT, M. (1971) [1965] *Madness and Civilization*. London: Tavistock.
FOX, R. G. (1970) 'Rurban Settlements and Rajput "Clans" in Northern India', in R. G. Fox (ed.) *Urban India: Society, Space and Image*. Durham, NC: Duke University Press.
FULLER, C. J. (1977) 'British India or Traditional India? An Anthropological Problem'. *Ethnos*, 42: 95–121.
—— (1984) *Servants of the Goddess: The Priests of a South Indian Temple*. Cambridge: Cambridge University Press.
—— (1989) 'Misconceiving the Grain Heap: A Critique of the Concept of the Indian Jajmani System', in J. Parry and M. Bloch (eds.) *Money and the Morality of Exchange*. Cambridge: Cambridge University Press.
FUSTEL DE COULANGES, N. D. (1956) [1864] *The Ancient City*. New York: Doubleday Anchor Books.
GABORIEAU, M. (1978) *Le Népal et ses populations*. Brussels: Éditions Complexe.
GALEY, J.-CL. (1989) 'Reconsidering Kingship in India: An Ethnological Perspective'. *History and Anthropology*, 4: 123–87.
GEERTZ, C. (1980) *Negara: The Theatre State in Nineteenth-Century Bali*. Princeton, NJ: Princeton University Press.
GELLNER, D. N. (1982) 'Max Weber, Capitalism and the Religion of India'. *Sociology*, 16(4): 526–43.
—— (1983) Review of C. Geertz (1980). *South Asia Research*, 3(2): 135–40.
—— (1988) 'Priesthood and Possession: Newar Religion in the Light of some Weberian Concepts'. *Pacific Viewpoint*, 29(2): 119–43.
—— (1992) *Monk, Householder and Tantric Priest: Newar Buddhism and its Hierarchy of Ritual*. Cambridge: Cambridge University Press.
GELLNER, D. N. and QUIGLEY, D. (eds.) (1995) *Contested Hierarchies: A Collaborative Ethnography of Caste among the Newars of the Kathmandu Valley, Nepal*. Oxford: Clarendon Press.
GELLNER, E. (1974) *Legitimation of Belief*. Cambridge: Cambridge University Press.
—— (1983) *Nations and Nationalism*. Oxford: Basil Blackwell.
—— (1988) *Plough, Sword and Book: The Structure of Human History*. London: Collins Harvill.
GHURYE, G. S. (1932) *Caste and Race in India*. London: Kegan Paul.
—— (1950) *Caste and Class in India*. Bombay: Popular Book Depot.
GONDA, J. (1965) *Change and Continuity in Indian Religion*. The Hague: Mouton.
—— (1966) *Ancient Indian Kingship from the Religious Point of View*. Leiden: E. J. Brill.
GOOD, A. (1982) 'The Actor and the Act: Categories of Prestation in South India'. *Man*, NS 17: 23–41.
GOODY, J. (1986) *The Logic of Writing and the Organization of Society*. Cambridge: Cambridge University Press.

GREENWOLD, S. M. (1974) 'Buddhist Brahmans'. *Archives Européenes de Sociologie*, xv(1): 101–23.

—— (1975) 'Kingship and Caste'. *Archives Européenes de Sociologie*, xvi(1): 49–75.

GUTSCHOW, N. and BĀSUKALA, G. M. (1987) 'The Navadurgā of Bhaktapur—Spatial Implications of an Urban Ritual', in N. Gutschow and A. Michaels (eds.) *Heritage of the Kathmandu Valley*. Sankt Augustin: VGH Wissenschaftsverlag.

HABIB, I. (1963) *The Agrarian System of Mughal India (1556–1707)*. Bombay: Asia Publishing House.

HALL, J. A. (1986) [1985] *Powers and Liberties: The Causes and Consequences of the Rise of the West*. Harmondsworth: Penguin.

HEESTERMAN, J. C. (1964) 'Brahmin, Ritual and Renouncer'. *Wiener Zeitschrift für die Kunde Süd- und Ostasiens*, viii: 1–31.

—— (1985) *The Inner Conflict of Tradition: Essays in Indian Ritual, Kingship, and Society*. Chicago: University of Chicago Press.

HOCART, A. M. (1927) *Kingship*. London: Oxford University Press.

—— (1950) [1938] *Caste: A Comparative Study*. London: Methuen.

—— (1954) *Social Origins*. London: Watts & Co.

—— (1970) [1936] *Kings and Councillors*. Chicago: University of Chicago Press.

—— (1987) *Imagination and Proof: Selected Essays of A. M. Hocart*, edited by R. Needham. Tucson: University of Arizona Press.

HÖFER, A. (1979) *The Caste Hierarchy and the State in Nepal: A Study of the Muluki Ain of 1854*. Innsbruck: Universitätsverlag Wagner.

HOLLIS, M. and LUKES, S. (eds.) (1982) *Rationality and Relativism*. Oxford: Basil Blackwell.

HOPKINS, E. W. (1931) 'The Divinity of Kings'. *Journal of the American Oriental Society*, 51: 309–16.

HUTTON, J. H. (1963) [1946] *Caste in India: Its Nature, Function and Origins*. Bombay: Oxford University Press.

INDEN, R. (1978) 'Ritual, Authority and Cyclic Time in Hindu Kingship', in J. F. Richards (ed.) *Kingship and Authority in South Asia*. Madison: University of Wisconsin South Asian Studies Publication Service.

—— (1986) 'Orientalist Constructions of India'. *Modern Asian Studies*, 20(3): 401–46.

—— (1990) *Imagining India*. Oxford: Basil Blackwell.

KETKAR, S. V. (1909) *The History of Caste in India*. New York: Ithaca.

KLASS, M. (1980) *Caste: The Emergence of the South Asian Social System*. Philadelphia: Institute for the Study of Human Issues.

KOLENDA, P. M. (1967) 'Toward a Model of the Hindu *jajmani* System', in G. Dalton (ed.) *Tribal and Peasant Economies*. Garden City, NY: American Museum of Natural History.

KOLENDA, P. M. (1978) *Caste in Contemporary India: Beyond Organic Solidarity*. London: Benjamin/Cummings.

KRAUSE, I.-B. (1988) 'Caste and Labour Relations in North West Nepal'. *Ethnos*, 53(1–2): 5–36.

LEACH, E. R. (1954) *Political Systems of Highland Burma*. London: Athlone Press.

—— (1960) 'Introduction: What Should We Mean by Caste?', in E. R. Leach (ed.) *Aspects of Caste in South India, Ceylon and North-West Pakistan*. Cambridge: Cambridge University Press.

LEVINSON, S. C. (1982) 'Caste Rank and Verbal Interaction in Western Tamilnadu', in D. McGilvray (ed.) *Caste Ideology and Interaction*. Cambridge: Cambridge University Press.

LEVY, R. (1987) 'How the Navadurgā Protect Bhaktapur. The Effective Meanings of a Symbolic Enactment', in N. Gutschow and A. Michaels (eds.) *Heritage of the Kathmandu Valley*. Sankt Augustin: VGH Wissenschaftsverlag.

—— with the collaboration of K. R. RĀJOPĀDHYĀYA (1990) *Mesocosm: Hinduism and the Organization of a Traditional Newar City in Nepal*. Berkeley: University of California Press.

LINGAT, R. (1973) *The Classical Law of India*, translated with additions by J. D. M. Derrett. Berkeley: University of California Press; originally published in 1967 as *Les Sources du droit dans le système traditionnel de l'Inde*, Paris: Mouton & Co.

LOCKE, J. (1989) 'The Unique Features of Newar Buddhism', in T. Skorupski (ed.) *The Buddhist Heritage*. Tring (UK): Institute of Buddhist Studies.

LUKES, S. (1975) [1973] *Émile Durkheim: His Life and Work. A Historical and Critical Study*. Harmondsworth: Penguin.

LYALL, J. B. (1889) *Report of the Land Revenue Settlement of the Kangra District*. Lahore: Civil and Military Gazette Press.

MACFARLANE, A. (1978) *The Origins of English Individualism: The Family, Property and Social Transition*. Oxford: Basil Blackwell.

MADAN, T. N. (1989) 'Caste and the Ordering of Hindu society', entry in F. Robinson (ed.) *The Cambridge Encyclopedia of India*, 364–6.

—— (1991) 'Auspiciousness and Purity: Some Reconsiderations'. *Contributions to Indian Sociology*, NS 25(2): 287–94.

MADAN, T. N. *et al.* (1971) 'On the Nature of Caste in India: A Review Symposium of Dumont's *Homo Hierarchicus*'. *Contributions to Indian Sociology*, NS 5: 1–81.

MALAMOUD, C. (1976) 'Terminer le sacrifice', in M. Biardeau and C. Malamoud, *Le Sacrifice dans l'Inde ancienne*. Paris: Presses Universitaires de France.

MANN, M. (1986) *Sources of Social Power*, i: *From the Beginning to A.D. 1760*. Cambridge: Cambridge University Press.

Marglin, F. A. and Carman, J. (eds.) (1985) *Purity and Auspiciousness in Indian Society*. Leiden: E. J. Brill.

Marriott, M. (1959) 'Interactional and Attributional Theories of Caste Rank'. *Man in India*, 39: 92–107.

—— (1965) *Caste Ranking and Community Structure in Five Regions of India and Pakistan*. Poona: Deccan College.

—— (1968) 'Caste Ranking and Food Transactions: A Matrix Analysis', in M. Singer and B. S. Cohn (eds.) *Structure and Change in Indian Society*. Chicago: Aldine.

—— (1976) 'Hindu Transactions: Diversity Without Dualism', in B. Kapferer (ed.) *Transaction and Meaning*. Philadelphia: Institute for the Study of Human Issues.

—— (1989) 'Constructing an Indian Ethnosociology'. *Contributions to Indian Sociology*, NS 23(1): 1–40.

Marriott, M. and Inden, R. B. (1977) 'Toward an Ethnosociology of South Asian Caste Systems', in K. David (ed.) *The New Wind: Changing Identities in South Asia*. The Hague: Mouton.

—— (1985) [1974] 'Social Stratification: Caste', entry in *Encyclopaedia Britannica*, 15th edn., vol. 27: 348–56.

Mauss, M. (1970) [1925] *The Gift: Forms and Functions of Exchange in Archaic Societies*. London: Routledge & Kegan Paul.

Mayer, A. C. (1960) *Caste and Kinship in Central India*. London: Routledge & Kegan Paul.

Moffatt, M. (1979) *An Untouchable Community in South India: Structure and Consensus*. Princeton, NJ: Princeton University Press.

Nepali, G. S. (1965) *The Newars*. Bombay: United Asia Publications.

O'Malley, L. S. S. (1932) *Indian Caste Customs*. Cambridge: Cambridge University Press.

Parry, J. P. (1979) *Caste and Kinship in Kangra*. London: Routledge & Kegan Paul.

—— (1980) 'Ghosts, Greed and Sin: The Occupational Identity of the Benares Funeral Priests'. *Man*, NS 15: 88–111.

—— (1986) '*The Gift*, the Indian Gift and the "Indian Gift" '. *Man*, NS 21: 453–73. √ *

—— (1991) 'The Hindu Lexicographer? A Note on Auspiciousness and Purity'. *Contributions to Indian Sociology*, NS 25(2): 267–85.

Pinney, C. (1988) 'Representations of India: Normalisation and the "Other" '. *Pacific Viewpoint*, 29(2): 144–62.

Popper, K. (1963) *Conjectures and Refutations*. London: Routledge & Kegan Paul.

Potter, K. (1989) 'Hinduism', entry in F. Robinson (ed.) *The Cambridge Encyclopedia of India*, 332–9.

Price, P. (1979) 'Raja-dharma in 19th century South India: Land,

Litigation and Largess in Ramnad Zamindari'. *Contributions to Indian Sociology*, NS 13: 207–40.

QUIGLEY, D. (1985) 'The *guthi* organisations of Dhulikhel Shresthas'. *Kailash*, xii(1–2): 5–62.

—— (1988*a*) 'Kings and Priests: Hocart's Theory of Caste'. *Pacific Viewpoint*, 29(2): 99–118.

—— (1988*b*) 'Is Caste a Pure Figment, the Invention of Orientalists for Their Own Glorification?' *Cambridge Anthropology*, 13(1): 20–36.

—— (1989) Review of Baechler (1988), in *British Journal of Sociology*, 40(1): 157–8.

—— (1990) Review of Raheja (1988*a*), in *Cambridge Anthropology*, 14(1): 78–81.

—— (1991) 'Hocart's Theory of Caste and Kingship'. *The Eastern Anthropologist*, 44(3): 315–44.

—— (1992) 'Le Brahmane pur et le prête impur'. *Recherches Sociologiques*, xxiii (2): 69–89.

RAHEJA, G. G. (1988*a*) *The Poison in the Gift: Ritual, Prestation, and the Dominant Caste in a North Indian Village*. Chicago: University of Chicago Press.

—— (1988*b*) 'India: Caste, Kingship, and Dominance Reconsidered'. *Annual Review of Anthropology*, 17: 497–522.

—— (1989) 'Centrality, Mutuality and Hierarchy: Shifting Aspects of Inter-Caste Relationships in North India'. *Contributions to Indian Sociology*, NS 23(1): 79–101.

RAMANUJAN, A. K. (1989) 'Is There an Indian Way of Thinking? An Informal Essay'. *Contributions to Indian Sociology,* NS 23(1): 41–58.

ROBINSON, F. (ed.) (1989) *The Cambridge Encyclopedia of India, Pakistan, Bangladesh, Sri Lanka, Nepal, Bhutan and the Maldives*. Cambridge: Cambridge University Press.

ROSE, L. E. and FISHER, M. W. (1970) *The Politics of Nepal: Persistence and Change in an Asian Monarchy*. New York: Cornell University Press.

ROSSER, C. (1966) 'Social Mobility in the Newar Caste System', in C. von Fürer-Haimendorf (ed.) *Caste and Kin in Nepal, India and Ceylon*. Bombay: Asia Publishing House.

RYAN, B. (1953) *Caste in Modern Ceylon*. New Brunswick: Rutgers University Press.

SAHLINS, M. (1985) *Islands of History*. Chicago: University of Chicago Press.

SCHNEPEL, B. (1988) 'In Quest of Life. Hocart's Scheme of Evolution from Ritual Organization to Government'. *Archives Européennes de Sociologie*, xxix: 165–87.

SHULMAN, D. (1985) *The King and the Clown in South Indian Myth and Poetry*. Princeton, NJ: Princeton University Press.

SJOBERG, G. (1960) *The Preindustrial City*. Glencoe, IL: Free Press.

SRINIVAS, M. N. (1956) 'Sanskritization and Westernization'. *Far Eastern Quarterly*, xiv(4): 481–96.

—— (1962) 'Varna and Caste', in *Caste in Modern India and Other Essays*. Bombay: Asia Publishing House.

—— (1975) 'The Indian Village: Myth and Reality', in J. H. M. Beattie and R. G. Lienhardt (eds.) *Studies in Social Anthropology*. Oxford: Clarendon Press.

STEIN, B. (1968) 'Social Mobility and Medieval South Indian Hindu Sects', in J. Silverman (ed.) *Social Mobility in the Caste System in India*. The Hague: Mouton.

—— (1975) 'The State and the Agrarian Order', in B. Stein (ed.) *Essays on South India*. Honolulu: University Press of Hawaii.

—— (1980) *Peasant State and Society in Medieval South India*. Delhi: Oxford University Press.

—— (1982) 'South India: Some General Considerations of the Region and its Early History', in T. Raychaudhuri and I. Habib (eds.) *The Cambridge Economic History of India*, i. 14–42. Cambridge: Cambridge University Press.

STEVENSON, H. N. C (1954) 'Status Evaluation in the Hindu Caste System'. *Journal of the Royal Anthropological Institute*, 84: 45–65.

—— (1970) 'Caste (Indian)', entry in *Encyclopaedia Britannica* vol. 5: 24–33.

STIRRAT, R. L. (1975) 'Compadrazgo in Catholic Sri Lanka'. *Man*, NS 10(4): 589–606.

STUTCHBURY, E. L. (1982) 'Blood, Fire and Meditation: Human Sacrifice and Widow Burning in Nineteenth Century India', in M. Allen and S. N. Mukherjee (eds.) *Women in India and Nepal*. Canberra: Australian National University.

TAMBIAH, S. J. (1976) *World Conqueror and World Renouncer: A Study of Buddhism and Polity in Thailand against a Historical Background*. Cambridge: Cambridge University Press.

THAPAR, R. (1966) *A History of India*, i: *From the Discovery of India to 1526*. London: Penguin.

TOFFIN, G. (1977) *Pyangaon: Une communauté Newar de la Vallée de Kathmandou*. Paris: C.N.R.S.

—— (1979) 'Les Aspects religieux de la royauté néwar au Népal'. *Archives de Sciences Sociales des Religions*, 48(1): 53–82.

—— (1984) *Société et religion chez les Néwar du Népal*. Paris: C.N.R.S.

—— (1986) 'Dieux souverains et rois dévots dans l'ancienne royauté de la vallée du Népal'. *L'Homme*, 99: 71–95.

—— (1990) 'Hiérarchie et idéologie du don dans le monde indien'. *L'Homme*, 114: 130–42.

TRAUTMANN, T. R. (1981) *Dravidian Kinship*. Cambridge: Cambridge University Press.

VATUK, S. J. (1975) 'Gifts and Affines in North India'. *Contributions to Indian Sociology*, NS 9: 155–96.

WEBER, M. (1958) *The Religion of India: The Sociology of Hinduism and Buddhism*, edited and translated by H. Gerth and D. Martindale. New York: Free Press.

—— (1968) *Economy and Society*, 3 vols., edited by G. Roth and C. Wittich. New York: Bedminster Press.

WILSON, B. (ed.) (1970) *Rationality*. Oxford: Basil Blackwell.

WINCH, P. (1958) *The Idea of a Social Science and Its Relation to Philosophy*. London: Routledge & Kegan Paul.

YALMAN, N. (1960) 'Caste Principles in a Kandyan Community', in E. R. Leach (ed.) *Aspects of Caste in South India, Ceylon and North-West Pakistan*, 78–112. Cambridge: Cambridge University Press.

INDEX